Black Nationalism and the Call of the Ancestors: Henry Highland Garnet, Alexander Crummell and Henry McNeal Turner

BEYOND THE BOOKCASE

James Arthur Holmes

Black Nationalism and Theodicy: Emphasizing Henry Highland Garnet, Alexander Crummell, and Henry McNeal Turner

BEYOND THE BOOKCASE

Accra - Albany - London

ISBN: 9781636520018

For bulk purchases email: bthebookcase@gmail.com

Black Nationalism and Theodicy: Emphasizing Henry Highland Garnet, Alexander Crummell, and Henry McNeal Turner

James Arthur Holmes

TABLE OF CONTENTS

Illustrations

*Please note that the image ownership of all the illustrations included in this publication are "Public Domain."

James Arthur Holmes

Dedication

This book is dedicated to my parents - James Arthur and Maranda Phillips Holmes, known as Charleston, South Carolina's "Mother Teresa" for her extraordinary humanitarian contributions. Besides, my parents nurtured me in the spiritual bosom of the African Methodist Episcopal Church and they instilled in their children and grandchildren the value and love for education. In addition, I would be derelict if I did not mention the genuine support of my sisters Inez Norris Jackson, Dr. Jeanette Maranda Holmes Steward as well as her husband William Steward and my sister, Linda Holmes Scott and nephew, Garry Demarco Norris..

Acknowledgments

Serious scholarship may be solitary and requires great care and thoroughness. All of which I experienced during the research and writing of this manuscript. I acknowledge the friends and well-wishers, too numerous to name, for their supportive efforts during this crucial period. My parents ,sisters, and nephew enamored me from the beginning to the completion of the project. Special thanks and appreciations are extended to Dr. Otis D. Alexander, Dean of the Faculty of Library Science at the International University for Graduate Studies. He edited and formatted the manuscript for publication.

Chapter I: **INTRODUCTION**

From the very beginning of the relationship between Black Religion and Black Nationalism, there has been a perplexing question of the meaning of undeserved suffering in a cosmos governed by a good, loving, and omnipotent God. Henry Highland Garnet (1815-1882), Alexander Crummell (1819-1898), and Henry McNeal Turner (1834-1915) wrestled with this question. How did Garnet, Crummell, and Turner account for evil in the world? How did they reconcile Black suffering with an omni-benevolent-omnipotent God? What was the meaning of undeserved suffering to these persons? This book compares and analyzes the differences and similarities in the thinking of Garnet, Crummell and Turner in terms of the emerging theodicies in their respective Black Nationalist positions.

For the past two centuries, Black Nationalism has been a cyclical idea in the United States, fading away at times and re-emerging with other forces at other times. Historically, Nationalistic Movements among Blacks have fared best when White resistance to Black progress has been most intense. Black Nationalism has been most subdued when there has been visible progress among Blacks.

10

However, when that progress is again impeded Black Nationalism undergoes a resurgence.[1]

While several books and numerous articles have examined Black Nationalism during the nineteenth century, no major work has focused upon the relationship between Black Nationalism and the theodicy question. Of the many Black Nationalist figures, several were ordained ministers, with three of the most prominent being Henry Highland Garnet, Alexander Crummell, and Henry McNeal Turner. While there are several biographies and books about these persons and their nationalistic ideas, there are no works that specifically focus upon the relationship between their theodicies and their Black Nationalist positions.

In general, this book will seek to find how the theodicy question influences Garnet's, Crummell's, and Turner's ideas of Black Nationalism. In comparing and analyzing Garnet's, Crummell's, and Turner's theodicies in relation to their Black Nationalist positions, this book will seek to answer whether one can be a Black Nationalist without a theodicy and whether it is necessary to address

---

[1]For a thorough discussion of the recurring varieties of Black Nationalism in America, see the introductory essay, John H. Bracey, August Meier, and Elliot Rudwick, *Black Nationalism in America* (New York, N.Y.: Bobbs-Merrill, 1970), i-ix.

theodicy if one is a Black Nationalist. In addition, this book will contribute to the Social Ethics literature of the Black Church by revealing the connection between theodicy and Black Nationalism in the thinking of three seminal nineteenth century Black Nationalist figures.

The research for book includes both library/archives work and scholarly research. The library and archives sources include Garnet, Crummell, and Turner writings, such as speeches, letters (personal and official), books pamphlets, scholarly articles, news articles, and official documents, such as conference minutes issued by Abolitionist Societies, the AME Church, and Negro Conventions. These sources are supported by works of Garnet, Crummell, and Turner researchers; news articles about Garnet, Crummell, and Turner; and works of church historians and theologians.[2]

Three researchers have provided the major speeches and writings of Garnet, Crummell, and Turner: Earl Ofari, *Let Your Motto Be Resistance: The Life and Thought of*

---

[2] AME is the abbreviation for African Methodist Episcopal, the name of the denomination founded by Bishop Richard Allen (1760-1831). See Harry V. Richardson, *Dark Salvation: the Story of Methodism as it Developed Among Blacks in America* (Garden City, N.Y.: Anchor Press/Doubleday, 1976), 80-81.

Henry Highland Garnet, Wilson Moses, *Destiny and Race: Selected Writings/Alexander Crummell*, and Edwin Redkey, *Respect Black: The Writings and Speeches of Henry McNeal Turner*. These works form the fundamental general sources for the study.

There are several specific collections for the study. The archives of the AME Publishing House in Nashville, Tennessee has copies of the *Christian Recorder*, the *Voice of Missions*, and the *Voice of the People* that are gold mines about Turner information. The Special Collections Department of the Interdenominational Theological Center has a valuable Turner pamphlet, *Bishop Henry McNeal Turner Speaks to This Generation* (Atlanta: AME Church, 1982) by Josephus Coan. The New York Public Library has several original Garnet letters and various Garnet documents in the Schomburg Collection.[3] The George W. Forbes Papers located in the Rare Book Department of the Boston Public Library offer various Crummell documents

---

[3] Arthur A. Schomburg (1874-1938), a famous curator, founded the Schomburg Collection, a large collection of materials on the African-American experience. Between 1926 and 1928 the Carnegie Corporation bought the Schomburg Collection and gave it to the Harlem Branch of the New York Public Library. The Schomburg Collection has grown to become the largest collection of African-American materials in the world.

that reveal information on Crummell's early life. The Moorland-Spingarn Research Center at Howard University (Washington, DC) has the Henry McNeal Turner Papers.[4]

Chapter One includes an Introduction, consisting of The Problem and Significance of the Study, Methodology, Previous Research, Sources of the Study, and Plan of this book.

The next chapter is an historic overview of the Black Church and Black Nationalism. This chapter traces the development of the Independent Black Church Movement from the founding of the Free African Society by Richard Allen and Absalom Jones in 1787, to the merger of the invisible and visible Black Churches after the Civil War. Providing the fundamental basis for Black social cohesion before the Civil War, the Black Church through its clergy became the prominent voice for the community. Nationalist

---

[4] The Moorland-Spingarn Research Center at Howard University is one of the largest repositories of African and African-American documents in America. In 1914 Dr. Jessie E. Moorland, a noted African-American theologian, donated his private library to Howard University. In 1946 Arthur B. Spingarn, a distinguished attorney and a prominent collector of African-American books, documents, and other materials, presented his collection to Howard University. Moorland's and Spingarn's collections provided the foundation for the development of a first-rate African-American research library. In 1973 the Howard University Board of Trustees voted to name the research library the Moorland-Spingarn Research Center in honor of its first two benefactors.

sentiments, once finding their way into the Black Church, were transported to the Negro Conventions and other prominent movements and debates through the Black clergy. This chapter will examine several of the historic relations between the Black Church and Black Nationalism.

Having set an historical and social context for the study, the next chapters focus on the lives and theodicies of Garnet, Crummell, and Turner, respectively. Chapter Three is an inquiry into Garnet's intense feelings of protest and hatred for slavery and his rejection of the White-controlled Negro Convention Movement. Drawing from the various sources previously mentioned, the study extrapolates and examines Garnet's theodicy: Providence and African-American Resistance.

The study turns next to Alexander Crummell, another prominent Black Nationalist of the nineteenth century. While born of free parents in New York City, Crummell was unable to escape the harshness of racial discrimination. Crummell and Garnet, life-long friends, were forced to leave Noyes Academy in New Hampshire because of their race. Returning home and graduating from high school, Crummell applied for admission to General Theological Seminary in New York City. He was again excluded because of his color. Experiencing a consistent pattern of racial discrimination throughout his life, Crummell developed a passion for the uplift and spiritual redemption of his race. Chapter Four examines Crummell's theodicy: Providence and Divine Retribution-Restoration.

The third prominent Black Nationalist of the nineteenth century was Henry McNeal Turner. Chapter Five focuses on this pivotal figure of Black Nationalism. While free born, Turner was compelled to work in the field alongside his slave brothers and sisters, under cruel overseers. The field work experience provided Turner with an indelible impression of the cruelty of slavery. Accepting the call to Christian ministry in his young adult life, Turner believed that Whites would gradually accord Blacks their full rights as American citizens. The declining status of Blacks during the two decades prior to 1900 disillusioned Turner, however, causing him to embrace militant nationalism and to propose a theodicy of Black Theology. The final pages of Chapter Five examine Turner's Black Theology.

Having set forth the theodicies of Garnet, Crummell, and Turner in the preceding chapters, Chapter Six provides a comparison of the three theodicies. In addition, the chapter, in the second and third sections, focuses on the thoughts of Garnet, Crummell, and Turner concerning their views on God and evil and the thoughts of the three men on the nature and destiny of the Black race. Finally, the last section provides an analytical summary of the three previous sections.

Having critically evaluated the theodicies of Garnet, Crummell, and Turner in the previous section, the study, in conclusion, focuses on their thoughts as they relate to the persistent problems of racism and oppression in the African-American community. In Chapter VII, the study develops meaningful implications for both the practice of a specific ministry of liberation to the African-American community, and a ministry of reconciliation and hope to the wider community in general.

The general methods used will include description, comparative analysis, and critical reflection. The theodicies of Garnet, Crummell, and Turner will be extrapolated from their writings and secondary sources and will be critically evaluated to ascertain their strengths and weaknesses. The theodicies of the three men will be compared and analyzed to ascertain their similarities and differences. In conclusion, the study seeks to answer whether one can be a Black Nationalist without a theodicy. In addition, we will provide implications for a theodicy to the Black Church for the twenty-first century.

Two previous Garnet researchers have focused mainly on his biography and his abolitionist thought and activities. *Sketch of the Life and Labors of Rev. Henry Highland Garnet* is basically a biography of Garnet's early life and says little about Garnet's theology, theodicy, or Black Nationalist position.[5] In Earl Ofari, *Let Your Motto Be Resistance: The Life and Thought of Henry Highland Garnet*, there are two chapters, "Prophet of Revolutionary Black Nationalism" and "Racism, Religion, and the Black Struggle" that examine Garnet's Black Nationalist position and theology of resistance.[6] Ofari does not make the connection between Garnet's theodicy and his Black Nationalist position, however.

Joel Schor's *Henry Highland Garnet: A Voice of Black Radicalism in the Nineteenth Century* provides a thorough examination of Garnet's role in the Abolitionist Movement between 1840 and 1882.[7] Schor's research reveals three major Garnet contributions to the Abolitionist Movement. First, Garnet found the constitution to be an

[5] James McCune Smith, *Sketch of the Life and Labors of Rev. Henry Highland Garnet* (Springfield, Massachusetts, 1891).

[6] Earl Ofari, *Let Your Motto Be Resistance: The Life and Thought of Henry Highland Garnet* (Boston: Beacon Press, 1972).

[7] Joel Schor, *Henry Highland Garnet: A Voice of Black Nationalism in the Nineteenth Century* (Westport, CT: Greenwood Press, 1977).

anti-slavery document for ideological purposes. Second, Garnet advocated civil disobedience and resistance on the part of slaves themselves. Third, Garnet advocated a selective emigration to Africa and the glorification of the Black race that included self-pride and self-reliance. If Frederick Douglass is placed in the moderate camp among Black leaders advocating moral persuasions, legislation, and judicial decisions, then Garnet's role is brought clearer into focus, according to Schor. Schor's research is valuable for Garnet's Black Nationalist ideas and projects between 1840 and 1882. His research may be distinguished from this study in that he does not make the connection between Garnet's Black Nationalist position and his theodicy, which is a main thrust of the present study.

There are two master's theses, Ernest Miller, "The Anti-slavery Role of Henry Highland Garnet" and William Hunton, "What a Negro Preacher Did in 1865" that focus mainly upon Garnet's anti-slavery activities.[8] Miller's and Hunton's research may be distinguished from that of this dissertation in that the earlier research did not focus on the

---

[8]Ernest Miller, "The Anti-Slavery Role of Henry Highland Garnet," (Master's thesis, Union Theological Seminary, 1969) and William Hunton, "What a Negro Preacher Did in 1865" (Master's thesis, Howard University, 1925).

19

direct relationship between Garnet's theodicy and his Black Nationalist position.

Wilson Moses, *Alexander Crummell: A Study of Civilization and Discontent* offers a well-researched biography of Crummell.[9] The main thrust of his work is to broaden the definition of nineteenth century Black culture and expose Crummell's ideas on the concepts of Civilization and racial destination. While Crummell's Black Nationalist position is revealed, as are parts of his theodicy, Moses does not examine Crummell's theodicy to a great extent or connect it with his Black Nationalist position.

Riggins Earl's doctoral dissertation entitled, *Toward a Black Christian Ethic: A Study of Alexander Crummell and Albert Cleage*, from Vanderbilt University in 1978, examined the moral dilemma faced by Crummell and Cleage who embraced the idea of Black Nationalism.[10] Earl focused on questions regarding whether one ought to place loyalty to race above loyalty to government and whether the Christian tradition provides answers. Earl's study is

---

[9]Wilson Moses, *Alexander Crummell: A Study of Civilization and Discontent* (New York, N.Y.: Oxford University Press, 1989).
[10]Riggins Earl, *Toward a Black Christian Ethic: A Study of Alexander Crummell and Albert Cleage*, (Doctoral dissertation Vanderbilt University, 1978).

different from the focus of this dissertation, which will examine the theodicy of Alexander Crummell and compare it with the theodicies of two other nineteenth century Black Nationalists.

Crummell wrote an essay, "The Destined Superiority of the Negro" in which he delineated a belief that African-Americans were chosen by God for greatness. Crummell claims that slavery resulted from sins committed by prior African generations. Specifically, African foreparents refused to worship the true God, the God of Christianity. The knowledge of the true God, the Christian God, became less known from generation to generation, until the knowledge was completely lost. Crummell claims that God ultimately would liberate the slaves and restore them to supremacy: "the mighty seizes upon superior nations [i.e., the Black race], and by mingled chastisement and blessings, [God] gradually leads them to greatness."[11] While this essay is fertile Crummell literature from which to extrapolate ideas concerning his theodicy, it does not go into detail and leaves Crummell's theodicy and Black Nationalist position unconnected.

---

[11] Alexander Crummell, "The Destined Superiority of the Negro," in *The Greatness of Christ and Other Sermons,* (New York: Thomas Whittaker, 1882), 336-377.

Many studies focus on various aspects of the life and thought of Turner. However, we are without studies exclusively concerned with Turner's theodicy in relation to his Black Nationalist position. Mongo Ponton wrote a biography of Turner, *The Life and Times of Henry McNeal Turner* two years after his death, but the work is "slim and uncritical" and says nothing directly of Turner's theodicy and very little about his Black Nationalist position.[12]

In his dissertation, *Henry McNeal Turner and Black Religion in the South, 1865-1900* (Doctoral dissertation, Vanderbilt University, 1988), Stephen Angell focuses on Turner's activities as a missionary to the South and as a church administrator. Angell's research reveals important political, social, and theological thoughts of Turner. Our research may be distinguished from Angell's in that we will focus on Turner's theodicy in relation to his Black Nationalist position.

Angell's dissertation became the basis for a well-researched biography, *Bishop Henry McNeal Turner and African-American Religion in the South* (Knoxville: University of Tennessee, 1992). In addition to a critical

---

[12]Stephen Angell, *Bishop Henry McNeal Turner and African-American Religion in the South,* (Knoxville: University of Tennessee Press, 1992).

interpretation of Turner's major activities between 1865 and 1915, Angell's work offers a serious analysis of Turner's theology. Angell's Epilogue: "The Growth of a Black Theologian," is the first major attempt to examine Turner's theology.[13] While the research of this dissertation will consider Turner's theology, our major focus will be Turner's theodicy in relation to his Black Nationalist position.

Two key terms in the title of the book will require definition: Black Nationalism and theodicy. In general, Black Nationalism refers to:

the belief that [B]lack people share a common culture and world view, have a common destiny, and have had a common experience: slavery, oppression, colonialism, and exploitation. Racial solidarity is perhaps the most basic form of [B]lack [N]ationalism. Presuming no movement, program, or ideology, it is simply a feeling that [B]lack people, because of their common descent, color, and condition, should act in unison. A higher and different level of consciousness is cultural

---

[13]In addition to Angell's Epilogue, the writer found David Wills' "Aspects of Social Thought in the AME Church, 1884-1910" (Doctoral dissertation, Harvard University, 1975). Wills' research examines Turner's social thought in the context of his religious and social times and compares him with other contemporary AME leaders. Wills claims that Bishop Turner was the chief exponent of Black Nationalist thought among his AME contemporaries and in the United States between Reconstruction and World War I. Wills' research is more social than theological and gives little attention to Turner's ideas about theodicy.

nationalism, the view that all [B]lack people share a common lifestyle, aesthetic, and world view, often expressed in a distinctively [B]lack idiom in literature, art, or music. Religious nationalism, a specific component of cultural nationalism, is the belief in a special [B]lack religious cosmology, including the idea that the deity is [B]lack. The highest expression and form of [B]lack [N]ationalism is Pan-Africanism. In its broadest sense, Pan-Africanism is the belief that African peoples share a community of interests. . . [and they must] unite in a common struggle for liberation. In a narrower sense, Pan-Africanism refers to the unity of African nations on the continent for mutual progress.[14]

A statement of this perspective is given by Mary Francis Berry and John W. Blassingame in their *Long Memory: The Black Experience in America*.[15] The specific use of Black Nationalism in this study refers to nationalist manifestations in culture, economics, race solidarity, race uplift, religion, and Pan-Africanism.

Traditionally, there were four prominent periods of American Black Nationalism: (1) from 1790 to 1820; (2) the late 1840's and the 1850's; (3) the 1880's into the

---

[14] Mary Frances Berry and John W. Blassingame, *Long Memory: The Black Experience in America*, (New York, NY: Oxford University Press, 1982), 388.
[15] Ibid.

1920's; and (4)since the early 1960's.[16] Throughout American history, there has generally been varied approaches to Black racial problems. Some thinkers tended towards integration and assimilation, while others tended towards nationalist and separatist ideology. When the latter dominated the former, a distinctive period of Black Nationalism emerged. While nationalist sentiments were generally present throughout the Black experience in America, nationalism tended "to be most pronounced when the Negroes' status had declined or when they had experienced intense disillusionment following a period of heightened but unfulfilled expectations."[17]

The period of the American Revolution between 1790 and 1820 lent itself to ideas of racial egalitarianism. Several Northern states and upper Virginia took steps to manumit their slaves. Beginning about 1800, the Baptist and Methodists made simplified appeals to lower classed Whites, who were socially excluded from the middle classes. The message of the evangelists held that Christ died for all, regardless of race or social condition.

---

[16] Bracey, Meier, and Rudwick, *Black Nationalism in America*, xxvi.
[17] Ibid.

Responding to the message of the evangelists, Blacks flocked to the Baptist and Methodist churches which then enabled them to enjoy some degree of White acceptance.[18]

By 1787 the prospect for African-Americans changed drastically. With its recognition of slavery, the United States Constitution set the tone for future discriminatory laws and devices. Baptist and Methodist Movements, hitherto relatively egalitarian in spirit, began to exclude and segregate their Black parishioners. In this context of legal slavery and declining status, the initial tendency towards Black Nationalism emerged. With a sense of alienation, African-Americans began developing separate institutions with predominately Black churches and denominations, fraternal organizations, and mutual aid societies coming into being. There was also a small contingent of African-Americans who proposed emigrating to Africa.[19]

---

[18] African-American and Black are used interchangeably, without any difference in status attached to either term. They refer to people of African descent living in America.

[19] See H. Sheldon Harris, *Paul Cuffee: Black America and the African Return* ,(New York, NY: Simon and Schuster, 1972).

During the last two decades before the Civil War, a second period of Black Nationalism emerged. There were several key developments that spawned the growth of Nationalism:

> The essential failure of the antislavery movement to liberate the slaves. . .the evidences of racism among White abolitionists who failed to accord Negroes positions of real influence in the antislavery societies, increasing trends toward disfranchisement and segregation in public accommodations in many of the Northeastern states, combined with the continuing pattern of discrimination in the Old Northwest that made. . .conditions there similar to that in the south; and the growing hopelessness of the economic situation. . . . At the same time, the compromise in 1850, with its new and more rigorous fugitive slave law, the Kansas-Nebraska Act, and the Dred Scott Decision, all made the outlook bleaker than ever.[20]

The gains of the Civil War and Reconstruction brought a sense of optimism to Black Americans. Blacks were freed, awarded citizenship, and given the right to vote through constitutional amendments. Congressional legislation and Reconstruction provided a period of Black political participation and clout. While Black Nationalism

---

[20] Bracey, Meier, and Rudwick, xxxv.

did not totally disappear, there was a feeling of non-nationalism.

The abrupt close of Reconstruction and its attendant consequences rekindled an interest in Black Nationalism. Primarily because of the desertion of the federal government, Reconstruction ended in 1877. Between 1880 and 1900, Blacks were exposed to the disappointment of disfranchisement and the hostility of "Jim Crowism" and lynching. Blacks were generally excluded from the skilled trades in the urban centers and regulated to farm tenancy and sharecropping in the rural South. It was from this context of violence, racial hatred, and declining status that the third period of Black Nationalism developed. The ideas of racial solidarity, racial pride, and self-help were integral parts of the movement. There was also a renewed interest in separate institutions, especially educational and religious. In addition, several leaders revived the idea of colonization.

Two prominent voices of this Black Nationalist period were Alexander Crummell and Henry McNeal Turner. Their speeches and writings overlap both the second and third periods of Black Nationalism. Because of Crummell's intellectual abilities he was called early in his life to join the Abolition Movement. In 1840, at age twenty-one, he began a life-long involvement with the anti-slavery crusade and other Black self-help projects. The study will focus mainly upon Crummell's sermons that reveal the theological basis of his social theories and a select group of statements of Crummell's social and political ideology recorded between 1840 and 1898, the year of his death.[21]

Henry McNeal Turner was a prolific writer, expounding upon such topics as Blacks and politics, Blacks and Christianity, church problems, emigration, and the race problem. The focus will be mainly upon those speeches and writings delivered and recorded between the years 1863 and 1898 that concentrate on Turner's views of the race problem and the relation between God and Black people.[22] Turner's influence began just after Emancipation and continued to dominate the national scene for the remainder of the century. His influence declined during the last fifteen years of his life because of ill health and his removal from the editorship of *Voice of Missions*, a strong national publication. By limiting the study to his works between

---

[21] See Wilson Moses, ed., *Destiny and Race Selected Writings/Alexander Crummell,* (Amherst: University of Massachusetts Press, 1992).
[22] See Edwin S. Redkey, ed., *Respect Black: the Writing and Speeches of Henry McNeal Turner* ,(New York, NY: The New York Times and Arno Press, 1970).

1863 and 1898, we may examine Turner's writings during his most influential years.[23]

With regards to the other key term, in general, theodicy "is the technical term for the problem of justifying the character of a good, creative, and responsible God in the face of such doubts as arise by the fact of evil. If God is good, why evil?"[24] In this context theodicy is not the general question. It is a group issue. It refers to a suffering of a people. It is not an attempt to speak to theodicy in general.

In this book when Garnet, Crummell, or Turner demonstrates the term theodicy, it refers to their attempts to reconcile slavery and racial oppression with an omnipotent and all-benevolent God.

---

[23] The fourth period of Black Nationalism emerged during the twentieth century and is beyond the limits of this study.
[24] Dagobert D. Runes, ed., *The Dictionary of Philosophy,* (New York, NY: Philosophical Library, 1942), 317.

Chapter II: **AN HISTORIC OVERVIEW OF THE BLACK CHURCH AND BLACK NATIONALISM**

The present chapter gives a terse account of the historical overview of the relation between the Black Church and Black Nationalism. This chapter will examine the following topics: (1) the Independent Black Church Movement; (2) Black Nationalism and the Black Church; (3) Black Nationalism and Resistance Literature; (4) Black Nationalism and the Negro Convention Movement; (5) Colonization-Emigration Responses; and (6) Martin Delany's (1812-1885) role as the Father of Black Nationalism. Using the analytical method, this chapter will isolate the radical Black tradition in each topic and trace its development. In so doing, the chapter will demonstrate the radical tendency in the Black Church of the nineteenth century.

The Declaration of Independence and the American Revolution produced a set of principles that upheld the equality of persons, the right of self-government, and the fundamental dignity of humankind.[25] African-Americans

---

[25] Gayraud Wilmore, *Black Religion and Black Radicalism: an Interpretation of the Religious History of African-American People,* (Maryknoll, NY: Orbis, 1983), 34.

used these principles to develop arguments against slavery and oppression.[26]   In *Anti-Slavery: The Crusade for Freedom in America*, Dwight Dumond listed four ideas from the Independence Period that were used to question slavery:

> Natural law is unchangeable and everlasting and the natural rights of [humankind] are above the power of the government to destroy or deny.   All [persons] are equaling their natural endowment of rights. Governments derive their authority from the people and their primary purpose is to make these natural rights of [humankind] secure, and to protect the individual in their enjoyment.   All citizens, therefore, are entitled under the law and in the administration of justice.[27]

The egalitarian principles were incorporated into legislative petitions, lawsuits, speeches and other resistance literature and protest efforts for African-American liberation. In There is a River: The Black Struggle for Freedom in America, Vincent Harding observes the creative use of the principles in the protest activities of free Northern African-Americans:

> Especially in the North, on many occasions during the War for Independence--in petitions to legislatures, freedom

---

[26] Ibid.

[27] Dwight Dumond, *Anti-slavery: The Crusade for Freedom in America*, (Ann Arbor: University of Michigan Press, 1961), 26.

cases in the courts, and speeches--Black people resolutely turned the processed revolutionary faith into outright challenges to the system of American slavery. The Deism of White Enlightenment, the Natural Rights doctrines of the White philosophers, the pietistic religion of the White [churchpersons] all were marshaled in verbal and legal attacks against the bases of Black bondage.[28]

There were profound feelings of hypocrisy and resentment among African- Americans directed toward the American government that declared itself free of all forms of tyranny while discriminating against its Black constituency. This hostility expressed itself both through the Independent Black Church Movement and the development of Black Nationalist sentiments. In *Ideological Origins of Black Nationalism*, Sterling Stuckey observes the tension that produced the Independent Black Church Movement and a spirit of Black Nationalism in saying that: considering the position of oppressed Blacks and the ambiguity of the major documents used by [Whites]

---

[28] Vincent Harding, *There is a River: The Black Struggle for Freedom in America,* (New York, NY: Harcourt Brace Jovanovich, 1981), 42. Liberation is defined as the shared experiences and efforts of Mrican-Americans to abolish unjust situations in order to create a more human society. See Edward Long, Jr., *A Survey of Recent Christian Ethics,* (New York, NY: Oxford Press, 1982), 62.

to rationalize rebellion and to begin their nation...to Black leaders...their people were not meaningfully included in the new nation...since the great majority of them were still slaves. Despite the fact that the Declaration of Independence (and the Constitution) helped to promote the countervailing value of freedom, the freedom at issue was freedom for [W]hites. Therein, but certainly not exclusively, lay the seed ground for [B]lack [N]ationalist organizations and sentiment. And it was precisely in such ironic soil that an ideology of [B]lack [N]ationalism would eventually take root.

Discrimination was a widespread practice in the Northern churches during the Antebellum Period. African-Americans were regulated to side, rear, or gallery seating, and other forms of subtle segregation. Subtleties notwithstanding, segregated worship was extremely disappointing and offensive to African-Americans. Leon F. Litwack, in *North of Slavery: The Negro in the Free States,* dramatized the practice in saying:

> To preserve proper decorum, church officials assigned an inconspicuous position to their [C]olored parishioners. When attending services, Negroes found themselves segregated, either in an "African comer," a "Nigger Pew," seats marked "B.M." (Black Members), or aloft in "Nigger Heaven." The Sabbath schools also

provided separate quarters for Negro and [W]hite children.

Religious bodies which offered the Lord's Supper generally compelled Negroes to wait until the [W]hites had partaken of the bread and wine...The "Nigger Pew" most dramatically symbolized the Negro's inferior status in the church. Property-minded [W]hites generally deeded their pews on condition that no Negro be permitted to purchase them, for this would depreciate the pecuniary value of nearby pews.

Two of the most vocally dissenting Black Methodists were Richard Allen (1760- 1831) and Absolom Jones (1746-1818).[29] They where both members of Saint George Methodist Church.

---

[29] or Allen biographic information see his autobiography, Richard Allen, *The Life Experience and Gospel Labors of the Rt. Rev. Richard Allen,* (Reprint: Nashville: Abingdon, 1960); Marcia Mathews, Richard Allen, (Maryland: Helicon Press, 1963).

Image Ownership: Public Domain
Absolom Jones

Image Ownership: Public Domain
Richard Allen

Methodist Church in Philadelphia comprised of Absolom Jones and Richard. Allen, the more popular of the two, was a licensed Methodist preacher, while Jones was a Methodist exhorter of some repute. Dissatisfied with the unfair treatment at Saint George, in 1786 Allen petitioned the elders of the church to allow him to begin a separate church.[30] Unsuccessful in this effort, Allen made several

---

[30] Allen, 25.

other attempts to build a church for African-Americans until the break came on a fateful Sunday in 1787. Writing in his autobiography, *The Life Experience and Gospel Labors of the Rt. Rev. Richard Allen,* Allen recalled the momentous event:

A number of us usually attended St. George's Church... [W]hen the [C]olored people began to get numerous, they moved us from the seats we usually sat on and told us to go in the gallery. We expected to take the seats over the ones we formerly occupied below.... We took those seats. Meeting had begun, and the elder said, "Let us pray." We had not been long upon our knees before I heard considerable scuffling. I saw one of the trustees...having hold of the Rev. Absolom Jones, pulling him up off of his knees, and saying, "You must get up--you must not kneel here." Mr. Jones repeated, "Wait until prayer is over. Mr. H------- M-------- said, "No, you must get up now, or I will call for aid and force you away." Mr. Jones said, "Wait until prayer is over, and I will get up and trouble you no more." With that he beckoned to one of the other trustees...to come to his assistance. He came, and went to William White to pull him up. By this time prayer was over, and we all went out of the church... and they were no more plagued with us in the church.[31]

The dissenters formed the Free African Society, a mutual aid society and the first such organization for African-Americans.[32] Typical of the organizations founded by newly arrived American immigrants, the Society provided for multiple needs of the African- American community, including care for the aged, the less fortunate, and assistance to family members during death. Gayraud Wilmore notes one fundamental difference between the Mexican-Americans and the newly arrived American immigrants. "The Free African Societies did not express the need for cultural unity and solidarity only, but the protest and resistance of a persecuted people as well. "[33]

In addition to providing for multiple needs, the Society established resolutions to regulate the morals of its members. By 1790, the society decided to begin worship services. In Black Religion and Black Radicalism: An Interpretation of the Religious History of African-American

---

[31] Ibid.,25-26.

[32] For an excellent discussion of the events leading up to the organization of the Free African Society and an examination of its sociology, see Wilmore, 80-84. The topic is further examined in the body of this section.

[33] Wilmore, 82.

People, Wilmore explained the Society's focus on religion and social welfare, as well as on Black solidarity:

Thus, in many respects the Free African' Society, which represented the first bid for independence among [B]lacks in the North, resembled an organized church without actually being one. Although Allen entertained hopes that a "preaching-house" would come out of it eventually, he never intended it to be a church as such, and yet he wanted it to serve the religious needs of those who joined. It was a fellowship of [B]lack citizens who craved independence and social progress without reference to the creeds and confessions used in most of the mainline [W]hite [C]hurches.

The interests of the Free African [S]ocieties were both religious and secular, and never became exclusively one or the other. They created, therefore, the classic pattern for the [B]lack [C]hurch in the United States--a pattern of religious commitment that has a double focus: free and autonomous worship in the Afro-American tradition, and the solidarity and social welfare of the [B]lack community.[34]

---

[34] Ibid., 82-83.

Image Ownership: Public Domain
Bethel African Church

In 1794 Allen organized the Bethel African Church, while Absalom Jones and a majority of the Free African Society organized the Saint Thomas Church of Philadelphia, the first African-American Episcopal church.[35] By 1816, Allen called several African- American congregations together from the Middle Atlantic states and founded the African Methodist Episcopal (AME) Church.

---

[35] 5George Bragg, *History of the Afro-American Group of the Episcopal Church*, (Reprint: New York, NY: Johnson Reprint Corporation, 1968).

Allen was consecrated its first Bishop While it became a typical response to exclusion, the Movement spawned by Allen and Jones represents one of many responses to oppression. In *There is a River: The Black Struggle for Freedom in America*, Harding identifies the struggle for African- American liberation with different streams of a continuous river, representing the various responses to slavery and oppression. The attitude of radical resistance began at the moment of capture in the African forest and continued through the middle passage, the Pre-Revolutionary, Revolutionary, and Antebellum Periods in the forms of individual acts of resistance and small- and large-scaled rebellions.

Oral streams of protest developed during and after the War for Independence, says Harding.[36] African-Americans took seriously the ideals articulated in the Declaration of Independence: that all persons are created equal. In addition, many legal petitions were based upon the ideas of Christian revelation and reflection.

The slave-owners, on the other hand, used the Bible to their advantage. They claimed special revelatory

---

[36] Ibid., 49.

experiences that provided truth about scripture.[37]   Since slaves were not permitted to read the Bible, religious instructions were mostly oral. The instructions extolled the virtue of Heaven and emphasized slave obedience.[38]

Revelatory ideas found their way into the minds and hearts of free Northern African-American who participated in White churches. African-Americans developed a liberation hermeneutics based in part upon a revelatory source within their theology. Revelation was a dynamic event operating in human history. African-Americans believed that God revealed God's self through the Exodus event of the Old Testament and in the person of Jesus in the New Testament. Jesus became the event of God, explaining God through God's activity on behalf of the oppressed.[39] Thus, African-Americans were unable to accept the White Church's hermeneutics that excluded Black liberation.

---

[37] Robert Cummings Neville, *A Theology Primer*, (Buffalo, N.: State University of New York, 1991), 19-24.

[38] Actually, Daniel Coker, a well-educated minister of Baltimore, was the first elected Bishop. For some reason he declined and Allen was elected the next day. In his Recollection of Seventy Years 9

[39] Cecil W. Cone, "The Black Religious Experience, "*Journal of the Interdenominational Theological Center* 2 (Spring 1975: 137-139

Indeed, the White-controlled churches to which many Blacks belonged became an important battleground because the Christian Religion had become the very center of African American life.[40] To hold a watered-down Christianity meant accepting both religious and secular inferiority. Hence, Harding put the Independent Black Church Movement in the radical stream in saying "when Black people moved beyond petitions to seize the time and break the White control over their lives in the religious institutions, they were obviously engaged in radical action on behalf of self-definition and self-determination."[41] Wilmore observes further that the Independent Black Church Movement was one of the initial steps toward Black Nationalism: "[t]he independent church movement among [B]lacks, during the following period of the Revolutionary War, must be regarded as the prime expression of resistance to slavery—in every sense, *the first Black freedom movement.*"[42]

Joseph Washington offers his view of the Independent Black Church Movement through his two-

---

[40] E. Franklin Frazier, *The Negro Church in America* (New York, N.Y.: Schocken Books, 1964), 49.
[41] Harding, 44.
[42] Wilmore, 78.

dimensioned classification of Black Religion.[43] In *Black Religion: The Negro and Christianity in the United States*, Washington observes that Black Religion began in the plantation fields amidst ethical confusion and a lack of clear racial identity.[44]

Adapting the salve-owners' sacred music to the experience of slavery, the slaves transformed the owners' religious tunes into folk-spiritual music emphasizing a yearning for freedom.[45] Fusing their spiritual music with their quest for physical liberation, the slaves gave themselves a sense of religious identity.[46] Washington explains Black Religion in this way:

> Born in slavery, weaned in segregation, and reared in discrimination, the religion of Negro folk was chosen to bear roles of both protest and relief. Thus, the uniqueness of Black Religion is the racial

---

[43] Washington distinguishes two streams in Black Religion: the White stream and the Black stream. The former began with the White missionaries and tended towards other-worldly hope. The latter began during the clandestine meetings of the slaves in the backwoods and other underground places. This stream developed a folk-religion that provided avenues for the protest and relief. See Joseph Washington, *Black Religion: The Negro and Christianity in the United States* (Boston: Beacon Press, 1964), 33-34.
[44] Ibid. 32-34.
[45] Ibid.
[46] Ibid.

bond which seeks to risk its life for the elusive but ultimate goal of freedom and equality by means of protest and action. It does so through the only avenues to which its members have always been permitted a measure of access, religious convocations in the fields or in the houses of worship.[47]

Washington calls this Folk Religion, an institution organized more for identity purposes and to serve as an outlet for protest and relief, and less as an authentic religion with moral teachings.

Washington identified two streams of Negro Folk Religion: the White stream and the Black stream. He distinguished the streams in this way:

(a)   The White Stream began with the missionaries who bear a path to the door of the slaves. Their main purpose was to extol the virtues of the next world.

(b)   The Black stream began under the camouflage of camp meetings during the day and singing at night in which the religion of the Whites and the concern of the salves were blended to create the Negro spirituals which provided a cover for Negro preachers to lead insurrections and escapes. The

---

[47] Ibid., 33

fermentation of the [F]olk [R]eligion began
in the shadows of the plantations.[48]

The Black stream continued into the leadership class
of ministers, like Richard Allen, who led the independent
Black churches during the Antebellum Periods. For
Washington, the movement was a "response to segregation
in, and later exclusion from, White congregational
communions, first in the North and then in the South."[49]
The impact of the segregated White Church produced the
independent Black Church that paralleled the White Church
in most respects except the name.[50] Washington concludes
that the Independent Black Church Movement was more a
sociological and less a theological phenomenon because the
movement fused African-American autonomy and Negro
Folk Religion and created centers for relief and protest.[51]

In his article, "They Sought a City: The Black
Church and churchmen in the Nineteenth Century" (1971),
Lawrence A. Jones reached the same conclusions as did
Washington concerning the motivation for the organization

---

[48] Ibid. 33-34.
[49] Ibid. 34.
[50] For example, we have the predominantly White, United Methodist Church and the predominantly Black, African
[51] Washington, 34-36.

47

of the mutual aid societies and the independent Black churches.[52] While Jones avoids Washington's element of Negro Folk Religion, he supports the position that the Independent Black Church Movement was more socially and less theologically motivated:

> Viewed from one perspective, the Blacks' [C]hurches and mutual aid societies were the means by which aggressive Blacks pursued their own possibilities. The first pulpits of the [men and women] who subsequently provided the leadership in the churches were in the mutual and societies. Moved by a strong evangelical commitment and perceiving themselves to have been called to preach the Gospel, the societies provided an alternative to the pulpits of the religious establishment to which they were denied fully accredited access.[53]

Jones finds the analysis distinctively applicable to the Philadelphia Free African Society:

> That this was in fact the case is illustrated in the history of the Free African Society in Philadelphia which was organized by

---

[52] Lawrence A. Jones, "They Sought a City: The Black Church and Churchmen in the Nineteenth Century" Union *Seminary Quarterly Review* 26:3 (Spring 1971): 253-272.
[53] Ibid. 259.

Richard Allen and Absalom Jones. These men formed the Free African Society only after they were frustrated in their attempt to form a religious society which they had desired to do, they report, from a love of the people of . . . [our] complexion whom . . . we beheld with sorrow because of their irreligious and uncivilized state. They failed in this venture because too free Blacks shared their concern and those who "differed in their religious sentiments."[54]

While Washington's view is consistent with Wilmore's and Jones' conception of the doubleness of Black Religion, Washington is unable to give Black Religion as high a degree of authenticity as do the other two men.[55]

In *The Social Teachings of the Black Churches*, Peter Paris contends that "the proponents of the two-dimensioned classification are in error because they fail to understand both the nature of religion in general and Black Religion in particular."[56] Paris observes that the general

---

[54] Ibid. 259-260.
[55] Washington, 50-52. Washington modified this position to some extent in his later writings. See Washington, *The Politics of God* (Boston: Beacon Press, 1967).
[56] Peter Paris, *The Social Teachings of the Black Churches* (Philadelphia: Fortress Press, 1985), 1.

relation between Black Religion and American Society can be classified as *compensatory* or *political*.[57] Paris' compensatory classification views Black Religion in basically other-worldly pre-occupations seeking relief from the harsh realities of daily existence. Paris' political classification views Black Religion as a dynamic force for social change. "The former implies a passive disposition towards social injustice while the other infers an attitude or vigorous resistance."[58]

Paris explains the rationale for the theory in saying:

The basis for this judgment lies in our view that it is the essence of every religion to be related to history in two ways: (1) to espouse a positive view of some distant future which serves as a lure for its adherents; and (2) to exhibit the basic sociocultural forms and values relative to its specific location. The former designates an eschatological vision of the final end of humankind, while the latter expresses the nature and meaning of historical experience. To deny either the former or the latter is to distort the nature of religion per se. Hence generalization on the basis of the one dimension of religious experience at the expense of the other constitutes the major error implicit in both of

---

[57] Ibid.
[58] Ibid.

those efforts to classify the [B]lack [C]hurches according to compensatory and political understandings.[59]

According to Paris, both views, when held in opposition to each other, have their evils. The compensatory view reduces "the [B]lack [C]hurch to a pathological institution emphasizing false futuristic hope and repudiating history."[60] The political view reduces the church to a purely secular institution that emphasizes politics and social change and denies sacred eternity.

Paris asserts that the Black Church has not held the two classifications antithetically. Indeed, they have been interrelated, bringing together the reality of an oppressed existence with a hope for a better future. Paris finds support in Vittorio Lanternari and other historians of religion:

> Probably there is no phenomenon which reflects more clearly than to do the religious movement among oppressed peoples the contradictory, yet indissoluble, bond between current reality and future goals, between history and eschatology, which lies

---

[59] Ibid.
[60] Ibid. 2.

at the root of almost every major human experience.[61]

Central to the goal is an ultimate value or sacred principle that believes that all persons ought to be in harmony with each other and with the Creator. Whenever African-American parishioners join this sacred principle with their activities to improve their daily existence, this forms for Paris "the integral relationship of religion and politics in the [B]lack [C]hurches."[62]

Richard Allen and the other leaders of autonomous Black churches institutionalized what Paris called the "Black Christian Tradition" in the Independent Black Church Movement.[63] Parish identified the Black Christian Tradition as the normative tradition for the Black Church and for the Black community.[64] The Black Christian Tradition is governed not so much by Western Christian Traditions, but by the principle of non-racism.[65] Paris finds the fundamental basis for the Black Christian Tradition in

---

[61] Ibid. 2. Paris cites Vittorio Lanternari, *The Religions of the Oppressed: A Study of Modern Messianic Cults* (New York
[62] Paris, 2.
[63] Ibid. 10.
[64] Ibid.
[65] Ibid.

the biblical doctrine of "the Parenthood of God and the kinship of all people."[66]

Richard Wright, however, posits that the birth of the AME Church marked the first time a new church came into existence for sociological rather than theological reasons. Writing in his *The Encyclopedia of the African Methodist Episcopal Church*, Wright contends that:

> Richard Allen brought forth something new
> ... [F]or the first time certainly in American history, there was a Christian denomination built entirely upon sociological grounds: to promote [brotherhood and sisterhood] and equality across racial lines. For Richard Allen and his followers made no protest against Methodist theology or polity . . . It was Richard Allen's interpretation of the "second great commandment"—"Thou shalt love they neighbor as thyself" – to mean "thou shalt give equality to [B]lack people"—[t]hat caused the organization of Richard Allen's AME Church. And this as

---

[66] Ibid. Paris borrowed the doctrinal statement "God our Father, Christ our Redeemer, and Man our Brother" from the AME Church and rephrased it to a gender-neutral form. For an excellent theological interpretation of the church's doctrinal statement, See James H. Cone, "God our Father, Christ our Redeemer, Man our Brother: A Theological Interpretation of the AME Church," *Journal of the Interdenominational Theological Center* 4 (Fall 1976): 25-33. For Cone, the motto represents the church founders' commitment to the liberation of all oppressed peoples.

the first time in the history of Western Christianity that a church included in a practical way, [B]lack people in terms of equality.[67]

Paris disagrees with Wright's observation contending that both the sociological and theological reasons were related:

> The theological grounding of this anthropological principle established its religious character while the anthropological focus specified its social relatedness. In other words, the [B]lack Christian tradition represents a formal union of the eschatological and the sociopolitical realism, never the one apart from the other. In summation, morality, religion, and politics are united whenever this formal principle is actualize in the thought and practice of those persons or institutions wherein racism has no reality.[68]

There are distinctions among Wilmore, Harding, Jones, Washington, Paris, and other scholars concerning their analysis of the Independent Black Church Movement.

---

[67] Paris, 17-18. Paris cites Richard r. Wright, *The Encyclopedia of the African Methodist Episcopal Church*, 2nd ed. (Philadelphia: AME Publishing House, 1947), 625. See Paris note five.
[68] Paris, 15.

To be sure, the movement marks a major milestone in Black History. The movement gave African-Americans a feeling of racial solidarity and pride through the establishment and operation of autonomous Black churches and the independent denominations. The successful operation of the independent Black churches gave African-Americans the confidence to begin other important institutions. In addition, the independent Black churches served as a developing ground for future leadership in the White world.[69]

Black Nationalism and the Black Church and the Debate Over the Insurrectionary Tradition

As revealed in the previous section, the Independent Black Church Movement primarily in the North was one of the first expressions of Black Nationalism. It was in one sense, an expression of racial solidarity: a desire of African-Americans to organize their own churches rather than accept segregated worship. In another sense, it was an expression of living out the true mission of the church that, as Lawrence Jones put it, "consisted of the task of freeing

---

[69] Henry Young, *Major Black Religious Leaders:* 1755-1940 Nashville: Abingdon, 1977), 39.

Black men's [and women's] souls from physical, political, and social bondage, and setting the conditions of existence so that they could achieve humanity.[70]

In still another sense, the Independent Black Church Movement was an expression of Cultural Nationalism that contends "that Black people in the United States—or throughout the world—have a culture, [a] style of life, [a] cosmology approach to the problems of existence and aesthetic values distinct from that of White Americans in particular and White Europeans or Westerners in general."[71]

In his article "Toward a Sociological Understanding of the Black Religious Experience," Preston Williams found the historical locus of African-American Cultural Nationalism in the Black Church.

> The [B]lack [C]hurch has been historically the locus of [C]ultural [N]ationalism among [B]lacks and it will continue to be so in the

---

[70] Jones, 262.

[71] See the introduction essay John H. Bracey, August Meier, and Elliot Rudwick, *Black Nationalism in America* (New York, N.Y.: Bobbs Merrill, 1970), xxvii. There are both mild and militant Cultural Nationalists. A mild Cultural Nationalist asserts that "the Afro-American subculture is one of many subcultures that make up a pluralistic American Society." Ibid. A militant Cultural Nationalist "maintains the superiority of Afro-American culture usually on moral and aesthetic grounds to Western civilization." Ibid.

future . . . It means that the [B]lack [C]hurch is to be analyzed as belonging predominantly to the church-type or denomination and not to the sect or cult-type. The [B]lack American, like the Jew, has always had a land problem, and at times he [or she] seeks to mobilize his [or her] community and resources around the desire for land. The [B]lack [person] however, is time-oriented, not space-oriented. History, not land, is the crux. The church has been preeminently the preserver of his [or her] culture and heritage and therefore it has never been purely a voluntary association. All [B]lacks have belonged to it even though they did not get baptized or attend regularly, and the church has even felt that every [B]lack [person] is a member of its parish. In myriad ways it has been the bearer of grace for [B]lack people, the conscience of the [B]lack community, and the matrix out of which self-awareness and identity, the [B]lack soul, grew.[72]

There was a Black Nationalist element which expressed itself through the relation between Black Religion and Black protest in the South. In his article, "Religion and Resistance Among Antebellum Negroes, 1800-1860," Vincent Harding examined Benjamin Mays' and E.

---

[72] Preston Williams, "Toward a Sociological Understanding of the Black Religious Community," *Soundings* 54 (Fall 1971): 261.

Franklin Frazier's views of Southern Black Religion.[73]
Harding's research revealed that the two men felt the
religion of the slaves kept them submissive and focused on
heavenly afterlives. In speaking of the submissiveness and
other-worldly focus of the slaves, Harding observes that:

> Much of the current historical opinion about
> the role of religion among Antebellum
> Southern Negroes still follows the classic
> lines set out in Benjamin Mays, *The Negro's
> God* which claimed that the Negroes' idea of
> God kept them submissive, humble, and
> obedient. [Benjamin Mays, *The Negro's
> God as Reflected in His Literature* (Boston:
> Chapman and Grimes, 1938), 26.] There the
> Antebellum Negroes—especially in the
> South—were identified with a religion that
> "turned their minds from the sufferings and
> privations of this world to a world after death
> where the weary would rest and victims of
> injustice would be compensated." [E.
> Franklin Frazier, *The Negro Church in
> America* (New York, N.Y.: Schocken
> Books, 1964). 45.]
>
> Repeatedly Mays referred to this religion
> as "otherworldly" and "compensatory,"
> inclining its votaries "to do little or nothing
> to improve their status here . . ." (Mays, 24.)

---

[73] Vincent Harding, "Religion and Resistance Among Antebellum
Negroes, 1800-1860" in August Meier and Elliot Rudwick, eds., *The
Making of Black America* Vol I (New York, N.Y.: Athenaeum, 1969),
180-181.

Even so shrewd and perceptive a scholar as E. Franklin Frazier later adumbrated the theme in his important work on the Negro Church (Frazier).[74]

Harding's critique does not negate their ideas but expands them to include the protest and rebellion dimension. Harding maintains that Mays' and Frazier's views were more likely accurate of religious instructions rather than descriptions of the religion itself.[75] Indeed, according to Harding, many slaves lived by religious instruction, as they generally "had no other choice than to give at least an impression that they did."[76]

While giving the impression that their religion made them docile and complacent about their oppressed condition, many slaves employed secretive resistance. To be sure, the slave-holding communities were not always convinced by the image of religiously inspired, peace-loving, contented slaves.[77] The Southern White community

---

[74] Ibid. 180.
[75] Ibid. 181.
[76] Ibid.
[77] For an excellent discussion of the slave-owners' fear of rebellion, see Herbert Aptheker, *American Negro Slave Revolts* (New York, N.Y.: International Publishers, 1969), Chapter II, 18-52.

revealed its fear of the relation between Black Religion and African-American rebellion through political warnings and legislative proscriptions. The legislatures developed laws against both unsupervised meetings and in some states, the education of slaves.

In 1800, the South Carolina General Assembly put double restrictions upon Black religious activities, limiting the actual meeting times to daylight hours and requiring White supervision.[78] In 1816, several thousand African-Americans organized an autonomous African church in Charleston, South Carolina. Fearing the African church's independence, the municipal authorities closed the church and razed the building in 1820.[79]

There was also the White community's immense fear of the Black preachers' influence that was heightened after Nat Turner's insurrection in 1831. In speaking of Nat Turner's revolt, Virginia's governor made these remarks, implicating the Black clergy in the plot: "From all that has come to my knowledge during and since this affair—I am

---

[78] Henry Meadoes Henry, *The Police Control of the Slave in South Carolina* (New York, N.Y.:" Negro University Press, 1914), 134-135.
[79] John Loften, *Insurrection in South Carolina: The Turbulent World of Denmark Vesey* (Ohio: Antic

fully convinced that every Black preacher in the whole country east of the Blue Ridge was in the secret, and again in relation to the extent of the insurrection 'I think it greater than will ever appear.'"[80]

W.E.B. Dubois found that Southern states moved quickly to restrict Black religious activity and to suppress future Black, religiously-inspired revolts. He reveals that:

> A wave of legislation passed over the South prohibiting the slaves from learning to read and write, forbidding Negroes to preach, and interfering with Negro religious meetings. Virginia declared, in 1831, that neither slaves nor free Negroes might preach, nor could they attend religious services at night without permission. In North Carolina slaves and free Negroes were forbidden to preach, exhort or teach "in any prayer meeting or other association for worship— slaves of different families are collected together on penalty of not more than thirty-nine lashes." Maryland and Georgia had similar laws. The Mississippi law of 1831 said, it is "unlawful for any slave, free Negro, or mulatto to preach the [G]ospel" upon pain of receiving thirty-nine lashes upon the naked back of the presumptuous

---

[80] Aptheker, 305. See also Governor Floyd's letter to Governor Hamilton, November 19, 1831, in the Papers of John Floyd, Library of Congress, Washington, D.C.

preacher . . . In the District of Columbia the free Negroes began to leave [W]hite [C]hurches in 1831 and to assemble in their own.[81]

While not overly zealous in publishing slave insurrection news, those few articles that were published by the White press reinforced the legislative position against Black Religion by connecting it to Black rebellion. In some instances, the press charged White preachers with sowing seeds of rebellion. The Baton Rouge *Gazette* reported such a position in 1841:

> We need not wonder if deeds of blood and murder should take place if incendiary preachers are allowed to hold forth with impunity at camp meetings and other places where our slaves congregate, and badly make appeals to the worst passions of human nature. A stop must be put to ranting and raving, of these wolves in sheep's clothing.[82]

---

[81] W.E.B. Dubois, *The Negro Church* (Atlanta: Atlanta University Press, 1963), 25-26.
[82] Quoted in Joe Taylor, *Negro Slavery in Louisiana* (Baton Rouge: Burns and MacEachern, 1963), 222.

In addition, Governor Floyd of Virginia felt that White Northerners, through their religious instructions, inspired rebellion among the slaves in his state. Governor Floyd expressed his feelings in a letter to James Hamilton, Governor of South Carolina, November 19, 1831:

> I am fully persuaded, the spirit of insubordination which has, and still manifests itself in Virginia, had its origin among, and emanated [sic] from the Yankee population, upon their first arrival amongst us, but most especially the Yankee peddlers and traders.

> The course has been by no means a direct one—they began first, by making them religious—their conversations were of that character—telling the [B]lacks, God was no respecter of persons—the [B]lack man [sic] was as good as the [W]hite—that all men [sic] were born free and equal—that they cannot serve two masters—that the [W]hite people rebelled against England to obtain freedom, so have the [B]lacks a right to do.[83]

In 1835 the South Carolina legislature passed a law forbidding slaves to be taught to read or write.[84] There were three basic provisions: (1) If a White person taught a slave,

---

[83] John Floyd to James Hamilton, Jr., November 17, 1831.
[84] Payne, 27F.

he or she would be fined and imprisoned for six months; (2) If a free African-American taught a slave, he or she would be whipped fifty lashes and fined; (3) If one slave taught another slave, he or she would be whipped fifty lashes.[85] Daniel Payne (1811-1893) a free African-American and later an AME Bishop, was forced to leave Charleston, S.C. for operating a school for African-American children.[86]

There were also newspaper reports linking the independent Black churches to insurrection activities. Concerning the African church in Charleston, where Denmark Vesey began his insurrection activities, *The Times* of Charleston reported that:

> Almost every night there is a meeting of these noisy, frantic worshipers . . . Midnight! Is that the season for religious convocation? Even allowing that these meetings were conducted with propriety, is that the accepted time? That the meeting of numerous [B]lack people to hear the scripture expounded by an ignorant and (too frequently) vicious person of their own color can be of no benefit either to themselves or the community is certain; that it may be

---

[85] Ibid. 27.
[86] Ibid. 27-28.

attended with many evils is, I presume, obviou8s to every reflecting mind.[87]

A Mississippi newspaper put "suspicion [around] itinerant preachers for the aborted Mississippi insurrection of 1835."[88] In 1839, a New Orleans newspaper identified a Black church as "the greatest of all public nuisances and a den for hatching plots."[89] To be sure, there were three notable religiously-inspired slave insurrections: Gabriel Prosser's plot, the Denmark Vesey conspiracy, and Nat Turner's rebellion.

Gabriel Prosser (1776-1800) was the slave of Thomas H. Prosser of Henrico County, Virginia. Gabriel was a "giant of six feet two inches, a fellow of courage, and an intellect above his rank in life."[90] In 1800, at age twenty-four, Gabriel and Jack Bowler, a twenty-eight year old co-conspirator, planned an attack upon the city of Richmond.[91] Gabriel's religious inspiration for the insurrection was

---

[87] Quoted in John Loften, 92.
[88] Quoted in Edwin A. Miles, "The Mississippi Slave Scare of 1835," *Journal of Negro History* I
[89] Quoted in Richard C. Wade, *Slavery in the Cities* (New York, N.Y.: Oxford University Press, 1963, 49.
[90] Aptheker, 219.
[91] Ibid. 220.

based upon his belief that God had chosen him to deliver African-Americans.[92]   He interpreted his plan for deliverance through various parts of the Bible, equating slave-owners to the Philistines and himself to Samson (Judges 15: 14-15; 20O.[93]   Prosser's and Bowler's insurrection plans were to involve several thousand slaves, have them rendezvous outside the city; engage and eliminate all Whites who were encountered; take control of the Richmond arsenal; seize the state's treasury; and negotiate with the remaining slave-owners for the freedom of all remaining slaves.[94]   Because of a storm that came to the staging area the day of the insurrection, the plans were aborted.   Prior to the day of the revolt, the plan was revealed to authorities by two slaves.   Processer escaped, but was eventually captured and executed.[95]

Another pivotal example of a religiously inspired insurrection was the plan of Denmark Vesey (1767-1822), a local minister in the AME Church of Charleston, South

---

[92] Wilmore, 54.

[93] Ibid.

[94] Ibid. In addition, Gabriel ordered that Quakers and Methodists be unharmed because of their support of abolition. This was another manifestation of Gabriel's deep religious conviction and his religious inspiration for the plot. Ibid. 55.

[95] Aptheker, 222.

Carolina. Born into slavery, he was later sold to Captain Vesey, a merchant sailor of Charleston who subsequently changed this name from Telemarque to Denmark Vesey. For the next twenty years, Denmark accompanied his master across the Atlantic to Europe and to the Caribbean.[96] Due to his wide travels, Denmark was unusually cultured and sophisticated.[97] His talents proved useful in planning the Charleston insurrection. After winning a lottery in 1800, Denmark purchased his freedom and opened a successful business.

Gayraud Wilmore found the sources of Vesey's radical dimension in his perusal of Black resistance literature and his contact with sailors who brought news of revolts from the country and in Haiti.[98] Another source of Vesey's radical dimension was that of Black Religion. In 1816, a number of African-American classes removed themselves from the White Methodist Church in Charleston and organized the African Church in Hampstead, a Northern

---

[96] Loften, 3-36.
[97] Ibid.
[98] Wilmore, 57.

suburb of the city. Fearing unsupervised African-American meetings, the city closed the church in 1818.[99]

Image Ownership: Public Domain
Morris Brown

The Reverend Morris Brown (1770-1849), pastor of the African Church and a free African-American, went to

---

[99] Lofton, 93. The authorities used the 1800 state law that prohibited the gathering of African-Americans without White supervision in order to jail the leaders of the African Church and to close its operation.

Philadelphia and petitioned Bishop Allen for membership in
the newly founded African Methodist Episcopal
denomination. In accepting the petition, Bishop Allen
brought over four thousand members into the connection,
including Denmark Vesey, who had become a local AME
minister.[100] Because the authorities closed the African
Church building, the AME's held secret meetings on the one
hand, and open meetings under the watchful eyes of the
Methodist Church on the other. At all times the AME's
maintained their loyalty to their own connection.[101]

In his article, "Religion and Resistance Among
Antebellum Negroes, 1800-1860" (1969), Vincent Harding
maintains that the importance of the events up to this point
was not whether an insurrection was being planned, but that
a relation between Black Religion and Black rebellion
developed:

> [I]t is of critical importance simply to see
> that organized rebellion on another level had
> already been built deeply into the structure
> of [B]lack [C]hurch life in Charleston. The
> agitation from 1815 to 1818 and the
> concerted withdrawal from the [W]hite

---

[100] Richardson, 69-70.
[101] Erskine Clarke, *Wrestling Jacob: A Portrait of Religion in the Sold South* (Atlanta: John Knox Press, 1979), 124-131.

congregations in the later year took significant courage for the slaves. The raising of an independent house of worship implied not only the gathering of financial resources, but it was clearly an act of defiance for the world to see. The municipal officials knew and responded accordingly with harassments, arrests, banishments, and finally with the closing of the church in 1821. Ulrich B. Phillips, *American Negro Slavery* (Baton Rouge, Louisiana: Louisiana State University, 1966), 476. It is essential to note that the sense of Black solidarity was imbedded in the organization of the Negro [C]hurch. Attempts to dilute this or break it down met inevitably with resistance which centered in that church's life.[102]

Vesey seized upon the resentment of the Blacks for the incursion upon their rare exercise of autonomy and began to preach the cause of African-American freedom and liberation. In *There is a River*, Harding further explains the radical spirit among Vesey and the Charleston African-Americans.

The spirit and struggle had been lodged deeply in the [B]lack community's religious life, and the [W]hite authorities were not the only ones who recognized its larger potential. Denmark Vesey and certain special companions of his had known it long

---

[102] Harding, 184-185.

before; indeed they had helped to nurture it. But the closing of the church was the stimulus for organizing [B]lack discontent and resistance into something more effective than anger. Vesey had been a member of the Hampstead church, as had his [friend] . . . "Gullah Jack" . . . They began meeting with some of the discontented members of the [B]lack community . . . sometimes in the areas for religious gatherings on plantations . . . Vesey and his comrades believed that the suppression of the church had provided the issue around which they could rally the Charleston-area [B]lack community in a full-scale rebellion against [W]hite power.[103]

Vesey took advantage of the religious meetings to plan a biblically-based revolt. In *Insurrection in South Carolina: The Turbulent World of Denmark Vesey*, John Lofton explains Vesey's thoughts on the advantages of the religious meetings and his creative use of the Bible:

> Vesey realized . . . that [religious meetings were held for an approved purpose, and that purpose could provide protection coloration for unapproved talk. Such meetings, where large numbers were gathered together, not only provided a convenient mode of indoctrination in the iniquities of slavery, but also provided a persuasive vehicle. For what lesson could be more convincing than one

---

[103] Harding, *There is a River*, 68.

taken from the Bible, presented, as it was, as the word of God which even the [W]hites were bound to obey?

Whenever an occasion presented itself, Vesey used the Bible and the religious forum to convince Negroes of the injustice of enforced servitude. Long before Abolitionism, with its scriptural overtones, became a movement to reckon with, Vesey was invoking the Bible in the interest of an even more aggressive movement.[104]

Vesey laid the plans for an insurrection on June 16, 1822. The plan called for three- to nine-thousand African-Americans to lay siege to the city of Charleston. The theatre of operation extended first to the peninsula city; next across the peninsula's two adjoining rivers to the sea islands of the South, and finally to Christ Church Parish of the North. The entire theatre covered approximately eighty square miles.[105]

Once the march began, other slaves and sympathetic Whites were to join. Based upon his direction from God, Vesey commanded that all Whites be eliminated except for those who joined the rebellion. In explaining such a harsh command, Wilmore observes:

---

[104] Loften, 133.
[105] Ibid., 140-143

72

As for the killing, not only did they have the biblical precedent before them and believed themselves to be instruments of God's terrible wrath, but they also knew, as David Walker pointed out later, that once they had begun, only total extermination, as lamentable as that may seem, could they hope to succeed in such an impossible situation. They could expect no mercy if they failed.[106]

A few days prior to the proposed start of the rebellion, a slave revealed the plot to his owner. Vesey and the leaders of the plot were rounded up, arrested, and hung. Because of their association with the African Church-AME denomination, the authorities closed the church and further repressed the free African-American community through more stringent laws and stricter enforcement of the slave codes.[107] The AME Church went to the underground and was not revived until Bishop Daniel Payne organized the South Carolina Annual Conference after Emancipation.[108] From the evidence in the trial it was obviously clear that

---

[106] Wilmore, 61.

[107] In effect, the laws closed the operation of the AME Church in South Carolina. The remnants of the African Church took to the underground and continued to worship in what Frazier calls "the invisible institution" (

[108] Payne, 163.

religious inspiration figured prominently in the minds of the defendants.[109]

Finally, Nat Turner (1800?-1831), the last of the three notable insurrectionists, was the slave of Benjamin Turner of Southampton County, Virginia.[110] Nat came to know Christianity through the prayer meetings for slaves sponsored by his owner. Nat was given the opportunity to learn to read and write. Because of his distinctive birth marks, Nat's parents felt that he was called to an African witch doctor or a conjurer and destined for a great purpose.[111] Nat believed himself to be liberate slaves in Southampton County, Virginia.[112] He enlisted approximately seventy slaves and set out to take the county seat and to supply themselves with weapons. The band of freedom fighters succeeded in killing at least fifty-seven Whites, but were repulsed by the state militia and dispersed. Nat was eventually caught ad hung.[113]

---

[109] Harding, "Religion and Resistance Among Antebellum Negroes 1800-1860," 184-184; Loften, 92-94; 132-133.
[110] Aptheker, 294-295.
[111] Frank Johnson, *The Nat Turner Insurrection* (Murfreesboro, N.C.: Johnson Publication Company, 1966), 16.
[112] Wilmore, 64.
[113] Ibid. 70-71.

There is an important connection between Turner's religious experiences and his liberation activities. In particular, his conversion experience completely transformed him into a new creature. Centering in the birth of a new self-hood, Turner emerged from his conversion free and no longer determined by the slave-system. Turner's conversion experience was fundamentally a theistic affirmation of himself.[114]

Wilmore contends that the liberating experience was an extremely important dimension of Turner's life. Wilmore criticizes William Styron's *The Confessions of Nat Turner* for focusing on Turner's biblical quotations and his spiritual life, yet failing to give the liberating experience its appropriate significance. In speaking of Turner' liberating religious experience and Styron's failure to underscore its significance, Wilmore said:

> The most important thing to know about Turner is that he was a representative of an important group of slave preachers who discovered something [W]hite Christians had attempted to conceal from the slaves for more than two hundred years. Nat Turner, like others whose names are buried under the debris of the citadel of American slavery, discovered that the God of the Bible

---

[114] Ibid. 64.

demanded justice, and to know [God] and [God's] Son Jesus Christ was to be set free from every power of dehumanizes and oppresses. Turner discovered his manhood in the conception of the Christian God as one who liberates. His fanatical attempt to authenticate that manhood in blood was the inevitable consequence of the fanatical attempt of [W]hites to deny it. Styron's frequent biblical quotations and references to Turner's inner life never lifted this essential fact about the man to the level of significance. Hence, what must be regarded as the major point in an attempt to write fiction tolerably faithful to history failed to come true.[115]

Notwithstanding the hypocrisy of the White Church, Prosser, Vesey, and Turner looked beyond the

---

[115] Ibid. Several prominent African-American writers concurred with Wilmore's analysis. Lerone Bennett reasoned that Styron robbed Turner both of his Blackness and his militant manhood. Bennett wrote:

According to the historical data, the real Nat Turner was a virile, commanding, courageous figure. Styron rejects history by rejecting this image of Nat Turner. In fact, he wages literary war on this image, substituting an impotent, cowardly, irresolute creature of his own imagination for the real [B]lack man who killed or ordered killed real [W]hite people for real historical reasons. The man Styron substitutes for Nat Turner is not only the antithesis of Nat Turner; he is the antithesis of [B]lackness. In fact, he is a standard Styron type: a neurasthenic, Hamlet-like [W]hite intellectual in [B]lackface.

John Henrick Clark, *William Styron's Nat Turner: Ten Black Writers Respond* (Boston: Beacon Press, 1968), 5.

inconsistencies and found the liberating essence of the Gospel. In *There is a River*, Harding explains the African-American adaptation of the new religion in saying:

> The Scriptures, the theology, the doctrine, the very places of worship were repeatedly transmuted in the alchemy of the Black Movement. This was seen in Gabriel's use of the preaching meetings and explains the laws against the independent Black gatherings for worship and the anger of Richard Byrd of Virginia in 1801 who felt that slave preachers used their religious meetings as veils for revolutionary schemes . . . [Prosser, Vesey, and Turner], like their ancestors on the slave ships, would hammer any object, any doctrine into a weapon for the struggle toward freedom. Indeed to love freedom so fully in the midst of slavery was religion and was radical.[116]

The Prosser, Vesey, and Turner insurrections are thus noted for their distinctive contributions to the Slave Insurrectionary Tradition. Prosser's insurrection captured the slave-owners attention and fired the radical imagination of African-Americans.[117] The slave-owners believed that their paternalistic system which pretended to be kind to the

---

[116] Ibid. 61.
[117] Ibid. 61.

slaves would also keep the slaves docile and complacent. Processer's insurrection, however, brought to the forefront the Black spirit of resistance and struggle that the slave-owners tried so desperately to suppress. Both Vesey and Turner caught Prosser's radical imagination and planned insurrections. Vesey planned the most comprehensive rebellion of the slave period, and Turner's revolt brought extreme fear throughout the South. The three men used religion as the center of hope for rallying their insurrection forces. Black Religion continued the hope for freedom and liberation, both through its survival and through racial traditions.[118]

Not all scholars agree on the significance of the Black Insurrectionary Tradition Eugene D. Genovese offers a less laudable appraisal of the Slave Revolutionary Tradition. In his article, "The Legacy of Slavery and Roots of Black Nationalism," Genovese claims that African-Americans are without a significant revolutionary tradition and have little evidence to support large-scale, well-developed oppositions to slave-owners.[119] He calls into question Herbert Aptheker's approximately 250 revolts

---

[118] Ibid.
[119] Eugene D. Genovese, "The Legacy of Slavery and the Roots of Black Nationalism," *Studies on the Left* VI (Nov-Dec 1966): 3-4.

chronicled and analyzed in his *American Negro Slave Revolts.*[120] Genovese questions the accuracy of the analysis of the three previously mentioned notable insurrection attempts in saying:

> As many of Aptheker's critics have pointed out, most of the 250 revolts probably never happened, being the imagination of hysterical self-serving [W]hites, insignificant plots that never matured, or mere local disturbances of a questionable nature. Of the three major revolts, one, Denmark Vesey's, was crushed before it came to fruition; only Gabriel Prosser's in 1800 and Turner's reached impression proportions. Even so painstaking and thorough a scholar as Aptheker has been unable to discover firm evidence of a major revolt between 1831 and 1865.[121]

In answering Aptheker's claim that the news of many smaller uprisings were suppressed, Genovese maintains that "the effect would have been to prevent the accumulation of a tradition to encourage and sustain revolt prone slaves."[122] Indeed, Genovese's research finds very little evidence to support a tradition of opposition or, at best, an extremely weak tradition.

---

[120] Aptheker.
[121] Genovese, 4.
[122] Ibid.

Genovese has four fundamental reasons for the extreme weakness of a tradition of opposition and resistance. First, the United States drew its slaves "from those portions of Lower Guinea which had a population previously disciplined to servitude and domination."[123] Second, because the slave-trade to the United States came to an end in 1808, the majority of the slaves thereafter were born in America and "received little enforcement from newly enslaved and aggressive Africans."[124] Third, in comparing the history of Brazilian and Caribbean revolts with revolts in the United States, the revolts of Brazil and the Caribbean had the ingredients of the division of the Whites into warring factions and the general weakness of the state apparatus."[125] Except for the Civil War Period and the abolitionist activities primarily in the Northern United States, the Southern United States were mostly unified towards the continuation of slavery and their states' apparatuses were mostly always intact. Last, the slaves were unable to develop an ideology and a leadership class presupposed in a substantial revolt movement.[126]

---

[123] Ibid. 5.
[124] Ibid.
[125] Genovese.
[126] Ibid.

Genovese has three basic reasons to explain why the leadership did not develop. First, the Christian Religion, from which most slaves developed leadership talents through their roles as preachers, kept slaves docile. Second, those slaves from both the secular as well as the religious stratum, who were strong enough to rebel against the system in more forceful ways, usually found the strength to escape. Last, "the free Blacks and Mulattoes in the United States had little opportunity for self-development and rarely could or would provide leadership to slaves.[127]

Genovese asserts that two factors decreased the slaves' desire to revolt and leave the plantation. One was the hostility of the non-slave-holders beyond the plantation borders, and the other was the small number of slaves living on the plantation in comparison to the large number of Whites living outside the plantation. Genovese explained the hostile environment beyond the plantation in saying: "the non-slave-holders were loyal, armed, and disciplined; the country immediately beyond the plantation areas was inhabited by armed Whites completely hostile to the Blacks. Death, not refuge, lay beyond the plantation."[128] For these

---

[127] Ibid. 110.
[128] Ibid. 6.

and many other reasons Genovese believes slaves often looked to owners to protect them.[129]

Owing to the residence and the homogeneity of the Southern planters, the protection of the slaves, according to Genovese, grew into a well-developed social system.[130] Because slaves were valued as work-producing property much like mules, oxen, or cows, laws and community sentiments were put into place to protect the investments and to strengthen the slave-systems.

A world view developed among the planters within which Genovese believes, [P]aternalism became the specific manifestation of class consciousness."[131] Genovese explained his idea of Paternalism as it affected both slave-owners and slaves:

> Paternalism did not mean kindness or generosity or love, although it embraced some of each; essentially it meant a special notion of duty and responsibility toward one's charges. Arbitrary power, harshness toward disobedience, even sadism, constituted its other side. For our immediate purposes, [P]aternalism and the trend of treatment are especially noteworthy in confronting the slave with a world in which

---

[129] Ibid.
[130] Ibid.
[131] Ibid. 6.

resistance could be quickly, severely and legitimately punished, whereas obedience placed him a position to benefit from the favor of [an owner] who more often than not had a genuine interest in [the salve's] welfare. The picture of the docile and infantilized Sambo, drawn and analyzed so brilliantly by Stanley M. Elkins, is one-sided, but he is not far from the mark when he argues that the Southern regime greatly encouraged acceptance of and dependence upon despotic authority. See Stanley Elkins, *Slavery: A Problem in American Institutional and Intellectual Life* (Chicago: University of Chicago Press, 1968), Chapter III. Elkins errs in thinking that the Sambo personality arose only in the United States, for it arose wherever slavery existed. He does not err in thinking that it was especially marked and extensive in the United States, where recourse to armed resistance was minimal and the tradition of [P]aternalism took such firm room.[132]

While most slaves were extremely accommodating, Genovese reasoned that slaves were very capable of acts of protest. Genovese discussed three very popular acts of rebellion: theft, arson, and the mishandling of tools. Genovese did not find theft particularly threatening because: "Every contortion necessary to do the job implied

---

[132] Ibid. 6-7.

inferiority. It proved the slave a clever [person]; it hardly proved him a man [or woman]. It gained a few privileges of crumbs but undermined [their] self-respect and confirmed the [owner's] sense of superiority."[133] Arson and the mishandling of tools, while more positively rebellion than theft, were in reality nihilistic, according to Genovese. In those few instances where damages ruined a planter, it was the slave who might be removed to another owner and separated from family and friends. On those occasions when a slave killed an owner, the slave in most probability would be hung.[134]

Genovese's review and analysis of the weakness of the Slave Revolutionary Tradition found "the formation of a tradition of recalcitrance but not revolution, action but not politics, dim awareness of oppression but not cumulative ideological growth . . . what was missing was the sense of group consciousness, collective responsibility, and joint political effort which is the essence of a revolutionary tradition."[135]

While Wilmore acknowledges the slave-owners' use of the idea of Paternalism, he focuses on the slaves'

---

[133] Ibid. 8.
[134] Ibid.
[135] Ibid. 9.

response to the idea. The essential idea of Paternalism meant "a special notion of duty and responsibility towards one's charges."[136] This duty and responsibility, according to most paternalistic theorists, was executed toward slaves in the most humane, kind, and gentle way.[137] Wilmore posits that slaves created responses contrary to paternalistic norms; thus, threats, force, and punishments were required to maintain the system.[138] For these reasons, both Wilmore and Genovese maintain that Paternalism "must not be interpreted as evidence of how good slavery was for most Blacks or how readily they acquiesced in it [because]" as Genovese put it:

> The slaves accepted the doctrine of reciprocity, but with a profound difference. To the idea of reciprocal duties they added their own doctrine of reciprocal rights. To the tendency to make them creatures of another's will they counterposed a tendency to assert themselves an autonomous human beings. And they thereby contributed, as they had to, to the generation of conflict and great violence.[139]

---

[136] Ibid. 7.
[137] See Eugene Genovese, *Roll, Jordan, Roll: The World the Slaves Made* (New York, N.Y.: Pantheon Brooks, 1974), 3-7 and Kenneth Stamp, *The Peculiar Institution: Slavery in the Ante-Bellum South* (New York, N.Y.: Alfred K. Knopf, 1969), 322-340.
[138] Wilmore, 221-222.
[139] Ibid.

Wilmore contends further that Paternalism functioned differently from its stated purpose:

> Paternalism, in fact, never really worked as it was supposed to. Slave-holders were obliged, sooner or later, to recognize that there was extreme insecurity in their situation. Only the most stupid could have mistaken the fact that they were not dealing with [B]lack "sons and daughters" who loved them as [seigniorial parents] and exchanged that love for protection, but the thinking, sensible human beings who could never be trusted, precisely on that account, to respond in the same manner as children. Moreover, whatever feelings of warmth or tenderness may have been engendered in day-to-day relationships, they would necessarily have to be subordinated to the hard, cold fact that the bottom line was economic value. In the final analysis that value was realistically considered and made secure by the imposition of discipline and the monopoly of violent power that legally and otherwise remained in the hands of the master.[140]

No matter how kind and humane a slave-owner, says Wilmore, slavery reduced men and women to chattel

---

[140] Ibid.

property, devoid of humanity and self-worth. While Genovese posits that Paternalism became the regulating norm for the slave community, Wilmore reasons that:

> The slaves' basic obsession was somehow "to make it," to hold body and soul together for as long as possible to engage in an unceasing interior struggle to preserve physical existence and mental sanity—in short, to survive. Survival, therefore, became the regulative principle of the slave community, particularly among field hands, and this single factor best explains tenacity and functionality of Black Religion in the plantation South.[141]

Wilmore makes two claims about the radical stream in Black Religion during the early nineteenth century: (1) it grew out of the survival tradition of Black Religion; and (2) it inspired many of the Antebellum insurrections.[142] Wilmore claims further that a second stream tending towards a hypocritical compromise, grew out of southern Black Religion during the Post-Reconstruction Period.[143]

Herbert Aptheker lists several motivating causes for the insurrections, concluding that the social system of

---

[141] Ibid. 222.
[142] Ibid. 220-228.
[143] Ibid. 225.

slavery itself and its attendant brutalities were the most prominent:

> Excitement of almost any kind, but especially that which more or less directly affected the slaves, such as the prevalence of slogans and propaganda about liberty and equality, or the knowledge of some not too distant haven or ally offering emancipation, tended to increase slave disaffection. A disproportionate growth of the Negro population as compared with the [W]hite also tended to increase the slaves' boldness, and move them to attempts to gain in action what seems never to have been totally absent from their dreams—freedom. Industrialization and urbanization were other forces producing similar results. Economic depression seems to have been even more important in evoking protest. Yet, the fundamental factor provoking rebellion against slavery was that social system itself, the degradation, exploitation, oppression, and brutality which it created, and with which, indeed, it was synonymous.[144]

For Wilmore, it was the clandestine teachings of the Whites that provided many Blacks with the skills to read and interpret the Bible towards a liberation theology.[145]

---

[144] Aptheker, 139.
[145] Wilmore, 45.

Wilmore is quick to point out, however, that this ought not mean that "Black preachers so lacked indignation that only the ethical revivalism of [E]vangelicals and the inspired teachings of 'White ministers and religious ladies' could have provided Blacks with a theology of revolution and the spiritual dynamism to act it out."[146] In explaining Black Religion as one important factor in the Insurrection Movement, Wilmore said:

> [T]he religious inspiration did not emanate from the [W]hite [C]hurches of the South, the North, or even from the disreputable Methodist itinerants and the Emancipating Baptists. It sprang rather from the religious imagination of the slaves themselves and from those former slaves who escaped to become pastors of churches, or to sit in the pews of the newly independent [B]lack congregations of Baltimore, Wilmington, Philadelphia, New York, and Boston.[147]

In answering Genovese's charge that there is little evidence to support the factual occurrences of the insurrectionary tradition, Wilmore gives three fundamental replies:

---

[146] Ibid.
[147] Ibid.

(1) Little is known about the content of slave preaching when [W]hites were not in the congregation;[148] (2) The compensatory nature of [B]lack preaching was revealed to [W]hites historians by the [B]lack preacher who hid the real message in order to make [B]lack preaching acceptable to the status quo; and (3) Much of our knowledge of preachers and churches during the [A]ntebellum [P]eriod comes from the reports of [W]hite missionaries who usually went to great pains to prove to the churches that Christianity was good rather than dangerous to [W]hites.[149]

While Genovese found traces of slave resistance he felt there was not a sense of group consciousness or enough of a joint effort to warrant a slave insurrectionary tradition. Aptheker disagrees, citing his research documenting over 250 slave revolts between the Pre-Revolutionary Period and Emancipation.[150]

Genovese faults Aptheker's research, attributing the report of the revolts to mass White hysteria or to self-serving Whites. While there may not be a great deal of factual

---

[148] Ibid. 32.
[149] Ibid. 33.
[150] See Aptheker.

evidence to support the insurrectionary tradition, Wilmore maintains that Black preachers suppressed the evidence in order to keep the movement alive.

Whatever one's view on the extent of which religion inspired slave revolts, or whether large-scale revolts occurred at all, to be sure, there was a strong Black Nationalist element in the early Black churches.[151] Black Nationalism in the Black churches emerged out of a conflict perspective challenging the view that the solution to the race problem was assimilation into White culture and White churches.[152] Once African-Americans came to understand themselves as a distinctive group bound together through African descent and the common experience of oppression, a movement evolved that defined the group and set the terms for the relationships with other groups.[153] During the nineteenth century the leaders of the independent Black churches developed a Black Nationalist ideology that expressed itself through five fundamental expressions: (1) racial solidarity; (2) resistance literature; (3) the Negro

---

[151] Wilmore, 45.
[152] James Turner, "Black Nationalism" in Henry J. Richards, *Topics in Afro-American Studies* (Buffalo, N.Y.: Black Academy Press, 1971), 64.
[153] Ibid.

Convention Movement; (4) "a Black theology of missionary emigrationism and racial destiny"[154], and (5) the demand for political freedom, social justice, and economic parity.

The study has examined the idea of racial solidarity in the previous sections concerning the Independent Black Church Movement. We will continue to examine the racial solidarity concept in the thinking of Garnet, Crummell, and Turner later in the study. Black Nationalism and Resistance Literature and the Negro Convention Movement will be examined in the next sections. The ideas of a Black Theology of missionary emigration and racial destiny, and the demand for political freedom, social justice, and economic parity, will be examined in later chapters in the study, and especially in those chapters that specifically focus on the three men.

Black Nationalism and Resistance Literature

Having examined Black Nationalism in relation to the Black Church in the previous sections, the study turns to an examination of Black Nationalism as manifested through resistance literature. Free African-Americans in the North,

---

[154] Wilmore, 109.

rather than African-Americans in the South, took the lead in working out Black Nationalist ideology. This is probably due to the broader freedoms in the North, less hostility towards African-Americans, and greater educational opportunities.[155] Indeed, by the turn of the nineteenth century, there was a strong Independent Black Church Movement in the North, with its attendant leadership class and a small group of Northern African-American intellectuals.

From the Revolutionary War to the Civil War, resistance literature played an important role in fueling religiously inspired insurrections, and promoting the various manifestations of Black Nationalism. Resistance literature came in a variety of forms, including pamphlets, tracts, sermons, addresses, newspaper articles, and legislative and court petitions.[156] The literature usually embodies religious, political, and philosophical rationale that undermined the slave-system.[157] Wilmore identifies a

---

[155] Harding, 60 and Stuckey, 6.
[156] For the texts of Robert Young's *The Ethiopian Manifesto* (1829) and David Walker's *Appeal to the Coloured Citizens of the World* (1829), see Sterling Stuckey, *The Ideological Origins of Black Nationalism*. I will discuss both pamphlets later in this chapter.
[157] Wilmore, 34.

part of the religiously inspired, resistance literature that developed during the Pre-Abolitionist Period:

> The majority of these documents from the [P]re-[A]bolitionist [P]eriod, and many that resulted from organized activity of [B]lacks in the North, indicate the extent to which the slaves appealed from their religious convictions to the consciences of [W]hite religionists. Some of the earliest statements were voted on and distributed by African societies, counterparts of the Free African Society organized in Philadelphia by Richard Allen and Absolom Jones in 1787. The antislavery pronouncements of the first independent [B]lack [C]hurches, the sermons and addresses against slavery by [N]orthern [B]lack preachers, are all a part of this dissident literature. There were also the speeches of Christian laymen, such as James Forten of Philadelphia, and the articles and editorials of the first [B]lack newspaper *Freedom's Journal*, published in New York City by the Reverend Samuel E. Cornish and John B. Russwurm in 1827.[158]

Because of the anti-Black environment of the 1830's, the literature spawned a tendency towards Black solidarity and militancy.

---

[158] Ibid. 35.

From a firm foundation of independent Black churches, hostility towards the idea of colonization, as espoused by the American Colonization Society, increased. With the Antislavery Crusade, the rising feeling of Black consciousness, and a Black intellectual tradition in place, Sterling Stuckey reasoned that the creation of a Black Nationalist ideology was inevitable:

> As America approaches the fourth decade of the new century with sectional differences about to explode into bitter hostilities, all that remained was for the nationalist perspective on the condition of Black people to be fashioned into theory. With a deep dedication to African peoples at the center of their consciousness, with the contradictions between American practice and preachment startlingly evident in the [P]ost Revolutionary [P]eriod, two Black men, Robert Alexander Young and David Walker, speculated on the status of American peoples in a way which broke beyond the shackles which America sought to impose on the African mind. [Through the publication of Young's *Ethiopian Manifesto* and Walker's *Appeal* they] created a Black Nationalism ideology.[159]

---

[159] Stuckey, 6-7.

Robert Young (1780-1835), a free African-American of New York, wrote and published *The Ethiopian Manifesto* in February 1829. The Manifesto contained several key Black Nationalist elements: a focus on the oppressed status of Africans around the world, a prophesy of the coming of a Black Messiah, and the responsibility of Blacks for their own freedom.[160] The document expressed some of the earliest ideas about the connectedness of African peoples around the world and a call for an African reassemblage. Young, much like Nat Turner, experiences mystical visions which inspired him to prophesy about a Black Messiah who would unite all African peoples and liberate them from slavery:

> Of the degraded of this earth, shall be exalted one who shall draw from tee as tough gifted of power [D]ivine all attachment and regard of the slave towards thee . . . As came John the Baptist, of old, to spread abroad the forthcoming of his master, so alike are intended these our words, to denote to the [B]lack African or Ethiopian people, that God has prepared for them a leader, who awaits but his season to proclaim to them his birthright. How shall you know this man? By indubitable signs which cannot be

---

[160] Ibid. 30-38v

controverted by the power of mortals, his marks being stamped in open visage, as equally so upon his frame, which constitutes him to have been particularly regarded in the infinite work of God to man.[161]

Young made clear the responsibility of Blacks to seek their own freedom: "we know in ourselves we possess a right to see ourselves justified therefrom, of the right of God knowing but of [God's] power hath [God] decreed to man [sic] that either in himself [sic] he stands or by himself [sic] he falls."[162] While Young did not draw much attention as did David Walker, he was no less drastic.[163] In addition, Young set the tone for Black messianic deliverance figures among future Black revolutionaries.[164]

Another seminal Black Nationalist publication was *The Appeal to the Coloured Citizens of the World* by David Walker. Born free in Wilmington, North Carolina, Walker (1785-1830) left the South for New England because of the hostility towards free Blacks and his disgust for the slavery system. Settling in Boston, Massachusetts, Walker

---

[161] Ibid. 33.
[162] Ibid.
[163] Franklin, 247.
[164] There were elements of Messianic deliverance figures in three of the notable Black insurrections: Nat Turner, Denmark Vesey, and Gabriel Prosser.

published *The Appeal* in September 1829: The central purpose of Walker's work was "to awaken in the breasts of my afflicted degraded and slumbering brethren [sic] a spirit of inquiry and investigation respecting our miseries and wretchedness in the *Republican Land of Liberty!!!*"[165] Walker addressed several major themes that included a call for the unity of all African peoples from around the world and three themes that Vincent Harding puts into summary form: (1) the unavoidable judgement which a just God would bring upon the White American nation unless it repented and gave up its evil ways of injustice and oppression; (2) the imperative for Black people to face their own complicity in their own oppression, and the need for them to end that complicity through resistance in very possible way, including the path of armed resistance; and (3) the need for an essentially Protestant Christian religious undergirding for the Black struggle for justice.[166]

In speaking of the religious aspects of *The Appeal* observes that:

> Even more than the *Ethiopian Manifesto*, Walker's *Appeal* is steeped in biblical

---

[165] Ibid. 142.
[166] Harding, 86-87.

language and prophecy. It is one of the most remarkable religious documents of the Protestant era, rivaling in its righteous indignation and radicalism Luther's "Open Letter to the Christian Nobility of the German Nation," published in Wittenberg in 1520. A comparative study of these two documents reveals striking similarities. Both men were addressing themselves to their own oppressed and beleaguered people out of a last-ditch, desperate situation that called for the most basic alteration of the religious and civil order. Both believed that God had commanded them to pronounce judgment against powers that seemed almost as indestructible as they were corrupt. Both were aware that such audacity might cost them their lives.[167]

In the view of Vincent Harding, Walker's *Appeal* made distinctive contribution to Black Nationalism and its relation to the protest element in Black Religion through its great "notoriety gained through advocacy of Black messianic armed resistance to White oppression and slavery."[168] In addition, *The Appeal* prefigured most of the important Black Nationalist aspects in the twentieth century

---

[167] Wilmore, 38.
[168] Harding, 37.

and influenced most of the important Black Nationalist religious thinkers of the nineteenth century.[169]

Resistance literature served to keep African-Americans informed of the struggle, to inspire insurrections and other protests against slavery, to put political and social pressure upon the government, and to arouse the conscience of White Americans to abolish the slave-system.[170] The religious and moral underpinnings added a powerful dimension to the persuasive force of the literature.

Black Nationalism and the Negro Convention Movement

As the research of this study revealed earlier, Richard Allen organized a National Negro Convention in 1830 composed mainly of the free African-American leadership class and especially the ministers of the independent Black churches.[171] The two main purposes of the convention were to protest against the American Colonization Society and to make plans to elevate the

---

[169] Stuckey, 12-13.
[170] Dumond, 264-274.
[171] Howard Bell, *A survey of the Negro Convention Movement 1830-1861* (New York, N.Y.: The New York Times and Arno Press, 1969).

African-American race.[172] The conventions met annually
through the Civil War.

Dominated by the independent Black Church, the
Negro Conventions adopted the spirit of Black Nationalism
which was typical of the Independent Black Church
Movement. Wilmore explains the interrelatedness between
the independent Black Church and the Negro Convention
Movement and the fusion of the Black Nationalist spirit:

> In a sense, the convention was the secular
> adjunct of the [B]lack [C]hurch. It became
> ideologically autonomous in the 1830's, but
> its contribution to the growing radicalization
> of abolitionism in the 1840's and 1850's
> cannot be separated from the influence of
> [B]lack [R]eligion. It was the spirit of uplift
> and self-reliance cultivated in the
> independent churches that originally infused
> the convention movement and, for a brief
> interim when a White agenda dominated it,
> served to secularize and institutionalize the
> [B]lack [R]eligious impulse. What the
> convention movement indicated was that the
> spirit of the religiously inspired
> insurrections, of Walker's *Appeal*, and of
> Allen's withdrawal from the Methodist
> Episcopal Church, was dislodged from

---

[172] Ibid. 10-18; Leon Litwack and August Meier, eds., *Black Leaders of the Nineteenth Century* (Urbana: University of Illinois Press, 1988), 17.

domination by ministers and taken over the
intelligent and capable lay persons who were
both within and outside of the churches. The
[B]lack clergy in the predominantly [W]hite
[C]hurches found its true métier in that
company.[173]

In addition, the Negro Conventions seized the
national stage to showcase African-American intelligence
which was one of the cornerstones of the Black Nationalist
Movement.[174] Knowing that their meetings were under the
watchful eyes of American society, the Negro Convention
of 1832 went on recording saying:

> But how beautiful must the prospect be to the
> philanthropist, to view us, the children of
> persecution, grown to [adulthood],
> associating in our delegated character, to
> devise plans and means for our moral
> elevation, and attracting the attention of the
> wise and good, over the whole country, who
> are anxiously watching our deliberations.[175]

From the 1830's to Emancipation, the Abolitionist
Cause, self-help, education, temperance, and colonization

---

[173] Wilmore, 92.
[174] Bell, 27.; *Minutes and the Proceedings of the Second Annual
Convention for the Improvement of the Free People of Color in these
United States* (Philadelphia, 1832), 34.
[175] Quoted in Bell, 28.

emigration-responses were popular concerns. During the early 1840's, the conventions moved steadily towards African-American control. One of the popular advocates of this position was the militant Presbyterian minister, Henry Highland Garnet. He addressed the National Negro Convention of 1843 in Buffalo, New York, giving the most famous speech of his career, "An Address to the Slaves of America," where he called on slaves to resist slavery and resist through violence if necessary.[176]

While Garnet's speech failed to win the endorsement of the convention, his spirit of militancy and Black self-determination captured the hearts of a significant minority of the delegates. Garnet's agenda caused him to lose favor with William Lloyd Garrison, the eminent abolitionist, and the Garrisonians who felt threatened by Garnet's call for African-American control of the Negro convention.[177] Notwithstanding the criticism and the biracial split in the convention, Garnet continued to push for a Black resistance and Black self-determination agenda. Because of Garnet's pivotal role in the Black Nationalist

---

[176] Earl Ofari, *Let Your Motto be Resistance: The Life and Thought of Henry Highland Garnet* (Boston: Beacon Press, 1972), 144-159.
[177] Franklin, 241-245; Litwack, *North of Slavery*, 65-112, 217-246; and Ofari, 33-50.

Movement of the nineteenth century, he will figure prominently in Chapter three.

The significance of the Negro Conventions cannot be understated because of their importance in bringing together the African-American intelligentsia to uplift their race and to rally against the American Colonization Society. Primarily because of the last reason, the Negro Conventions will figure prominently in the next section.

Colonization-Emigration Responses

The idea of colonization began during the second decade of the nineteenth century. It was basically the presence of free African-Americans that spawned the idea of colonization among slave-owners.

Free African-Americans were anathema to slave-owners because a free African-American class called the slave-system into question and gave hope to slaves for their freedom. Free African-Americans were a constant threat for rebellion and offered proof of a successful and free African-American existence. Dwight Dumond explains the slave-owners' fear of free African-Americans:

The mere existence North or South of free Negroes was a constant torment to slaveholders. Their presence in a slave community increased the individual slaveholder's problem. Marriages between slaves and free Negroes, though not recognized by law or by the churches, created all sorts of difficulties, particularly absences and running away. The mere presence of Negroes who were free, increased the slave's desire for freedom. They constituted a potential source of conspiracy and insurrection. They were proof of the Negroes' ability to profess a denial of [their] animal status. The slave states simply refused to countenance any program of assistance to these people. They tried to discourage manumissions. They tried to force free Negroes to move out. They finally tried to get them back into slavery. The objective always was to strengthen slavery, not to aid the Negro.[178]

Not only were free African-Americans anathema to slave-owners, but a problem to Northern Whites as well. Both the White politicians and the White working class kept a suspicious watch over the free African-American community, fearing Black political clout and competition for industrial employment.[179] It is out of this background

---

[178] Dumond, 127
[179] Wilmore, 101.

that free African-Americans were anathema to slave-owners in the South, and a cause for White hysteria in the North, and herein Wilmore finds motives for White American's idea of colonization:

> In the North the specter of [B]lack franchise and competition for industrial jobs was combined with racial prejudice. In the South the [W]hites feared [B]lack inundation a consequent rebellion of slaves. The very existence of a community of free [B]lacks, such as in Charleston and Richmond, reminded those who were still in bondage that slavery was not a natural and necessary condition of all; [B]lacks, and "uppity" and querulous free [B]lacks represented a potential seedbed of conspiracy and insurrection. The problem of what to do with the [B]lacks was, therefore, conveniently if fraudulently solved by the idea of African of West Indian colonization. Both those [W]hites who favored slavery and those who were genuinely opposed to it found common cause in the proposal to remove this source of embarrassment and danger and, perhaps, salve their consciences about Africa at the same time.[180]

---

[180] Ibid.

Wilmore makes the claim, however, that colonization or repatriation was an African-American idea inspired by the continuity of ex-slaves who escaped American slavery and returned to Africa. Wilmore explains:

> Almost from the beginning of slavery in the New World, a process of repatriation and colonization back to Africa made it possible for a few slaves, who by one means or another had secured their freedom, to return to their homeland from South America and the Caribbean, and later from the English colonies in North America. The reverse movement facilitated the development of an early relationship between [B]lacks in the New World and those who remained in Africa. During the Revolutionary War thousands of slaves who escaped to the British forces, or who had been liberated by loyalists, made their way to Canada and Nova Scotia, to the West Indies, or to the coastal areas of the South American mainland. Some of them later recrossed the Atlantic to take up their lives again in West Africa.[181]

In *Black Exodus: Black Nationalism and Back to Africa Movements, 1890-1910*, Edwin Redkey agrees with

---

[181] Ibid. 99.

the spirit of Wilmore's idea that the African Emigration Tradition began long before the founding of the American Colonization Society in 1816.[182] Redkey's research, however, revealed very little evidence to support the claim:

> Because most slaves were illiterate, few documents tell of their desire to return to Africa. Some Africans, however, had been educated in the tradition before being enslaved and sent across the Atlantic, and several such [persons] left autobiographies in Arabic. Each of them considered Africa [their] true home and a promised land of freedom from slavery.[183]

Redkey sides with Frazier in the Frazier-Herskovitz debate as to how much Africanism survived American acculturation and the extent to which African-Americans held ties to Africa. Redkey reasoned that very few ties persisted among later generations of slaves and free Africa-Americans.[184]

Samuel Hopkins (1721-1803), a White New England minister, was one of the first to devise a colonization plan. In 1759 he proposed to send educated

---

[182] Organized by a group of leading citizens from Washington, D.C. and Virginia, the Society was formed for the purpose of colonizing free African-Americans. See p. 60 of this study.

[183] Redkey, *Black Exodus*, 16.

[184] Ibid. 17.

African-Americans to Africa to spread the Christian Gospel among the unconverted.[185]

One of the first African-Americans to put the idea of colonization into form was Paul Cuffee (1759-1817), a New England ship owner.[186] Cuffee approached the colonization idea through a dual focus: looking at commerce between African-Americans and Sierra Leoneans and expecting commerce to lead to repatriation of a significant number of free African-Americans. Consequently, Christianity would gain an important threshold in West Africa. Cuffee brought the plan to fruition in 1815 by taking nine families and thirty-eight persons to Sierra Leone.[187]

In his efforts to establish links with the independent Black churches, Wilmore maintains that Cuffee's venture was a result of his relationship with the Philadelphia Free African Society. Wilmore identified Cuffee with a "small group of Blacks in Massachusetts who made contact with the Free African Society of Philadelphia and founded the first African Baptist and Methodist churches in Massachusetts and Rhode Island."[188] Infused with a spirit

---

[185] Wilmore, 101.
[186] Ibid. 100.
[187] Ibid.
[188] Wilmore, 100.

of Black Nationalism gained through the relationship with the Free African Society, coupled with his own business talents, Cuffee began the mission work in Africa.[189] In addition to a relation with Black Nationalism, Wilmore maintains that Cuffee's activities were a prelude to twentieth century Pan-Africanism:

> Influences flowing from men such as Captain Cuffee, from the missionary aspirations of the new [B]lack [C]hurches in the United States and the West Indies, from political developments and anti-slavery agitation on both sides of the Atlantic, circulated back and forth and generated quite early a spirit of incipient [B]lack consciousness and anti-colonialism more than a hundred years before what came to be known as the Pan-African movement against European colonialism.[190]

Wilmore thus maintains that there is a clear relation between the radical tradition in Black Religion and the origins of Black Nationalism, colonization, and Pan-Africanism.

---

[189] Ibid.
[190] Ibid.

Redkey makes the claim, however, that color became the most obvious inheritance from the parentland.[191] He reasoned that both skin color and persistent, pervasive oppression served to remind African-Americans of their marginal connection to American society. While wanting to be an integral part of the American nation, skin color and pervasive discrimination reminded African-Americans that Africa was their distinctive heritage.[192] Hence, when liberation came to many slaves during and after the American Revolution, a return to the parentland became a popular idea based more upon vestigial emigration sentiments, rather than on Wilmore's idea of a direct connection to Africa.[193]

Wilmore maintains that the American Colonization Society, and the founding of Liberia in 1822, grew out of Samuel Hopkins' plan to repatriate Blacks to Africa and proselytize the Christian Religion.[194] John Hope Franklin observed that Cuffe's African venture brought the idea of emigration to the national forefront:

---

[191] Redkey, 17.
[192] Ibid.
[193] Ibid.
[194] Wilmore, 101.

Perhaps nothing brought colonization before the country more dramatically than the carrying of the thirty-eight Negroes to Africa in 1815 by Paul Cuffee, at his own expense. His act suggested what might be done if more people, or even the government, became interested. It suggested, too, that Negroes themselves were interested in leaving the United States.[195]

Both the federal and a state government tried to inaugurate colonization between 1777 and 1800 through ideas proposed by Governor James Madison of Virginia and President Thomas Jefferson, but the ideas failed and were dormant until Henry Clay revived them during the second decade of the nineteenth century.[196] In 1816 the Virginia legislature initiated the legal effort for colonization by requesting its governor to make representation to the President of the United States for a distinct U.S. territory for African-Americans or for a place abroad, but Congress failed to act on the request. It was unclear whether the move was to be coerced or voluntary. A short time after the formal request, several leading citizens of Washington, D.C. met to form the American Society for Colonizing the Free

---

[195] Franklin, 235.
[196] Dumond.

People of Color of the United States, which came to be called the American Colonization Society, or the ACS.[197] The Society's constitution stated its purpose as being:

> To promote and execute a plan for colonizing (with their consent) the free people of color, residing in our country, in Africa, or such other places as Congress shall deem most expedient. And the Society shall act to effect this object in cooperation with the general government and such of the states may adopt regulations upon the subject.[198]

While there were varied responses to colonization among African Americans, a strong opposition movement developed among free African-Americans in the North. Two of the most vocal colonization opponents were Bishop Allen and Reverend James Forten (1776-1842).[199] John

---

[197] Ibid.

[198] Quoted in Dumond. See also "The First Annual Report of the American Society for Colonizing the Free People of Color of the United States," (Washington, D.C., 1818).

[199] Born of free Black parents in Philadelphia, James Forten (1777-1842) became a wealthy sailsmaker. Forten used his fortune to promote equal rights for African-Americans. He vigorously opposed the ACS and became a leading member of the Abolitionist Movement. For a brief Forten biography, see "James Forten" in Charlotte Forten, *The Journal of Charlotte Forten: A Free Negro in the Slave Era* (London: Collier-MacMillan, 1969), 6-14.

Hope Franklin described a meeting of the Allen-Forten opposition party in saying:

> Three thousand Negroes of Philadelphia led by Richard Allen and James Forten met in 1817 and registered their objections to colonization urging humane and benevolent inhabitants of Philadelphia to reject the scheme altogether. They branded it an outrage having no other object in view than the benefit of the salve holding interests of the country.[200]

Leon F. Litwack observed the concerns of the same meeting:

> One month after the organization of the Colonization Society, approximately three thousand Negroes crowded into Philadelphia's Bethel Church to give their reply: the colonization scheme violated professed American principles, it sought to stigmatize the free Negro population, and it countenanced the perpetuation of human bondage and encouraged it by seeking to remove the free [B]lacks. Under these circumstances, it deserved to be repudiated by all Negroes, who should, instead, reaffirm their determination never to part voluntarily from their enslaved [brothers

---

[200] Franklin, 237.

and sisters]. As for those Negroes who
endorsed the idea, a subsequent protest
meeting denounced them as "a few obscure
and dissatisfied stranger among us . . . in
favor of being made president, governors,
and principals in Africa."[201]

Because their ancestors were among the pioneer

laborers who helped to build America and because the

Republic stood on the principles of freedom and equality,

the convention resolved that:

> We view with deep abhorrence the
> unmerited stigma attempted to be cast upon
> the reputation of the free people of color, by
> the promoters of this measure, "that they
> are a dangerous and useless part of the
> community," when the state of
> disenfranchisement in which they live, in
> the hour of danger they ceased top
> remember their wrongs, and rallied around
> the standard of their country . . . That we
> never will separate ourselves voluntarily
> from the slave population in this country;
> they are our [brothers and sisters] by the
> ties of consanguinity, of suffering, and of
> wrong; and we feel that there is more virtue
> in suffering privations with them, than
> fancied advantages for a season.[202]

---

[201] Litwack, 24-25; Quoted in *The Liberator.*
[202] Lerone Bennett, *The Shaping of the Black American* (Chicago:
Johnson Publishing Co., 1975), 133.

Many African-American religious leaders were militant in their posture towards the Society. The opponents threatened violent resistance if forced to leave America and reminded the Society that African-American military persons fought during the Revolutionary War. Benjamin Quarles gives two examples:

> Peter Williams, pastor of St. Phillips Episcopal Church in New York, [said] . . . "We are natives of this country, we only ask that we be treated as well as foreigners. Not a few of our fathers and mothers suffered and bled to purchase its independence; we ask only to be treated as well as those who fought against it." . . . In a speech at the African Masonic Hall in Boston, the deeply religious Maria W. Stewart . . . strongly rebuked the colonization society vowing that before she would be driven to a strange land "the bayonet shall pierce me through."[203]

While not militant like Peter Williams or Maria Stewart, Bishop Allen articulated a patriotic argument: "[t]his land which we have watered with our tears and our blood, is now

---

[203] Benjamin Quarles, quoted in Carter G. Woodson, *Negro Orators and Their Orations* (Washington, D.C.: Associated Publishers, 1925), 80. For Mrs. Steward, see Lillian O'Connor, *Pioneer Woman Orators: Rhetoric in the Antebellum Reform Movement* (New York, N.Y.: Columbia University Press, 1954), 54-58.

our mother country and we are well satisfied to stay where wisdom abounds and the [G]ospel is free."[204]

The hostility towards the Society spread quickly throughout free African-American communities in the North. Benjamen Quarles explains some of the colonization concerns that troubled the opponents of the Society:

> As initially voiced by the Philadelphia Negroes, and adopted quickly by those elsewhere, the opposition to African colonization resulted from the evil effects it would have on all Negroes, slave and free. Colonization would cause a rise in the price of slaves, thus making it less likely that they would be freed. Colonization would make slavery more secure by removing the free Negro—a source of discontent to the slave and his possible ally in Rebellion. Moreover, free Negroes who went to Africa would be turning their backs on the slave."[205]

---

[204] Albert J. Raboteau, "Richard Allen and the African Church Movement," in Litwack and Meier, 16. Ironically, Richard Allen, one of the co-conveners of the first National Negro Convention, where he vigorously opposed ACS's colonization scheme, was the principal endorser of a revolution adopted by the 1830 Negro Convention favoring the forming a settlement in upper-Canada for fugitive slaves.
[205] Quarles, 5-6.

In addition to the rationale that Quarles explains, Wilmore reasons that the Paternalism of the Society in thinking that they could think for African-Americans and the refusal of the Society to reject slavery on its face based upon biblical, moral and humanitarian grounds so outraged free African-Americans:

> It was the arrogance of the [W]hites, their miscalculations of the self-esteem of free [B]lacks and their feeling of solidarity with the slaves, rather than aversion of the idea of emigration that made [B]lack leaders repudiate the ACS. It was the talk of "Negro inferiority" and "degradation," the obvious attempt by the colonization to dodge the question of the immorality of slavery, and the overenthusiastic participation of the slaveholders themselves in what purported to be a benevolent scheme, that turned the free communities in the North against the colonization proposal. They were well aware of the illogic of [W]hites wanting to do "a great good" for a people they despised while continuing to hold their relatives and friends in chains.[206]

As noted earlier, in 1830 Bishop Allen organized a National Negro Convention composed mainly of the Free

---

[206] Wilmore, 102.

African-American leadership class and especially the ministers of the independent Black churches. This was the first of several National Negro Conventions that would be held through the Civil War.[207] Harry V. Richardson reveals the two main purposes of the convention: first to issue a "positive statement against the American Colonization Society, that is the movement that was started in 1816 to send Negroes back to Africa," second to plan means "for "the speedy elevation of ourselves and brothers and sisters to the scale of standing [men and women]."[208] To call such a convention was an audacious venture but because of Bishop Allen's national stature and his positive relationship with the independent Black churches, the effort was a large success.

The Negro Conventions served as a national forum to display African-American leadership and as a pulpit to rally against the Society. By 1839 there was a large class of intelligent and articulate free African-Americans who were willing to address Black concerns in an open forum. Howard Bell explains:

---

[207] Howard Bell, ed., *Minutes of the Proceedings of the National Negro Convention, 1830-1864* (New York, N.Y.: The New York Times and Arno Press, 1964).
[208] Richardson, 94-95

One of the important aspects of the first few
years of the conventions was the emergence
of the Negro on the national stage, where
his [or her] hopes and aspirations could be
known, and where the intelligent part of the
community could have a chance to evaluate
their accomplishments and their slow but
steady climb toward commanding the
respect of [their White brothers and sisters].
The [Negroes] used the convention to
display [their] wares knowing that they
were being watched.[209]

The convention dominated by Black Church men
and women had particular condemnation for the ACS.
Bishop Allen presented a well-developed argument against
the idea of colonization. Noting that the Society planned to
use African-Americans, Allen reasoned that African-
Americans were lacking both religious and secular
education to perform the tasks. Allen saw growth in
American's future through the settlement and domestication
of the frontier region and ever-expanding industries that
called to Europe for farm and industrial labor. The idea of
sending away a ready-made labor force which had

---

[209] Howard Bell, ed., *A Survey of the Negro Convention Movement,*
1830-1861 (New York, N.Y.; The New York Times and Arno Press),
27.

performed much of the initial work was, for Allen, unfair, unchristian, and illogical and without prudent business sense.   While the Society maintained that its purposes were the education and evangelization of Africa, Allen felt that the true purpose of the Society was to promote a colonization scheme and to rid the country of free African-Americans so that slaves would not be inspired by them.[210]

There was strong consistent opposition to the Society until Liberia became an independent colony in 1847.[211]   By 1831 the Negro Convention equated the Society's colonization efforts with forced slavery. Moreover, many African-Americans reasoned that the colonization scheme sullied their contribution to the Revolutionary War effort.   An excerpt from a resolution adopted at the convention expressed the delegates' disgust with the Society:

> The Convention has not been unmindful
> of the operations of the American
> Colonization Society, and it would . . .
> suggest to that . . . body . . . that, in our
> humble opinion . . . they are pursuing the
> direct road to perpetuate slavery . . . and, as

---

[210] Litwack and Meier, 15-16.
[211] Bell, 27.

citizens . . . whose best blood is sapped to gain popularity for that Institution, we would . . . beg of them to desist. Many of our [parents] and some of us, have fought and bled for the liberty, and independence, and peace which you now enjoy; and surely, it would be ungenerous and unfeeling in you to deny us an humble and quiet grave in that country which gave us birth![212]

In 1833 the convention reiterated its opposition to the Society, finding the Society's efforts inconsistent with the Christian doctrine of universal brotherhood and sisterhood:

After having divested ourselves of all unreasonable prejudice, and reviewed the whole ground of our opposition to the American Colonization Society . . . we still declare to the world, that we are unable to arrive at any conclusion, than that the life-giving principles of the association are totally repugnant to the spirit of true benevolence.[213]

The Negro Convention gave half-hearted support to a Canadian emigration project in 1831 and every year

---

[212] Bell, *Minutes of the Proceedings*, 15.
[213] Ibid. 27.

thereafter the emigration movement lost support. In 1832 the Convention decided to adopt the position taken by the Reverend Samuel Cornish (1795-1858), co-editor of *Freedom's Journal*, who three years earlier found that "any extensive emigration would weaken the position of those who remained behind."[214] By 1833 emigration to Haiti was as undesirable as emigration to Africa. The convention concluded that "there is not now and probably never will be actual necessity for large emigration of the present race of free coloured people."[215] The Convention gave priority to Canada over Haiti for those seeking asylum.[216]

While the early Negro Conventions condemned the Society, there was always a desire on the part of the African-American clergy to carry the Gospel abroad to their African brothers and sisters. Dr. Josephus Coan, the foremost

---

[214] Bell, *Survey of the Negro Convention*, 32.

[215] Ibid. African-Americans were not as negative to the idea of emigration to the Western United States, Canada, or parts of the Caribbean as to the idea of colonization to Africa (Bell, 29). The idea of emigration may be distinguished from the idea of colonization in that the former was a Black Nationalist response to White oppression, while the latter was the White community's plan to eliminate African-Americans from the United States (Redkey, 16). There were strong sentiments at the first Negro Convention to secure a safe haven for fugitive slaves seeking asylum outside the United States and to secure land for African-Americans who desired emigration to places where slavery was illegal (Bell, 29).

[216] Ibid. 27-32.

African Methodist Episcopal missiologist, found two compelling convictions that motivated African-Americans to participate in Christian missions:

(1) The sense of obligation to respond in obedience to the mandates of our Lord Jesus Christ as found in the four Gospels and the book of Acts.

(2) The sense of a special duty to spread the Gospel among the people of African descent wherever they could be reached.[217]

Central to the idea of redeeming Africa was the theory that African-Americans were in an excellent position to civilize and evangelize the continent because of the benefits gained through contact with American society. There was also the idea that African-Americans were better suited than their White brothers and sisters to perform missionary work among the indigenous people.

There were a few African-American ministers who supported the idea of colonization independent of the Society and a small cadre worked closely with the Society.

---

[217] Josephus Coan, "Redemption of Africa: The Vital Impulse of Black American Overseas Missionaries," *Journal of the Interdenominational Theological Center* (Spring 74): 27.

The former group included Paul Cuffee and John Kizzel.[218]

James Forten, who had co-convened with Richard Allen the first Negro Convention, held privately to the idea of the inevitability of emigration because America would not allow African-Americans to reach racial equality.[219] These persons were not so much opposed to the idea of emigration as they "resented the belittling attitude of the Society and could not leave their brothers and sisters who would be left to fight oppression alone."[220] In Wilmore's view, Richard Allen and the other leaders resented:

> the coercive, high-handed methods of the [W]hites—who once again wanted to speak and act for [B]lacks. Although they recognized the need of many African-Americans to be relocated in a land where the laws and prejudices of society [would] have no effect in retarding their advancement to the summit of civil and religious improvement, they refused to be settled "in any place which [was] not the object of their choice."[221]

---

[218] Wilmore, 99-100.

[219] Bracey, Meier, and Rudwick, 46.

[220] Ibid.

[221] Wilmore, 103.

The latter group that included Lott Carey, Daniel Coker and Alexander Crummell, circumvented the Society's Paternalism and the public notion that emigration abandoned the slaves and developed a cooperative relation with the Society. Wilmore reveals this group's motivation and intrigue:

> Black [C]hurch leaders could never quite divorce their desire to carry the Gospel to their unconverted brothers and sisters in the West Indies and Africa from a candid recognition of the intolerable condition of [B]lack life in America and the chance that there might be a better life abroad. Despite their public opposition to the idea of running away from the challenges at home, the missionary implications of the offers held by the ACS and other state and local colonization groups continued to intrigue many.[222]

One of the Society's first agents was the Reverend Lott Carey (1780?-1828) of Richmond, Virginia.[223] Born of slave parents, Carey purchased his freedom in 1813 through wages earned from work in a tobacco shipping

---

[222] Ibid.
[223] William Poe, "Lott Carey: Man of Purchased Freedom," *Church History* 39 (March 1970): 49-61.

company. He received a license to preach in 1815 through a White church—the First Baptist Church in Richmond, Virginia. Coming into contact with Luther Rice, a distinguished White Baptist missionary, Carey was inspired to help form the Richmond Baptist Missionary Society.

Carey's African interest was aroused through his association with the Baptist General Convention and the Richmond African Missionary Society. His African interest was further stimulated through reading the *Journal* (1819), a publication by Samuel Mills, Jr., an agent of the American Colonization Society who detailed his daily experiences as a missionary to Sierra Leone.[224] Carey had little enthusiasm for the colonization polices of the ACS, but he recognized the excellent opportunities to promote African evangelism through the resources of the Society. Carey was inspired to perform missionary work among the Africans through his longing "to preach the way of life and salvation to the poor Africans."[225]

Carey sailed in 1821 with a small group of African-Americans to West Africa. Carey's group sailed under the

---

[224] Logan and Winston, *American Negro Biography*, 96.
[225] Ibid. 52.

cooperative sponsorship of the American Colonization Society, the Richmond Missionary Society, and the Triennial Baptist Convention.[226] Carey worked untiringly in Sierra Leone and Liberia, carrying the Gospel to indigenous Africans and building American settlements among the African-American emigrants until his death in 1828.[227]

Another early agent of the Society was Daniel Coker (1780-1846), a highly intelligent AME pastor.[228] Born of mixed parentage on the Eastern shore of Maryland, Coker was classified as a slave. He received a good elementary education while accompanying his free half-brother to school as his servant. Coker escaped to New York State, where he enhanced his education and became a licensed Methodist minister. In 1800 Coker moved to Baltimore and became pastor of the independent African Methodist Bethel Society. In 1816 he joined with Richard Allen to organize the AME denomination.

---

[226] Ibid. 51-52.
[227] Ibid. 61.
[228] Josephus Coan, "Daniel Coker 19th Century Black Church Organizer, Educator, and Missionary," *Journal of the Interdenominational Theological Center* 3 (Fall 1975): 17-31.

Elected the church's first Bishop, he declined the honor the next day in favor of Richard Allen.[229]

Coker and a small group of African-Americans landed in Sierra Leone in 1820. Coker saw colonization as both an opportunity for a better way of life and a chance to being the Christian Gospel to Africa.[230] For the next fifteen years, until his death, Coker worked untiringly in those regards.

> Coker revealed his hopes for Africa
> in a letter to a Baltimore friend:
> What darkness has covered the minds of the
> people . . . There are hundreds of people
> who are as ignorant of God as the brutes
> who perish . . . I do believe it will be a great
> nation, and a powerful and worthy nation;
> but those who break the way will suffer
> much.[231]

Another prominent supporter of African emigration was Alexander Crummell (1819-1898), the intellectual

---

[229] There are two views concerning the reason why Coker declined the Bishopric. According to one view, Coker felt that Allen deserved the office more than he. See Charles Wesley, *Richard Allen: Apostle of Freedom* (Washington, D.C.: The Associated Publishers, 1969), 152. According to another view, the delegates thought Coker too fair-skinned to lead a Black Organization. See Payne, 100-101.

[230] Wilmore, 104.

[231] Quoted in Bracey, Meier, and Rudwick, 47.

Episcopal priest.[232] Born in 1819 in New York City to free parents, Crummell enjoyed a secure, comfortable life. He received a good elementary, high school, and college education. It was a Queen's Collee in England that Crummell received the call to the Episcopal priesthood.

Crummell vacillated between support and opposition for his idea of colonization during his early public career. In 1840 he opposed a resolution condemning the idea of emigration to Africa. "By 1844 he had become a vigorous opponent of colonization efforts, arguing that Blacks in the United States had been brought there by God, with the result that they had become 'citizens of this land integral portions of this republic.'"[233]

During the first part of his stay in England, Crummell continued this disdain for the idea of colonization of the American Colonization Society in particular. By 1853 Crummell made a significant shift in support of the Society. Crummell chose not to return to the United States but to emigrate to Liberia under the auspices of the Society.[234]

---

[232] Alfred Moss, "Alexander Crummell: Black Nationalism and Apostle of Western Civilization," in Litwack and Meier, 247-251.
[233] Ibid. 242.
[234] Ibid.

There was a combination of reasons that led to
Crummell's emigration to Liberia. Prominent among them
were Crummell's association with President Roberts of
Liberia and with other Liberian citizens while studying in
England.[235] Founded by the American Colonization
Society in 1816, Liberia, West Africa, and American
Colony established for African-Americans who wanted to
emigrate to the parentland, became an independent country
in 1847.[236]

Crummell's theological motivation for emigration
focused on the regeneration and Evangelization of Africa.
He reasoned that God chose the talented tenth of people of
African descent living in the Americas for the work of
African evangelism. Making this point in a sermon,
"Emigration, an Aid to the Evangelization of Africa," he
said:

> This continent [Africa] is to be reclaimed
> for Christ. The faith of Jesus is to
> supersede all the abounding desolation of
> heathenism . . . In this work the [C]olored
> populations of America are largely to
> participate. They, whether living on the

---

[235] Wilson Moses, *Alexander Crummell: A Study of Civilization and Discontent* (New York, N.Y.: Oxford University Press, 1989), 85.
[236] See Christian Cassel, *Liberia: History of the First African Republic* (New York, N.Y.: Fountainhead Publishers, 1970); Franklin, 238-239.

mainland, in the states; or residing as inhabitants of the Antilles; or dwelling in the Brazilian Empire; are to be active agents of God for the salvation of Africa.[237]

Crummell devoted twenty years of his life to Liberia as a missionary and a school teacher, and to the cause of African Nationalism. Because of his importance for this study, Crummell will figure prominently in Chapter Four.

Notwithstanding their ties to the American Colonization Society, the first group of the Society's missionaries to Africa planted there the foundation for future Black churches. The early missionary efforts served to broaden horizons and introduce new visions and bold endeavors for the next wave of African-American missionary efforts to Africa. In addition, the early missionaries built the foundation upon which a "Black Theology of missionary emigration and self-determination" would be developed.[238]

Martin Delany (1812-1885): The Father of Black Nationalism

---

[237] Alex Crummell, *Africa and America: Addresses and Discourses* (Springfield, Massachusetts: Wiley and Co., 1981), 421.
[238] Wilmore, 109.f

Born in West Virginia May 6, 1812, Martin Delany was the son of Samuel Delany, a slave, and Pati Delany, a free African-American. The five Delany children were taught to read by a Yankee peddler. When the Whites in the community discovered this, they threatened the Delany's with imprisonment. Because of the persecution, the Delany's moved to Chambersburg, Pennsylvania, a Northern city.[239]

At age nineteen, Delany moved to Pittsburgh where he studied in a school sponsored by a local AME church. He immediately became a leader in the Black community, working with the Pittsburgh Anti-Slavery Society and the Underground Railroad. Elected a delegate to the New York Negro Convention in 1836, Delany began a close association with the influential clergypersons of the day.[240]

In 1843, Delany married Catherine Richards, granddaughter of one of the wealthiest African-Americans in Pittsburgh. Shortly after the marriage, Delany began publishing the *Pittsburgh Mystery*, a weekly publication of African-American news in the Pittsburgh area. The

---

[239] Nell Irvin Painter, "Martin R. Delany: Elitism and Black Nationalism," in Litwack and Meier, *Black Leaders of the Nineteenth Century*, 150-151.
[240] Ibid. 151-154.

newspaper was short-lived, however, because of lack of financial support. Delany then moved to Rochester, New York, and co-edited the "North Star" with Frederick Douglass. During 1847 Delany toured the mid-west, speaking to anti-slavery societies. It was both the co-editorship of the *North Star* and the speaking tour that vaulted Delany into national prominence.[241]

Because the paper was unable to support two editors, Delany resigned in 1848 to resume his medical studies. He returned to Pittsburgh to study medicine under two of Pittsburgh's leading physicians. Rejected by medical schools both in New York and Pennsylvania, Delany was later admitted to the medical program at Harvard. Not more than a month into his studies, Delany met stiff opposition from several students and faculty who resented an African-American. Forced to leave Harvard, Delany returned to Pittsburgh and resumed his medical practice.

By 1850 Delany was a disappointed man. He had seen the Fugitive Slave Act of 1850 strengthen the position of the slave holders. He had experienced dismissal from Harvard and the failure of White abolitionists to protest the

---

241

expulsion. He began to question whether Blacks ought to continue to live in the United States.

Delany's frustration drove him to a room in New York where he re-evaluated the Black status. The period of seclusion provided the opportunity to write *The Condition and Elevation Emigration and Destiny of the Colored People of the United States Politically Considered*, Delany's first full-length formulation of Black Nationalism. *The Condition* set forth Delany's ideas of elevation, emigration, and Black Theology.[242] Borrowing from the Jacksonian ethic of the self-made person that had infused the National Negro Convention Movement, Delany advocated a philosophy of self-reliance for African-American improvement. He, like Alexander Crummell, reasoned that African-Americans had to elevate themselves through cultural, business, and religious achievements.[243]

In his article, "Martin R. Delany: Elitism and Black Nationalism," Nell Irvin Painter explained Delany's idea of elevation:

---

[242] Martin R. Delany, *The Condition Elevation Emigration and Destiny of the Colored People of the United States Politically Considered* (Philadelphia: 1852).
[243] Litwack and Meier, 152; see Crummell's idea of elevation in Chapter Four of this study.

He defined elevation to include the acquisition of gentlemanly culture and correct speech, of upright morals, independent thought, and "manly" religion (as opposed to religiosity, which he distained as servile). Elevation meant achievement that would earn the world's applause, such as owning a successful business or governing a prosperous nation. Delany wanted for his people the sort of collective self-respect that he thought only education, wealth, and recognition would secure."[244]

For free African-Americans, Delany proposed elevation through business success: "let our young men and women prepare themselves for usefulness trading and other thing s of importance . . . educate them for the store and the counting house . . . to do every day practical business."[245] For slaves, Delany proposed that they dare to strike the first blow for freedom.[246] The self-assertive act would allow slaves to rise in Delany's view "a captive redeemed from the portals of infamy to the true dignity of their nature . . . elevated [freed persons]."[247]

---

[244] Litwack and Meier, 152.
[245] Lerone Bennett, *The Shaping of Black American,* 295.
[246] Litwack and Meier.
[247] Ibid.

Reasoning that the African-American intelligentsia were ordained to help elevate the race, Delany's ideas of intelligence and elevation were closely related. Painter explains:

> He never questioned his assumption that the most intelligent of the race—however defined—should decide what the masses should do, and he saw unquestioning acceptance of "intelligent" leadership as the duty of the masses . . . "intelligent" was the most common adjective in Delany's vocabulary . . . he used it to connote common sense, leadership, education, cultured deportment, and independence of mind, the same qualities that characterized a people who had achieved "elevation." Intelligence was the means of acquiring elevation on the individual level; it was the psychological precondition for elevation. Intelligence and elevation ensured respect that gained the respect of others, which Delany valued tremendously.[248]

There were two important dimensions of Delany's Black Theology: (1) self-help and self-reliance and (2) the idea of racial redemption.[249] While a Christian, Delany

---

[248] Ibid. 156.
[249] Wilmore, 111-113.

separated the ideas of the spiritual and the practical. Though believing in the power of prayer, Delany advocated working towards one's goals as well. He had little use for praying, do-nothing Christians. Wilmore explained Delany's prayer-work ethic in saying:

> Delany reasoned that the right use of religion required an understanding of its function and limitations as ordained by God . . . [For Delany] "God helps those who help themselves" . . . Hence, said Delany, a spiritual blessing is to be prayed for, a moral good sought by exercising one's sense of justice, and a physical end requires the use of might and muscle.[250]

Delany promoted the idea of racial redemption which expressed the liberating activity of God in favor of the oppressed. The idea of racial redemption joined the power of God with liberating activity of the oppressed to restore Black people to a position of greatness. This perspective has long been a part of the Black Religious experience because Africans recognized the power of religion and brought the idea to America.[251] The Africans

---

[250] Ibid. 110.
[251] John S. Mbiti, *Introduction of African Religion* (London: Heinemann Educational Books, Ltd., 1969), 44-46.

fused the power inherent in religion with the call for a just

social order by the prophets of the Old Testament. Delany

prefigured the National Council of Black Churchpersons

who composed this comprehensive definition of Black

Theology in 1980:

> Black Theology is a theology of liberation .
> .. The message of liberation is the
> revelation of God in Jesus Christ. Freedom
> is the Gospel. Jesus is the liberator! The
> demand that Christ the Liberator imposes
> on all [persons] requires all Blacks to affirm
> their full dignity as [human beings] and all
> Whites to surrender their presumptions of
> superiority and abuses of power.[252]

Indeed, Delany was highly critical of the Black

Church for accepting a White interpretation of Christianity

that tended to thwart Black progress. Delany reasoned that

the African-Americans were capable of developing their

own hermeneutics to fit their existential situation. Writing

in his book, *The Condition*, Delany said:

> We no longer slaves, believing any
> interpretation that our oppressors may give

---

[252] James Cone and Gayraud Wilmore, *Black Theology A Documentary History, 1966-1979* (Maryknoll, N.Y.: Orbis Books, 1979), 101.

the word of God, for the purpose of
deluding us to the more easy subjugation;
but [free people], compromising some of
the first minds of intelligence and
rudimental qualifications, in the country.
What then is the remedy, for our
degradation and oppression? This appears
now to be the only remaining question—the
means of successful elevation in this our
native land? This depends entirely upon the
application of the means of Elevation.[253]

Because Delany recognized the crucial role of the
church in empowering the masses of African-American
people, he was unable to support other-worldly teachings or
spiritual means that did little to equip African-Americans to
deal with their existential situation. Delany made a
distinctive contribution of Black Religion and Black
Nationalism through fusing the ideas of self-help, self-
reliance, and radical redemption in order to move African-
Americans toward liberation.

Refusing to allow his disappointments to stifle his
active participation in the Abolition Movement, Delany

---

[253] Wilmore, *Black Religion and Black Radicalism*, III who quotes
Delany's *The Condition*, 38.

traveled abroad in 1858.[254] He went both to West Africa and London seeking help for the American Abolition Movement and a place for freed African-Americans. Delany secured a place in what is now Nigeria for a colony and support of British officials for intercontinental trade between London and the new colony.

The beginning of the Civil War in 1861 brought Delany back to Canada. While wanting to be involved in the war effort, he refused to live in the United States while it supported slavery. It was not until President Lincoln signed the Emancipation Proclamation that Delany decided to return home. Offering his skills and popularity to the Union, he became a recruiter for the Fifty-Fourth Massachusetts Regiment and the Black units. In February 1865, Delany met with President Lincoln to present a plan to arm slaves behind the enemy lines. While the plan was rejected, the President offered Delany a commission in the Army. Accepting the rank of Major, he thus became the first Black field officer.

Assigned to Charleston, South Carolina, Major Delany raised two units of ex-slaves. Remaining in South

---

[254] Rayford W. Logan and Michael R. Winston, eds., *Dictionary of American Negro Biography* (New York, N.Y.: W.W. Norton and Company, 1982), 169-172.

Carolina at the end of the war, he became a commissioner with the Freedpersons Bureau assigned to Hilton Head Island. Delany mustered out of the service in 1868 and immediately plunged into South Carolina Reconstruction politics. Rising to power in the Republican Party, he received several important governmental appointments, including Trial Justice, Customs Inspector, and Colonel in the state militia.

Delany threw both his political support and immense popularity behind the Liberian Exodus Joint Stock Company, a business enterprise formed in 1868 to transport emigrants to Liberia. After two transatlantic trips, the venture failed, and mostly due to mismanagement.[255]

During his work with the Liberian Exodus Company, Delany wrote *Principia of Ethnology: The Origin of Races and Color*, a mixture of Black history, archeology, and anthropology.[256] While not a scholarly work by current standards, it focused on the role of Blacks in the development of Egypt and Ethiopia. From the biblical account of creation, Delany traced the descendants of Ham

---

[255] George Brown Tindall, *South Carolina Negroes 1877-1900* (South Carolina: University of South Carolina Press, 1970), 153-167.
[256] Martin R. Delany, *Principia of Ethnology: The Origin of Races and Color* (Baltimore, Maryland: Classic Press, 1991).

from Egypt and Ethiopia to their diffusion throughout Africa. Using Egyptian sculpture and hieroglyphics and the Ethiopian alphabets, Delany sought to demonstrate that the builders of the pyramids were Black.

Delany died in 1885 after nearly fifty years as a fighter for Black liberation. He distinguished himself as an Army officer, abolitionist, medical doctor, self-taught scholar, writer, and an early intellectual voice of Black Nationalism.

Summary

This chapter gave a brief examination of the historical development of the Independent Black Church Movement, focusing upon the relation between the Black Church and Black Nationalism, the African-American religious contribution to resistance literature, the role of African-American church men and women in the Negro Convention Movement, and the Black Church's response to colonization and emigration. In each topic, the chapter demonstrated that there were at least two streams in the Black Church. The first tended toward societal compromise, complacency, and Heavenly hope, and the second tended toward radical behavior, seeking African-

American solidarity and liberation. In addition, the chapter examined Martin Delany's role as the "father and Black Nationalism," extrapolating the basic tenets of his radical ideas about Black Theology, African-American solidarity, and liberation. Having accomplished this, the historical and social context for the remainder of the study has been said.

Chapter III: HENRY HIGHLAND GARNET (1815-1882): PROVIDENCE AND AFRICAN-AMERICAN RESISTANCE

This chapter provides a biographical sketch of Garnet, focusing on the life experiences that influenced his ideas of theodicy. The chapter traces the development of Garnet's conception of Black Nationalism and examines its sources. In addition, the chapter examines Garnet's ideas of Black Nationalism in his philosophies of economic justice and emigration. Finally, the chapter critiques Garnet's idea of theodicy, Providence and African-American Resistance, by illuminating its strengths and weaknesses.

144

Image Ownership: Public Domain
Henry Highland Garnet

One of the most influential Black Nationalists of the Antebellum Period was Henry Highland Garnet. Born on December 23, 1815, in Kent County, New Market, Maryland, Garnet traced his lineage to the Mandingo people where his grandfather was an African chieftain.[257] Captured in an inter-tribal war, the grandfather was sold into slavery in Virginia and later to Colonel William Spencer in Maryland.[258]

Image Ownership: Public Domain
James McCune Smith
first African-American
degreed medical doctor

---

[257]William Brewer, "Henry Highland Garnet," *Journal of Negro History* 13 (January 1928): 38; Alexander Crummell, *Africa and America Discourses by the Rev. Alex Crummell* (Springfield, Massachusetts: Wiley and Company, 1891), 272-273; James McCune Smith, *Sketch of the Life and Labors of Henry Highland Garnet* (Springfield, Massachusetts, 1891), 17.
[258]Crummell, 273; Smith.

James McCune Smith, a friend of the Garnet family, observed that the grandfather "was as noble an ancestor as [humankind] could desire, [who brought] moral and religious power. . .to New Market."[259] He earned the name "Joseph Trusty"-Joseph from his gifts in exhorting, praying, and praising the Lord and Trusty from his unbending character.[260] Joseph died between 1822 and 1823, leaving seven sons.

Upon Colonel Spencer's death in 1824, his descendants made plans to divide Joseph Trusty's offspring.[261] Because of the immediate threat to divide the family, coupled with the daily abuses attendant to slavery, the Trustys plotted an escape. Using the pretext of attending a funeral, George Trusty (Henry Garnet's father) secured passes for the family to leave the plantation and used them for safe passage to Wilmington, Delaware.[262] There were eleven in the escape party: Henry's father, mother, sister, and seven others, including himself."[263] In Wilmington they

---

[259]Smith, 17.
[260]James McCune Smith, *Introduction to a Memorial Discourse by Rev. Henry Highland Garnet* (Philadelphia: Joseph M. Wilson, 1865), 17-18.
[261]Ibid., 18.
[262]Brewer, 38 and Smith, *Sketch of Garnet*, 19.
[263]Brewer.

made contact with Thomas Garret, a Quaker-abolitionist, who assisted them in safe passage to Bucks County, Pennsylvania. George and his family settled in New York City in 1825.[264]

The bold decision to leave slavery, and the intricate details and precise execution of the plan of escape, provided Henry Garnet a basis upon which to develop his future ideas of Black self-reliance and self-improvement. In their article, "Henry Highland Garnet: Nationalism, Class Analysis, and Revolution," Nathan Huggins, Martin Wilson, and Daniel Fox (hereinafter Huggins), commented on the skill, self-determination, and self-belief required to strike such an audacious blow for freedom, and its attending influence upon Henry Garnet:

> The factors that lead to the decision to flee were more important than any others in the development of Garnet's sense of why slavery had to be overcome. Beyond that, the way they escaped deeply influenced his views regarding whose responsibility it was to overcome slavery. It was a complex operation, one that George Garnet's being a skilled slave greatly facilitated, for it would have been virtually impossible for him to plan and carry

---

[264]Ibid. William Simmons, ed., *Men of Mark: Eminent, Progressive, and Rising* (New York, N.Y.: The New York Times and Arno Press, 1968), 21.

out the escape if he had not had the relative mobility that being skilled afforded, and that helped him tap clandestine sources so that the family might negotiate the dangerous passage to. . .Delaware. The success of the plan required nerve and discipline, in addition to intelligence, far more than was required of a runaway with only a single life to protect. Responsibility touched all, but the greatest responsibility was that of the men, especially that of George Garnet, whose command of the details and direction of the overall plan was superb. . . . His example strongly influenced Henry's later views about how the younger generation must not abandon the self-reliant course of those of their people who had gone before.[265]

Once George Trusty settled in New York, he assembled the family in a baptism to liberation celebration, a rite of passage from a slave to a freed person. He then changed the family's surname from Trusty to "Garnet."[266] The ceremony, according to Sterling Stuckey, was a "conscious effort on the part of the Garnets to reclaim their identity--a certain power of definition for the family."[267]

---

[265]Nathan Huggins, Martin Wilson, and Daniel Fox, eds., *Key Issues in the African-American Experience* (New York, N.Y.: Harcourt, Brace, Javonovich, 1971), 140.

[266]Sterling Stuckey, "A Last Stern Struggle: Henry Highland Garnet and Liberation Theory" in Leon Litwack and August Meier, *Black Leaders of the Nineteenth Century* (Urbana: University of Illinois Press, 1988), 130.

[267]Ibid.

The link with Africa through his family provided a basis for Henry Garnet's future Black Nationalist expressions.

George Garnet bore little resemblance to a former slave. He was stately in character and stature.[268] According to Alexander Crummell, who lived next door to the Garnet's in New York City, "George was as tall as his more celebrated son; a perfect Apollo, in form and figure; with beautifully molded limbs and fine and delicate features; just like hundreds of grand Mandingoes I have seen in Africa whose full blood he carried in his veins."[269]

Crummell's close contact with the Garnet's allowed him to observe the characteristics and demeanors of the family members. Crummell's observations of George and Henry revealed two distinctive demeanors:

Unlike his son, he [George] was grave and sober in his demeanor, but solid and weighty in his words; not given to talk and reminding one of the higher Quaker character; deeply religious; and carrying in his every movement strength and dignity. I remember well the self-restraint his appearance always evoked among my playmates, and a certain sense of

---

[268]Crummel, 274.
[269]Ibid.

awe which his majestic presence always impressed us with.[270]

Crummell offered this description of Henry's mother:

> His mother was as notable a person as his father, both in personal presence and traits of character; a most comely and beautiful woman; tall and finely molded with a bright, intellectual face, lit up with lustrous, twinkling, laughing eyes--which she gave as an inheritance, to her son; and the very soul of fun, wit, frolic and laughter.[271]

It was from both parents that Crummell reasons that Henry got that readiness, humor, intellectual fire, steadiness of character, and strong native thought which were his grand characteristics. They came from both parents; but like most great [persons] they were especially the gift of that grandmother.

From such a stock, with both physical and mental greatness in both lines of his ancestry, Henry Garnet inherited that fine physique, that burning vitality, that large intellectual power, that fiery flame of

---

[270]Ibid.
[271]Ibid.

liberty, and those high moral and spiritual instincts, which are generally characteristic of the great.[272]

In his article *Henry Highland Garnet*, William Brewer sheds light on Henry's personality:

> For the peculiar task of leading the slaves to freedom Garnet was especially fitted. There was something about his personality which few leaders possess--the commanding presence which inspires courage and the will to fight through difficulties. In his personality were reflected the fire and genius of African chieftains who had defied the slave catchers and later had rankled in Southern bondage. No disappointment could crush such a spirit as that which Garnet manifested in behalf on his people.[273]

In 1829, during Henry Garnet's work as a ship's cabin boy, a group of slave-hunters scattered the Garnet family.[274] Crummell watched the events and gave an eyewitness account:

> One evening a White man, a relative of the late Colonel Spencer, the old owner, walked up to Mr. Garnet's dwelling. "Does. . .George Garnet live here?" was the question put. "Yes," was Mr. Garnet's reply; and immediately he recognized one

---

[272]Ibid., 275.
[273]Brewer, 36.
[274]Smith, *Sketch of Garnet* 25 and Brewer, 39.

of his old owner's relatives. The slave-hunter, however, did not recognize George Garnet. "Is he at home?" was the next question, to which with quiet self-possession, Mr. Garnet replied: "I will go and see." Leaving the open door Mr. Garnet, without saying a word to his family, passed into a side bedroom. . .and leaped from the side window of the bed-room into my father's yard. Mr. Garnet escaped through Orange Street, and the slave-hunter's game was thus effectively spoiled.[275]

The only person arrested was his sister, who pleaded a case of mistaken identity, saying that she lived free in New York City during the time of her purported slavery in Maryland. Her defense persuaded acquittal.[276]

Upon returning to New York City and learning of the slave-scattering incident, Garnet bought a large clasp knife for protection and walked around New York City hoping to be accosted by slave-hunters.[277] The family-scattering incident was a transforming experience for Garnet that brought him to a new level of consciousness, reminding him of his slave past and his precarious quasi-free existence. Huggins explained:

---

[275]Crummell, 275-276.
[276]Smith, 25.
[277]Smith, 26; Brewer, 39.

The possibility that one or more members of his family would be enslaved once more--that he would be hunted down himself--brought to Garnet's consciousness, as nothing since the circumstances that had led the family to escape to freedom some years earlier and the vulnerability of the status of Blacks in the North. Having resisted slavery to gain freedom, Garnet was determined never to be enslaved again. And now that he was older, the effect on him of marauding slave-catchers seared his conscience and gave him new strength.[278]

William Brewer reveals that the scattering of Garnet's family produced in him one of the greatest opponents of slavery during the thirty years prior to the Civil War:

Slavery had produced in him one of the greatest foes which the crisis from 1830 to 1860 would ever face. To the liberation of fellow slaves Garnet's life was now firmly dedicated. Douglass and others had escaped from bondage, but few if any of them suffered in mind and body the agony of Henry Highland Garnet. Naturally he placed responsibility for his condition at the door of slavery, to the destruction of which he was resolved to lend his utmost of intellect and

---

[278]Huggins, 146. Earl Ofari claims that the destruction of the Garnet family by the slave-system left an indelible impression upon him. Garnet promised that he would never submit to slavery again; nor would he allow a White person to insult or mistreat him. Ofari, *Let Your Motto Be Resistance: the Life and Thought of Henry Highland Garnet* (Boston: Beacon Press, 1972), 15-20.

character. To this tremendous task he brought strength and courage which the stormiest difficulties of the conflict never daunted.[279]

Garnet indentured himself to Captain Epenetus Smith of Long Island, New York in 1829.[280] While vigorously opposed to slavery, Garnet took the best opportunity available to better himself financially. The Captain's son, Samuel, offered this description of Garnet:

> The appearance of the boy was prepossessing; his eyes were bright and unclouded, and above them was a massive forehead, which might have been chosen as a model for an artist. His perceptions were quick, and the ingeniousness of his nature soon won the hearts of the entire family.[281]

It is unclear as to the number of years Garnet contracted, but the indenture came to an end because of a leg injury sustained in an athletic contest.[282] After thirteen years of unsuccessful therapy, Garnet had the leg amputated at the hip.[283] Garnet, according to Joel Schor, "was probably

---

[279]Brewer, 40.

[280]Huggins, 147; Brewer, 46.

[281]Samuel Smith, "Letter to the *Signal*," December 3, 1983. Quoted in Joel Schor, *Henry Highland Garnet: A Voice of Black Radicalism in the Nineteenth Century* (Westport, CT.: Greenwood Press, 1977), 9.

[282]Schor

[283]Ibid.

altered emotionally for life" (Samuel Smith, *Letters to the Signal*, 3 December 1883); "the useless appendage became his personal thorn challenging and goading him onward into relentless attack upon the twin monsters of his people: subordination and slavery."[284]

Having served as an indentured servant and born into slavery, Garnet experienced what Huggins reveals as the "whole range of oppression attending to slavery and indenture."[285] These experiences strengthened Garnet's hatred of oppression and gave him an early state of Black consciousness. Indeed, Garnet was often a visionary in relation to his Black contemporaries, who took longer periods to arrive at a more self-reliant and independent Black state of consciousness.[286] Crummell reasoned that both the slave-scattering incident and the leg injury produced in Garnet a prophetic sense of mission to fight against oppression:

> So the anguish of this family calamity gave birth to a giant soul! From this terrible ordeal Henry Highland Garnet came forth like gold thoroughly refined from fire! The soberness which comes from trial, the seriousness which is the fruit of

---

[284]Ibid.
[285]Huggins, 147.
[286]Ibid., 151; Ofari, 43-44.

affliction, the melancholy and the reflection which spring from pain and suffering, for he was not a cripple, soon brought Garnet to the foot of the Cross.[287]

New York African Free School No. 2 built a century ago

Image Ownership: Public Domain
African Free School in New York City

In 1826 Garnet enrolled in the African Free School in New York City, an institution founded by the New York Manumission Society.[288] The school provided an atmosphere for the free expression of ideas that included the

---

[287]Crummell.
[288]Brewer, 40; Schor, 5; Smith, 26.

alleviation of oppression with a Pan-African prescription.[289]

Garnet was in a group of young scholars that included Alexander Crummell, "who became an eminent pastor; Ira Aldridge, who gained fame abroad as a Shakespearean tragedian, Thomas S. Sidney, a precocious young scholar, who died at an early age; and Samuel Ringgold Ward, who established a reputation as a logician of liberty."[290] This was a radical group who decided against celebrating the fourth of July in protest of slavery.[291] Crummell explained the group's position in saying:

> For years, our society met on that day [July the Fourth], and the time was devoted to planning schemes for the freeing and up building of our race. The other resolve which was made was, that when we had educated ourselves we would go South, start an insurrection and free our [people] in bondage. Garnet was a leader in these rash but noble resolves; and they indicate the early set and bias of his soul to that quality of magnanimity which Aristotle says "exposes one to great dangers

---

[289]Charles Andrews, *The History of the New York African Free Schools* (New York, N.Y.: Negro University Press: 1969), 1-25.

[290]Stuckey, 132. Brewer identified Garnet's principle mentor as Charles Andrews, an Englishman, who inspired Garnet with the desire to learn. In addition, Andrews laid the intellectual foundation for Garnet's Pan-Africanist views. See Brewer, 40-41.

[291]Schor, 5.

and makes a man unsparing of his life," thinking that life is not worth having on some terms.[292]

Continuing his education, Garnet studied in an African-American high school in New York City.[293] In 1835 Garnet, Crummell, and Sidney were recommended to the Noyes Academy in Canaan, New Hampshire, by the Reverend Theodore S. Wright, a prominent Presbyterian minister.[294] The Noyes Academy was an abolitionist school that vowed to admit African-Americans and Whites equally. The trip between New York City and Canaan, New Hampshire, was a treacherous, four hundred miles. There were two modes of transportation: over land by carriage and up the Atlantic by ship. Because African-Americans were not allowed equal interstate accommodations, the three men were required to sleep on the ship's deck, exposed to the elements, without dining and other private privileges. They were also required to sit atop the stagecoach, separated from the White passengers beneath. Crummell wrote recalling the experience:

> On the steamboat from New York to Providence no cabin passage was allowed [C]olored people,

---

[292]Crummell, 300.
[293]Ibid., 278.
[294]Ibid.

and so, poor fellow, he was exposed all night, bedless and foodless, to the cold and storm. Coaches then were in use, and there were no railroads; and all the way from Providence to Boston, from Boston to Concord to Hanover, and from Hanover to Canaan, the poor invalid had to ride night and day on the top of the coach. It was a long and wearisome journey, of some four hundred and more miles; and rarely would an inn or a hotel give us food, and nowhere could we get shelter.[295]

Because of his amputated leg, Garnet suffered a terrible ordeal. In speaking of Garnet's distinctive difficulties Crummell wrote:

Sidney and myself were his companions during the whole journey; and I can never forget his sufferings-sufferings from pain, sufferings from cold and exposure, sufferings from thirst and hunger, sufferings from taunt and insult at every village and town, and off times at every farm-house, as we rode, mounted upon the top of the coach, through all this long journey. In seems hardly conceivable that Christian people could thus treat human beings traveling through a land of ministers and churches! The sight of three Black youths, in gentlemanly garb, traveling through New England was, in *those days, a most unusual*

---

[295]Ibid., 279.

sight; started not only surprise, but brought out universal sneers and ridicule.[296]

Not long after Garnet's arrival at Noyes Academy, a mob of White farmers opposed to abolition and the education of African-Americans hitched a team of sixty oxen to the school and dragged the building off into the swamp. Under the leadership of Garnet, the African-American students armed themselves anticipating an attack. That night, a mob gathered, and one of their number fired a shot, hoping to begin a charge towards the boarding house. Garnet answered the shot with a shot of his own and turned the mob in retreat. The African-Americans left Noyes Academy the next day, but were fired upon as they made their departure.[297] Crummell remembers Garnet's bold leadership during the crisis:

> Under Garnet, as our leader the boys in our boarding-house were molding bullets, expecting an attack upon our dwelling. About eleven o'clock at night the tramp of horses were heard approaching, and as one rapid rider passed the house and fired at it, Garnet quickly replied by a discharge from a double-barreled shotgun which blazed away from the window. That musket shot

---

[296]Ibid., 279-280.
[297]Ibid., 280-281.

by Garnet doubtless saved our lives. The cowardly ruffians dared not attack us.[298]

Following Garnet's departure from Noyes Academy in 1836, he enrolled in the Oneida Institute, Whitesboro, New York. Although his studies were constantly interrupted by long periods of illness, Garnet acquired a good command of the materials. Crummell observed that "[Garnet's] early long continued illness broke up the systematic training of the schools and so he was never the deep plodding laborious student."[299] Crummell thought Garnet an impressive original thinker, however. Crummell further observed that:

> [h]is superiority and refinement was more the result of instinct and genius than it was of scholarship. . . . His originality was astonishing. Other eminent [persons] of our acquaintance were, of necessity, readers, investigators, students; Garnet, beyond all other [persons], drew from the deep wells of his own nature the many stores of his thought and speech. He brought into public life all the largeness and richness of one of the rarest and most beautiful minds I have ever met.[300]

---

[298]Ibid., 283.
[299]Ibid.
[300]Ibid.

In 1837 while an Oneidan student, Garnet joined the Christian Young Men's organization, becoming one of its vice-presidents. The Christian Young Men opposed the New York property holder qualification, reasoning that it diluted the African-American vote.[301] Garnet was appointed to a committee that wrote a petition to the New York legislature asking for a repeal of the property holder provision. A part of the petition reflects Garnet's idea of Black self-improvement:

> Whatever lawful measures we may take, their efforts cannot politically degrade us more than we now are. But if anything can produce a favorable change, it will be a knowledge of our being seriously and earnestly engaged in endeavoring to effect our own elevation. Early indications on our part, of a determination to seek our own elevation, will also have a beneficial influence upon many of our Law-Makers; and it will also turn their minds to the subject preparatory to the presentation of our petitions.[302]

To further prepare for ministry, Crummell applied to New York City's General Theological Seminary, but because of the school's segregation policy his application

---

[301]"Anti-Slavery Standard," September 11, 1845, 3.
[302]*The Colored American*, January 28, 1838, 11, quoted in Schor, 20.

was denied. Chosen to co-author a letter to Crummell on behalf of the African-American Oneidans, Garnet expressed their outrage with General's discriminatory practices and commended Crummell for his firm stand against racial humiliation. They wrote in 1839:

Esteemed sir,--

It is with deep regret that we learn by the last number of *The Colored Americans* of the proceeding of the above mentioned Seminary, in relation to yourself. And we take this early opportunity to express our feelings in regard to so glaring an outrage against humanity, religion, and the Almighty.

We congratulate you for the [outstanding] and commendable stand which you have taken, in not consenting to bow and succumb to time nurtured, hoary-headed prejudice--and for thus showing to the world that moral principle disdains to yield to the influence of slavery either directly or indirectly.[303]

The firm stand against prejudice and racial discrimination would become a consistent theme throughout Garnet's future speeches and writings.

---

[303]Ibid., September 28, 1839, 3, quoted in Schor, 23.

Graduating from Oneida in 1840, Garnet became a salesperson for the *Colored American* and co-editor of the *National Watchmen* in Troy, New York. In 1841 he married Julia Williams of New York.[304]

Between 1840 and 1850 Garnet became one of the leading Black Nationalist spokespersons. Internationalizing the Abolitionist Cause, Garnet traveled to Europe in 1850 to lecture and solicit funds and support for the Abolition Movement. By 1853 Garnet sailed to Jamaica as a missionary and teacher. The deteriorating situation between the Northern and Southern states brought Garnet back to the United States in 1856. During the Civil War, Garnet served as a recruiter of African-American troops for the Union Army. He was among the first to demand that President Lincoln issue an Executive Order lifting the ban to African-American enlistment, in spite of the draft riots in New York that threatened his life. In 1881 Garnet was appointed Minister and Consul General to Liberia. Garnet died a year later in Africa after having contracted a fever.

---

[304]Julia Williams predeceased Garnet; they had no children. Garnet then married Sarah Smith Thompson, a widow with two children who died at a very young age. Sarah died in 1911.

A stalwart member of the American Anti-Slavery Society, Garnet supported the idea of moral suasion as a means to achieve abolition. In his "Speech Delivered at the Seventh Anniversary of the American Anti-Slavery Society, 1840," Garnet made two fundamental points.[305] First, while asking God to liberate the slaves he pleaded for the slave-owners to:

> Avenge thy plundered poor, oh Lord!
> But not with fire, but not with sword;
> Avenge our wrongs, our chains, our sighs,
> The misery in our children's eyes!
> But not with sword--no, not with fire,
> Chastise our country's locustry;
> Nor let them feel thine heavier ire;
> Chastise them not in poverty;
> Though cold in soul as coffined dust,
> Their hearts as tearless dead, and dry
> Let them in outraged mercy trust
> and find that mercy they deny.[306]

Central to Garnet's love-your-enemy position was his belief in the redemptive power of love. Using the creative force of love, Garnet sought to appeal to the heart

---

[305]Schor, 30. For a complete text of the speech see Ofari, 127-135.
[306]Quoted in Schor, 30 and Ofari, 134.

and conscience of White America to move them towards abolition. As will emerge in this section, Garnet proposed Negro Conventions and abolitionist literature to demonstrate the plight of the slaves, and political and legal reforms to repeal the slave-system. He hoped to bring White America to a deeper understanding of humanity through the transforming power of love, thus enabling them to liberate the African-American community.

Second, Garnet gave an impassioned plea for the liberation of the slaves based upon his special kinship to his African brothers and sisters:

> I speak in the behalf of my enslaved people and the nominally free. There is. . .a higher sort of freedom which no mortal can touch. That freedom thanks be unto the Most High, is mine. Yet I cannot be entirely free. I feel for my people as a member of [humankind]. I am bound with them as a [human being]. Nothing but emancipating my [people] can set me at liberty. . . . For although my habitation were fixed in the freest part of Victoria's dominions, yet it were worse than vain for me to indulge the thought of being free while three millions of my people are waiting in the dark prison house of oppression.[307]

---

[307]Quoted in Schor, 31 and *The Colored American*, May 30, 1840, 1.

From the 1840's through the 1860's Garnet put the blame for the continuation of slavery on the descendants of the founding parents of America. He reasoned that the founding constitutional parents permitted slavery as a compromise, leaving the resolution of the matter to the next generation.[308] Extremely disappointed with the descendants, Garnet criticized them through his "Speech Delivered at the Seventh Anniversary of the American Anti-Slavery Society, 1840," in saying:

> We do not question the sincerity of purpose, and devotion to freedom, which seemed to wield the swords of most of the [parents] of the revolution. But we complain, in the most unqualified terms, of the base conduct of their degenerate [children]. If, when taking into consideration the circumstances with which the revolutionists were surrounded, and the weakness of human nature, we can possibly pardon them for neglecting our [peoples'] rights-- if, in the first dawning of the day of liberty, every part of the patriot's duty did not appear plain, now that we have reached the mid-day of our national career--now that there are ten thousand suns flashing light upon our pathway, this nation is guilty of the basest hypocrisy in withholding the rights due to millions of American citizens.[309]

---

[308]Huggins, 152.
[309]Ofari, 128.

The harshness of both Garnet's slave- and free-life experiences influenced his criticism of the second generation of White Americans. In the article, *Henry Highland Garnet: Nationalism, Class Analysis, and Revolution,* Nathan Huggins explains:

> While criticism of the offspring of the founders was characteristic of abolitionists of his day, Garnet arrived at a position on the question via a more specific path than most, and at an earlier stage in his development. Their descendants at New Hampshire, by wrecking Canaan Academy and threatening his life and those of others, affected his consciousness and physical being in a very direct way. The meanness with which he and his friends were greeted as they traveled to Canaan, to say nothing of the slave-hunting episode in New York and his having been a slave as late as 1824, helped establish his relationship to the sons [and daughters] of the Founding [parents] in ways not possible for a [W]hite colleague. He and his family knew and were owned by [W]hites in Maryland who were determined to maintain oppression into the indefinite future, and that was more than a generation following the drafting of the Constitution.[310]

By 1840 there was a major division in the Abolition Movement as to which strategy could best alleviate slavery.

---

[310]Quoted in Huggins, 152.

Dominated by William Lloyd Garrison, the esteemed abolitionist, the American Anti-Slavery Society proposed moral suasion. Garrison advocated full citizenship for free African-Americans and sought to achieve the means of abolition and elevation through anti-slavery literature, lectures, boycotts, and support of a world-wide pan-abolitionist movement.[311] Reasoning that both the Constitution and White religious institutions were in support of slavery, Garnet thus had little to do with political activism or White churches.[312] Three days after Garnet gave the 1840 speech to the American Anti-Slavery Society, the organization divided into the American Anti-Slavery Society and the Foreign Anti-Slavery Society. Formed during the convention, the Foreign Anti-Slavery Society was basically composed of those who did not agree with Garnet's leadership.[313]

Prominent among the causes of the division was the issue of political activism. Following the leadership of the Garrisonians, the American Anti-Slavery Society did not

---

[311]Schor, 34.   Russel B. Nye, *William Lloyd Garrison and the Humanitarian Reformers* (Boston: Little Brown, 1955).
[312]Schor.
[313]Howard Bell, *Minutes of the Proceedings of the National Negro Conventions 1830-1864* (New York, N.Y.: The New York Times and Arno Press, 1969), 72-77.

favor political involvement. The newly formed Foreign Anti-Slavery Society allowed political activism, but stopped short of endorsing a political party.[314] A significant number of American Anti-Slavery Society defectors were already members of the Liberty Party, including Garnet.[315]

Garnet held a deep sense of Black consciousness. He refused to support the widely held view that an integrated movement was the best means towards liberation. For Garnet, "who would be free themselves must strike the first blow."[316] Having experienced the hypocrisy of Whites in regard to social equality, and having served in abolitionist organizations where Whites presented paternalistic or racist

---

[314]For background information concerning both the American Anti-Slavery Society and the American and Foreign Anti-Slavery Society, see Gilbert H. Barnes, *The Anti-Slavery Impulse 1830-1844* (New York, N.Y.: D. Appleton Century Co. Inc., 1934); Dwight Dummond, *Anti-Slavery* (Ann Arbor: University of Michigan Press, 1961); and Louis Filler, *The Crusade Against Slavery 1830-1860* (New York, N.Y.: Harper and Row, 1963).

[315]The Liberty party was born as a result of the philosophical differences between the American Anti-Slavery Society and the American and Foreign Anti-Slavery Society. Organized in the fall of 1840, the Liberty Party was a national-state party dedicated to the immediate abolition of slavery. The members of the new society formed the nucleus of the party. See David Ruggles, ed., *The Mirror of Liberty* (New York: David Ruggles, 1838); *The Liberty Almanac for 1849* (New York: American and Foreign Anti-Slavery Society, 1899); and Charles Wesley, "Negroes in Anti-Slavery Political Parties" *Journal of Negro History* 29 (Jan 1944): 32-74.

[316]*Minutes of the State Convention of Colored Citizens* (New York: Piercy and Reed, 1840), 14.

attitudes, Garnet felt the need for a Black-controlled convention of the state of New York.[317]

Garnet and several leading African-Americans of New York state called for such a meeting that assembled in Troy, New York, during the middle of June 1840.[318] The main purpose of the convention was to discuss the issue of African-American suffrage. It was from the Black conventions that the fundamental stratagem developed to pressure the state of New York to delete property ownership as a requirement for the franchise. The free soil dispute was an extremely important battle for Garnet because it barred African-Americans from the legislative process on economic grounds and, in a subtle sense, because of their race.[319] The free soil dispute thus became both a Black Nationalist and an economic issue.

---

[317]The assistance given the Garnet's in their escape North provided by the Quaker-abolitionist Thomas Garret, coupled with the abolitionists' influences acquired through Garnet's educational experiences, led him to accept Whites as allies in the struggle for Black liberation. On balance, however, Garnet found more White oppression and White insincerity towards social justice than he found White initiative to bring about social equality. These findings encouraged Garnet to find a spirit of liberation in himself and to develop a Black Nationalist theory of self-reliance and self-assertiveness.
[318]Ibid.
[319]Huggins, 153; Ofari, 18.

While Garnet received criticism from the Garrisonians, who argued that the separate convention promoted segregation and damaged the African-American cause, Garnet countered in saying that the difficulties over African-American suffrage necessitated the separation.[320] From thencefore, a spirit of militant African-American independence infused the future state Negro Conventions.[321] Because of Garnet's call for the organization of the convention and his opposition to the Garrisonians, he began to grow in national stature. Although beginning a Black Convention with a predominately African-American leadership, Garnet did not sever ties with the Liberty Party. He continued to pressure the Libertarians to lobby the New York legislature to remove the hindrance to African-American suffrage.[322]

While Garnet viewed slavery and its twin sibling-- discrimination against free African-Americans--as two different classes of oppression, he proposed fundamentally the same remedies for redress. Garnet recognized the power in the legislative process and decided to use political action

---

[320] Jane and William Pease, "Black Power: The Debate in 1840," *Phylon* 29 (Spring 1968): 19-26.
[321] Ofari, 18-23.
[322] Wesley, 44.

to achieve the goal of abolition and the alleviation of racial discrimination. For Northern free African-Americans, Garnet sought to change the laws through pressure upon the local and state governments. For the slavery issue in the South, Garnet sought abolition through a constitutional amendment. In addition, Garnet used the Negro Conventions, the Foreign Anti-Slavery Society, resistance literature, lectures, and support from abroad to challenge the slave-system and to alleviate African-American discrimination.

It is unclear as to why Garnet put so much faith in the legislative process. In part, his plan of action was based upon the inalienable rights delineated in the Constitution and the Declaration of Independence. Moreover, he hoped that the second generation of White Americans would extend to African-Americans the rights guaranteed in the Constitution. This thinking kept Garnet from promoting the idea of violence to achieve liberation. Garnet projected this unusual faith in the effectiveness of political activity in a speech to the Liberty Party Convention in 1842:

> I cannot harbor the thought for a moment that their deliverance will be brought about by violence. No, our country will not be so deaf to the cries of the oppressed; so regardless of the commands of God

and [her] highest interests. No the time for a last stern struggle has not yet come, may it never be necessary. The finger of the Almighty will hold back the trigger and [God's] all powerful arm will shea the sword till the oppressor's cup is full.[323]

Within a year after his speech to the Liberty Party Convention, Garnet entertained the thought of violence as a means to achieve liberation. Of several factors that led to Garnet's change of mind, impatience was prominent. While there was a relatively short span of time between his change of position, it may be reasonably concluded that the slow pace towards abolition, between the ratification of the Constitution in 1789 and the call for a National Negro Convention in 1843, may have influenced Garnet's change of tactics.

The change may have resulted from a logical progression of thought: an eroded faith in the belief that Whites would liberate African-Americans and the futility of political activism. Both failures may have contributed to Garnet's reasoning that violence was the better means to achieve liberation. In addition, Garnet's suffering during his enslavement, his oppression by Northern Whites, and the

---

[323]Ofari, 143. The formal title of the speech, *Speech Delivered at the Liberty Party Convention Massachusetts, 1842.*" For the complete text, see Ofari, 138-144.

suffering of African-Americans in general, may have pushed him to a more militant posture. Both Stuckey and Huggins reasoned that Garnet's reading of David Walker's *Appeal* was also a decisive influence.[324]

In *Henry Highland Garnet: A Voice of Radicalism in the Nineteenth Century*, Joel Schor reveals that by 1843 Garnet had come to believe "political parties were merely one means towards liberation."[325] The slave-owners were unimpressed with West Indian liberation and did not seem inclined to repeal slavery through conventional political means.[326] Garnet began to look at the three million number of slaves as a powerful threat to slave-owners.[327]

Schor revealed another possible Garnet influence. In 1842 the United States Supreme Court's decision in *Priggs v. Pennsylvania* upheld the federal government's right to maintain slavery. By dictum the court upheld the right of slave-owners to retrieve fugitive slaves. The *Priggs* decision left to interpretation the legality of the Fugitive

[324]Stuckey, 135; Huggins, 154.

[325] Schor, 53.

[326] Ibid.

[327] Ibid. Garnet borrowed the idea of using the three million number of slaves as a threat to slave-owners from Walker's *Appeal*. See Laren Katz, ed., *Walker's Appeal and Address to the Slaves of America* (New York, N.Y.: The New York Times and Arno Press, 1969), 96.

Slave Laws. The most prominent spokespersons for the Liberty Parties were either defeated in their elections or not vigorous enough in their opposition to slavery and the Fugitive Slave Laws, for Garnet. Disillusioned with the federal government, the Supreme Court, and members of his political party, Garnet's despondency may have led to a greater acceptance of the possibility of violence as a means to achieve liberation.[328]

There were, nevertheless, a number of important events that developed as a result of the loose coalition between the New York Liberty Party and the New York Negro Conventions between 1840 and 1843. While the coalition tried unsuccessfully to repeal the property restriction in New York state, they were impressive with other victories. Schor recounts their achievements:

> Although the suffrage fight was lost, abolitionists did achieve a few victories in New York before the Civil War. One success was the repeal of the "nine months law" which required a slave to remain in the state for nine months with his [or her owner's]

---

[328] It was not until the *Dred Scott* decision in 1857 that the court gave finality to its interpretation of the Fugitive Slave Law. The *Dred Scott* decision held that slaves were merely property without standing to sue and would be returned to their owners. This no doubt added to Garnet's radicalism as the decade continued.

knowledge before he [or she] could legally become free. Another was the cooperation of Governor William Seward in refusing to deliver fugitives wanted in the South and his approval of an act establishing trial by jury in runaway cases.[329]

In speaking of the Negro Conventions of New York state, Schor revealed three unprecedented achievements:

In retrospect, the New York conventions of 1840 and 1841, while not the first such state movements among [B]lacks were the first held with the chief emphasis on suffrage. These were in all likelihood the first state Negro Conventions to send an appeal to the state legislature. Finally, they were the first to go on record as being independent of [W]hite domination. In that sense they were the harbinger of a new age in Negro thought and action.[330]

In addition, there was an ever-increasing awareness of discrimination that came to light with every succeeding New York Liberty Party Convention after 1840.[331] Garnet's Black Nationalist influence figured prominently both in the Liberty Party and at the Negro Conventions. Through his speeches, articles, and influence in Black religious circles, Garnet put pressure upon the Liberty Party to keep the free

---

[329] Schor, 48.
[330] Ibid.
[331] Ofari, 15-32; Wesley, 32-74.

soil and other abolitionist issues alive. Garnet was one of the major proponents of Black control of the Negro Conventions.

In 1843 the African-Americans of New England, Philadelphia, and New York state met in a National Black Convention in Buffalo, New York.[332] Of the delegates, there were Libertarians, American Anti-Slavery Society members, Foreign Anti-Slavery members, and a number of prominent abolitionists, including Frederick Douglass, Henry Highland Garnet, and William Lloyd Garrison. Influenced by Liberty Party ideals, the convention looked to involve itself more in direct action and politics rather than moral persuasion. In his article *National Negro Conventions of the Middle 1840's: Moral Suasion vs. Political Action*, Howard Bell explained the historic relationship between the Liberty Party and militant abolitionists:

> By 1840 militant abolitionism was a way of life widely accepted by many people in the North. To that date those championing moral persuasion as the best means of abolishing slavery had been the dominant group. But with the advent of the Liberty

---

[332] See Bell, *Minutes of the Proceedings of the National Conventions 1830-1864.*

179

Party many turned to political action as more effective in accomplishing that end. By 1843 many Negro leaders, especially in the areas outside New England, were ardent admirers of the new party since it offered an opportunity for a type of action which had previously been denied them. It was therefore to be expected that national conventions meeting in upstate New York during the middle 'forties would be influenced by Liberty Party ideals.[333]

Infused with the spirit of Black Nationalism, several African-American delegates held key convention posts, and most of the African-American delegates pushed for the adoption of a Black Nationalist agenda. Most of the convention's 28 resolutions were pro-Libertarian, denouncing slavery and the Fugitive Slave laws, and denouncing both the National Whig and Democratic Parties as pro-slavery institutions.[334] Ofari's observation about the agenda offers proof of a genuine Black convention:

> Clearly the delegates to this convention were concerned with devising programs to increase Black self-determination. The resolutions centered around the real needs of Northern [B]lacks. There was a marked absence of the

---

[333] Howard Bell, "National Negro Conventions of the Middle 1840's: Moral Suasion vs. Political Action," *Journal of Negro History* XLII (October 1957): 315.

[334] *Minutes of the National Conventions of Colored Citizens*, 22.

rhetoric that had tended to characterize previous conventions. The delegates did not get sidetracked into debates over abstractions such as freedom and justice. Reports were precisely worded so as not to cause any confusion over goals. An intense feeling of cooperation among the delegates was shown in the proceedings. The convention was a product of the combined resources of the participants. It received almost no publicity in the regular commercial press and only scattered notices in the abolitionist press. As a result, the convention was, in every sense, a genuine [B]lack convention.[335]

The resolution that stirred the most debate was Garnet's proposal that the convention accept in principle the slaves' right to resist.[336]

The climax of the convention was Garnet's speech, "An Address to the Slaves of the United States of America, Buffalo, N.Y., 1843."[337] By the time Garnet made the speech he had become a leading Black Nationalist advocate and a leader of national stature.[338] The "Address to the

---

[335] Ofari, 49.

[336] Carleton Mabee, *Black Freedom: The Non Violent Abolitionists from 1830 Through the Civil War* (New York, N.Y.: The Macmillan Co., 1970), 64.

[337] For the complete text of the speech see Ofari, 144-153.

[338] Ernst J. Miller, as does Benjamin Quarles, suggests that it was Garnet's *Address to the Slaves* in 1843 that brought him into national prominence. Prior to 1843 Garnet was an outspoken Black Nationalist known only in New York State and in neighboring parts of New

Slaves," like most pivotal speeches, was basically a simple document. It held three fundamental provisions. First, it equated the acceptance of slavery to sin: "To such to such degradation it is sinful in the extreme for you to make voluntary submission."[339]

Second, it admonished slaves to take the initiative for their freedom: "If hereditary bondsmen [and women] would be free they must themselves strike the first blow,"[340] Slaves were to ask, then plead, with their owners for freedom: "[G]o to your lordly enslavers and tell them plainly that you are determined to be free. Appeal to their sense of justice and tell them that they have no more right to oppress you. . . ."[341] Upon gaining freedom, the former [bondspersons] were to work diligently for their wages: "[p]romise them (the former slave-owners) renewed diligence in the cultivation of the soil if they will render to you an equivalent for your labor."[342] If the pleas of the slaves fell on deaf ears, then they were to strike, refusing to work: "[d]o this and

---

England. See Miller, "The Anti-Slavery Role of Henry Highland Garnet," (Master's thesis, Union Theological Seminary, 1969) and Quarles, *Black Abolitionist* (New York, N.Y.: Oxford University Press, 1969).

[339] Ofari, 147.
[340] Ibid., 148-149.
[341] Ibid., 149
[342] Ibid.

forever after cease to toil for the heartless tyrants who give you no other reward but stripes and abuse."[343] Finally, Garnet called on slaves to resist slavery through whatever means they found expedient:

> Let your motto be resistance! *resistance!*
> *resistance!* No oppressed people have ever
> secured their liberty without resistance. What kind
> of resistance you had better make, you must decide
> by the circumstances that surround you, and
> according to the suggestion of expediency.
> Brethern, adieu! Trust in the living God. Labor
> for the peace of the human race, and remember that
> you are *four millions.*[344]

In addition to his own opinion about the speech, Ofari gave the opinions of William McAdoo, a twentieth century historian, and James McCune Smith, a Garnet contemporary, and a likely member of the convention:

> Garnet's speech, a milestone in the Abolitionist
> Movement, ranks as one of the major documents
> of the entire pre-Civil War period. William
> McAdoo, in his *Pre-Civil War Black Nationalism,*
> states that Garnet's address ushered in the era of
> revolutionary nationalism and "undermined the
> corrupt role of those [W]hite liberal managers in

---

[343] Ibid., 150.
[344] Ibid., 153.

[B]lack conventions and in other gatherings of [B]lack people" (PL Magazine, July-August 1966, p. 29). Closer to the scene, James McCune Smith, an active participant in the conventions of the 1840's, said this "document elicited more discussion than any other paper brought before that or any other deliberate body of colored persons and their friends."[345]

William Brewer, a Garnet researcher, concurs with the three men's impressions of the speech:

The address to the slaves at the Convention of Colored Citizens at Buffalo, New York, in 1843, was unquestionably a milestone in the Abolition Movement. Garrison and other abolitionists had previously spoken frankly and fearlessly concerning the institution of slavery. Certain Negroes had voiced such sentiments. Before this time, however, no Negro had dared express himself [or herself] in the language which Garnet used in this appeal.[346]

It should be noted that Garnet did not specifically call slaves to insurrection. Fundamentally, Garnet made two distinctive contributions to resistance literature: (1) the development of a theory of slave resistance; and (2) the development of an unlimited theory of resistance that

---

[345] Ibid., 145.
[346] Brewer, 44.

allowed slaves to rebel in those ways that were appropriate for their situation. Garnet, however, was not original in the idea of slave resistance. David Walker's *Appeal* (1829) and Robert Young's *Ethiopian Manifesto* (1829) were militant documents that pre-dated Garnet's "Address to the Slaves."[347] From *The Appeal* Garnet borrowed three of Walker's ideas: (1) slavery was an evil frowned upon by God; (2) God sided with the oppressed; and (3) slave-owners made deliberate attempts to keep slaves degraded and uninformed.[348]

The ideological origins of Garnet's call to resistance are based upon his ideas of Black Nationalism. Fundamentally, Garnet's Black Nationalism expressed itself through a call to Black unity asking that people of African descent come together to break the bonds of common oppression.[349] One of the basic sources of Garnet's Black Nationalism was his hatred of slavery, oppression, and

---

[347] For a good discussion of Walker's *Appeal* and Young's *Manifesto* see Chapter Two of the dissertation, "Black Nationalism and Resistance Literature."

[348] See Katz. So impressed was Garnet with Walker's *Appeal* that he went to Boston to speak with Walker's widow, hoping to gain insights into Walker's personality and his militant idea of Black Nationalism. Between 1847 and 1848 Garnet had his own *Address to the Slaves* and Walker's *Appeal* published in a single volume. See Ofari, 41 and Quarles, 227-228.

[349] Ofari, 144.

second-class treatment of African-Americans. There were several experiences, discussed earlier, that brought these feelings to the forefront of Garnet's Black Nationalist thinking: (1) his escape from slavery in Maryland; (2) the scattering of his family by slave-catchers in New York City; and (3) the racist experiences at Noyes Academy in New Hampshire.[350] Impressed by these experiences, Garnet was thus motivated to work for the liberation of the oppressed.

Another important source of Garnet's Black Nationalist thinking was his realization that the fate of free Northern African-Americans and Southern slaves were in reality not unlike. They were bound together by the Southern plantation system that produced cotton and other goods, the Northern need for slave produce, and the experience of African-American oppression that was correlative to their Black skin color. Capturing this spiritual kinship in his "Address to the Slaves," Garnet said: "[w]hile you (the slaves) have also been oppressed we (free African-Americans) have also been partakers with you nor can [we] be free while you are enslaved. We therefore write to you as being bound with you."[351]

---

[350] See this chapter of the dissertation: "Biographical Sketch of Garnet," 95-96, 98-99, 103.
[351] Ofari.

Garnet was also inspired by the stories heard about the free African existence told to him by former slaves, who longed for their old lives in the parentland.[352] Using the life experiences of the slaves, who were brought to American with broken hearts against their wills, Garnet formulated a reciprocal idea, fusing the experiences of the living with their deceased ancestors, to provide a powerful vehicle from which to call slaves to resistance.[353] Speaking in his "Address to the Slaves," Garnet said:

> Look around you and behold the bosoms of your loving wives heaving with untold agonies! Hear the cries of your poor children! Remember the stripes that your father bore. Think of the torture and disgrace of your noble mothers. Think of your wretched sisters' loving virtue and purity as they are driven into concubinage and are exposed to the unbridled lusts of incarnate devils. Think of the undying glory that hangs around the ancient name of Africa and forget not that you are native born citizens and as such you are justly entitled to all the rights that are granted to the freest.[354]

Garnet may have come to the knowledge of the free African existence and African religious spirituality through

---

[352] Huggins, 155-156.
[353] Ibid.
[354] Ofari, 149.

his father. Henry Garnet's father was the son of a Mandingo chief who came to America as one of the spoils of an intertribal war.[355] It is likely that the chief told his son about the free African existence and practiced Traditional African Religion. Thus, through both the oral tradition and through practice, the knowledge of the free African existence and African religious spirituality may have passed through three generations of Garnets. Focusing upon the religiosity of Garnet's grandfather and father, Huggins saw this as a logical process:

> Being an adult when captured, and an African chief, his grandfather was deeply grounded in African religious values--that is, he communed with the ancestors, a process that Christianity could not have brought to an end, especially since this dimension of the African's faith was hardly comprehended by Christians. And since Garnet's father was also a man of religion, close to his father even in slavery and living in a Maryland environment under powerful African ancestral influences, regard for the ancestors almost certainly was a legacy passed down from one generation of Garnets to another, enabling young Henry to embrace it as well.[356]

---

[355] Crummell, *Africa and America*, 273; Smith, *Sketch of the Life of Garnet*, 17.
[356] Quoted in Note 52, Huggins, 382-383.

A second source of contact with the African past was Garnet's opportunities for contact with runaway slaves in New York state. In speaking of those opportunities Huggins said:

> As late as the 1840's, there were enough old Africans in New York State and elsewhere in the North for him to have come by such knowledge. Then, too, by 1843 Garnet had had contact with slave runaways passing through or remaining in Troy. Opportunities for discussing slave religion were actually abundant to him through association with runaways. Even more intriguing is the possibility that he may have learned something of African ancestral concerns from his father, who may have learned them from *his* father.[357]

Another source of Garnet's contact with his African heritage was his association with the New York African Society. The New York African Society was a mutual aid organization with a strong spirit of Black Nationalism. In addition to the New York African Society, several African-American organizations celebrated an annual African Heritage Day in New York State.[358] Stuckey's research

---

[357] Ibid., 156.
[358] See Charles Wesley, "The Negroes of New York in the Emancipation Movement," *Journal of Negro History* 29 (January 1939): 65-103.

found Garnet at one of the parades in 1827.[359]   James
McCune Smith, one of the parade's participants, gave a
picture of the festive event and emphasized the Pan-
Africanist connection:

> The side-walks were crowded with wives,
> daughters, sisters, and mothers of the celebrants
> representing every state in the Union, and not a few
> with gay bandana handkerchiefs, betraying their
> West Indian birth: neither was Africa itself
> unrepresented, hundreds who had survived the
> middle passage. . .joined in the joyful procession.
> The people of those days rejoiced in their
> nationality and hesitated not to call each other
> African or descendants of Africa.[360]

Garnet's fusion of African spirituality with political
and social liberation created a powerful, militant liberation
strategy.   Indeed, Garnet did not separate the two.
Throughout his public career, Garnet synthesized spiritual
and physical liberation.[361]   Huggins, explains the powerful
appeal of Garnet's creative synthesis:

> What is beyond doubt is that by arguing from
> ancestral ground he offered a powerful appeal for
> winning slaves to his militant strategy.   Since the
> principal religious ceremonies of the slaves were

---

[359] Stuckey, 131.
[360] Quoted in Stuckey, 131.
[361] Young, 100.

devoted to the renewal of contact with the ancestors, the ancestors at times entering their very being at the highest point of communion in the ring shout, his references to the continuing responsibility of the slave to them is a brilliant illustration of cultural thought being put to revolutionary purposes.[362]

This was not an entirely new concept because Prosser, Vesey, and Turner combined African spirituality and the radical dimension of Christianity to inspire slave rebellions.[363] While the three men put Garnet's creative union into practice, Huggins maintains that Garnet was one of the first to intellectualize the idea in formal Black Nationalist thought: "[w]hether by accident or design the confluence of cultural and political theory in his thought, the level at which the two meet marks a rare instance of such creative union in nineteenth century nationalist thought."[364]

Garnet's focus upon cross-generational Black suffering was an original formulation according to Huggins and a distinctive contribution to nineteenth century Black

---

[362] Huggins, 156.
[363] See Chapter Two of the dissertation, section entitled "Black Nationalism and the Black Church in the South," 36-48.
[364] Huggins

Nationalist thought.[365] In speaking of the near endless cycle of oppression, Garnet said:

> Years have rolled on and tens of thousands have been borne on streams of blood and tears, to shores of eternity. . .nor did the evil of their bondage end at their emancipation by death. Succeeding generations inherited their chains and millions have come from eternity into time and have returned again to the world of spirits caused and ruined by American slavery.[366]

For Huggins, Garnet's focus upon cross-generational suffering was the first to establish the need for revolution based upon this idea.

Garnet seized the opportunities to speak before African-American assemblages to advocate his ideas of Black self-reliance and self-assertiveness. Both ideas were practiced by Garnet's father and uncles who used the qualities to escape slavery.[367] The self-reliant qualities of both Garnet's father and uncles left a self-assertive impression on Garnet, who incorporated it into his Black Nationalist thinking. Thus, thought Garnet, if slavery was to be obliterated, then slaves had to take the major

---

[365] Ibid.
[366] Quoted in Huggins, 155; see also Ofari, 145.
[367] See pages 85-86 of the dissertation.

responsibility for its demise: "[Brothers and sisters] the time has come when you must act for yourselves. . .you can plead your own cause and do the work of emancipation better than others."[368] Garnet sought to tap the inner spiritual strength of African-Americans and motivate them towards liberation. Self-reliance and self-assertiveness would become cornerstones of Black Nationalist thinking in the nineteenth century.

Garnet's speech sparked much debate and touched the fundamental heart of the Abolition Movement. Was the movement to continue the moral suasion stratagem or was the movement to change to violence? Frederick Douglass opposed Garnet's speech because he felt "too much physical force in both the address and the speaker."[369] Douglass feared that the adoption of the speech might ignite mass insurrection which would be counter-productive to the Abolition Movement. He asked that moral suasion be used a little longer.[370] Douglass knew, as did Garnet, that there was an extreme indignant streak in the slaves' Black consciousness that could ignite a revolt. The difference in

---

[368] Garnet, 148-149.
[369] *Minutes of the National Convention of Colored Citizens Buffalo, N.Y., August 1843*, 13-14.
[370] Ibid.

the two men's thinking was the anticipated results of a revolt. While Garnet saw positive gains through a revolt, Douglass saw immediate disaster, such as a crushing slave defeat.[371] Several historians reasoned that both men were probably of the same mind, Douglass in the short perspective and Garnet in the longer.[372]

William Lloyd Garrison's *Liberator* described the speech as "inflammatory, provocative, and a flight of fancy."[373] Because of Douglass' and Garrison's influence, the resolution to adopt the speech was defeated by one vote.[374] Although it was defeated, the speech made a lasting impression.[375] In speaking of the effect of the address on the Abolition Movement, Ofari observed that:

> Garnet was not the first [B]lack to openly call for a mass slave rebellion, but the impact of his speech was more profound than that of previous declarations because he forcefully expressed an ideal that was beginning to gain acceptance within the [B]lack communities of the North. Further,

---

[371] *Minutes of the National Convention of Colored Citizens*, 12-13. Robert Abzug, "The Influence of Garrisonian Abolitionists' Fears of Slave Violence on the Anti-Slavery Argument, 1829-1840," *Journal of Negro History* 55 (January 1970): 15-26.

[372] See Stuckey, 138; Huggins, 158.

[373] *The Liberator*, September 8, 1843, 1.

[374] *Minutes of the National Convention of Colored Citizens*.

[375] Ofari, 37; Schor, 57; Quarles, *Black Abolitionists*, 227-238.

Garnet spoke before a national assemblage and therefore received maximum attention by the general public. The convention's failure to adopt the speech was not really important. The fact that is was presented and seriously discussed legitimized it. The main measure of its value, however, was its overall effect on the actions of [B]lacks.[376]

In the years following the address, many State and National Negro Conventions endorsed the idea of radical liberation.[377] Indeed, several years after his initial statement condemning Garnet's speech, Douglass revised his opinion and expressed a view consistent with Garnet's address. Speaking to a Boston anti-slavery audience in 1849, Douglass said:

I should welcome the intelligence tomorrow, should it come, that the slaves had risen in the South, and that the sable arms which had been engaged in beautifying and adorning the South were engaged in spreading death and devastation.[378]

Another source of Garnet's Black Nationalism was his focus on Black history. His focus on Black

---

[376] Ofari, 42-43.
[377] Ibid., 45.
[378] Quoted in Ibid., 44.

achievements served to combat the myths of Black inferiority and to give Africans and African-Americans a sense of pride and a Black identity.[379] In his speech before the Female Benevolent Society of Troy, New York, 1848, Garnet focused on the history of ancient Africa.[380] Garnet placed both the blame for slavery and the destruction of African civilization on the Europeans:

> By almost common consent the modern world seems determined to pilfer Africa of her glory. It were not enough that her children have been scattered over the globe clothed in the garments of shame-humiliated and oppressed-but here merciless foes weary themselves in plundering the tombs of our renowned sires and in obliterating their worthy deeds which are inscribed by fame upon the pages of ancient history.[381]

Garnet extolled the achievements of ancient Africa emphasizing that during Africa's glory, Europe was much less advanced:

> At this time when these representatives of our race were filling the world with amazement the ancestors of the now proud Anglo-Saxons were

---

[379] Ofari, 76.

[380] The formal title of the speech was "The Past and Present Condition and the Destiny of the Colored Race, Troy 1848." For a full text of the speech see Ofari, 160-182.

[381] Ibid., 161.

among the most degraded of the human family. They abode in caves underground either naked or covered by the skins of wild beasts. Night was made hideous by their wild shouts, and day was darkened by the smoke which arose from bloody alters, upon which they offered human sacrifice.[382]

Another important source of Garnet's Black Nationalism was his emphasis upon an enlightened people and the need for an African-American intelligentsia. Indeed, one of the essential pillars of ethnic nationalism is the love of knowledge and the need for an educated leadership class.[383] Garnet was a person of great intellectual ability and proposed that African-Americans use education as a means of uplift:

> The good institutions of the land are well adapted to the development of the mind. So far as the oppressed shall make their way towards them. . .so far shall they succeed in throwing off their bitter thralldom, in wrenching the scrouge from the hands of tyranny.[384]

---

[382] Ibid., 166.

[383] Vincent Franklin, *Black Self-Determination: A Cultural History of African-American Resistance*, 2nd ed. (Brooklyn, N.Y.: Lawrence Books, 1992), 161-166; W.E.B. Dubois, "The Talented Tenth" in Booker T. Washington and Others, *The Negro Problem: A Series of Articles by Representative Negroes of Today* (New York, N.Y.: James Pott and Company, 1903), 33-75.

[384] Ofari, 172.

Garnet thus anticipated Dubois' theory that a talented tenth of an oppressed group must equip itself and provide the leadership towards elevation.[385] Indeed, intellectual strength was a principle source of Garnet's Black Nationalism.

Continuing his speech before the Female Benevolent Society, Garnet praised the revolutionary efforts of Black rebels in Haiti, Cuba, and the Americas. Garnet was saddened by the disunity among African-Americans, however. He mentioned his disappointment with a small group of clergypersons who were insincere about Christianity: "[s]ome who officiated in the temples said to be dedicated to God, are idolaters to sectarianism."[386] Garnet was particularly upset over discrimination of African-Americans against each other based on skin color: "[a]nd some too would draw a line of blood distinction and would form factions upon the shallow basis of complexion."[387]

---

[385] W.E.B. Dubois, "The Training of Negroes for Social Power" in Phillip Foner, ed., *W.E.B. Dubois Speaks* (New York, N.Y.: Pathfinder Press, 1970), 33.
[386] Ofari, 171-173.
[387] Ibid., 173.

Notwithstanding the Southerner's obstinacy in their slave-holding position, Northern oppression against free African-Americans, and divisions in the African-American community, Garnet saw hope that slavery would be abolished: "There are blessings in store for our patient, suffering race-- there is light and glory. The star of our hope is slowly and steadily rising above the horizon."[388]

Garnet gave several prescriptions to hasten the liberation event:

> By following after peace and temperance, industry and frugality, and love to God and to all men [and women], and by resisting tyranny in the name of Eternal Justice. We must also become acquainted with the arts and sciences, and agricultural pursuits. These will elevate any people and sever any chain.[389]

Self-elevation through diligence, thrift, love, and learning were prominent features in Garnet's Black Nationalist thinking.

Two weeks after the National Negro Convention in Buffalo, August 1843, the Liberty Party of New York held a state convention, also in Buffalo. Garnet and a significant

---

[388] Ibid., 182.
[389] Ibid.

number of the African-American delegates to the first convention were also delegates to the second convention. They continued the sense of Black independence and Black militancy from the Negro Convention into the Liberty Convention. Consistent with his idea of direct action, Garnet co-sponsored several resolutions calling for political action repealing slavery and condemning the government for its role in supporting the institution.[390] According to Charles Wesley, this was an extremely important milestone in African-American political participation:

> The Buffalo Convention of the Liberty Party was the most significant convention in the history of the Negroes' political life in the United States prior to the Civil War. . . . This was the first time in American history that Negro citizens were actually in the leadership of a political convention.[391]

What began in the early 1840's as Garnet's idea of a revolt against the property qualification for the franchise in New York, within a few years blossomed into several important Black Nationalist achievements. They included Garnet's militant speech calling slaves to resistance, Black

---

[390] Ibid., 23-25.
[391] Quoted in Ofari, 24. Charles Wesley, *Neglected History* (Xenia: Central State College Press, 1965), 62.

control of the Negro National Conventions, and the re-birth of a sense of Black consciousness. Garnet's spirit of self-reliance, self-assertion, and independence would spill over into his other ventures and philosophies, such as economics, emigration, Black Religion, and theodicy.

Black Nationalism and Economic Justice

Another important expression of Garnet's idea of Black Nationalism was his focus upon the goal of economic justice. Borrowing from Walker's *Appeal*, Garnet reasoned that Africans were not so much influenced by the love of power and the notion of greed as were the Europeans.[392] These tendencies caused the Europeans to plunder the African continent and to put its people into slavery. Indeed, the notion of economic greed was one of the driving forces of the slave-trade. Garnet reasoned that it was through this process that "the great nations were enriched."[393]

Garnet combined the economic, nationalistic, and Christian elements of his thoughts to form the fundamental bases for his idea opposing the forced use of humans for profit. He reasoned that the slave-system put a high value

---

[392] Ofari, 181.
[393] Ibid., 168.

upon Africans because of their superior performance in manual labor: "one Black [person] could do as much labor as four Indians."[394] African prejudice was thus founded both upon skin color and the profit motive. He further reasoned that the cotton industry and the slave-system provided for their mutual needs: the former needed a cheap labor force, while the latter provided it. Because the lives of both institutions were dependent upon political-economic support, Garnet made his opposition strategy both political and economic.

---

[394] Ibid., 167.

Image Ownership: Public Domain
David Walker

Garnet, as did David Walker, combined the movement from economic justice with the welfare of the entire world.[395] Because of America's significant economic

---

[395] Stuckey, 142.

influence, its injustices had an almost universal effect. Indeed, the rejection of the evil spirit of capitalism was a necessary prerequisite for a new world order.[396] Garnet cited the situation in the American South as an example of economic justice. Of eight million persons in the South, three hundred thousand owned the overwhelming majority of the land and held exclusive control of the government. Writing in Frederick Douglass' *North Star* Garnet spoke about universal economic democracy:

> The chains of the last slave on Earth may be broken in twain and still while the unholy system of landlordism prevails nations and people will mourn. But the moment that this wide-spread and monstrous evil is destroyed the dawn of the [G]ospel day will break forth and the world will have rest.[397]

Garnet thus reasoned that the destruction of the prevailing system of land ownership was an essential prerequisite for a new life of freedpersons who expected parity with their former owners. Continuing his thoughts in the *North Star* Garnet wrote:

---

[396] Huggins, 171.
[397] Quoted in Huggins: *The North Star*, September 15, 1848.

Again, let slavery be abolished in this country, and let the land and the labor monopolists have three or four hundred years of the emancipated, and still the free [people] will be heavy laden with an uphill course before them. Herein lies the secret of the trouble in the British West Indies. The old slaveholders are the landlords, and such they intend to be.[398]

Between 1847 and 1849 Garnet proposed an economic boycott of goods produced through slave labor. In Garnet's view the Free Produce Cause (as the economic boycott of goods produced by slaves came to be called) was one of the single best means by which pressure could be put upon the United States to outlaw the slave-trade.[399] In 1850 Garnet internationalized the economic struggle by traveling to London to seek support for the Free Produce Cause.[400]

---

[398] Ibid. The free persons refer to Whites as well as African-Americans. Garnet prefigured what Marx would articulate in his *Capital* (1867) by nearly twenty years that: "[l]abor in the White Skin can never be free as long as labor in the Black Skin is branded." Karl Marx, *Capital: Critique of Political Economy* (Reprint: New York, N.Y.: International Publishers, 1979), 705-774.

[399] Ofari, 58.

[400] Ten years before Garnet's arrival the English workers had begun to recognize the disastrous effects of slavery on their employment. The English workers realized that slave-produced goods undersold English products and would eventually cost English jobs. Industrialist owners were also concerned that lower-cost goods would force them to lose business and cause reductions in the English labor force. Fear of lost jobs, labor unrest, decreased profits, and an increased climate of abolition, created a strange marriage of workers, industrialist owners,

For two years Garnet spoke to groups throughout the British Isles championing both the Abolitionist and the Free Produce Causes. He was in great demand as an abolitionist speaker. Ofari observes that "Garnet's schedule was so packed with engagements that he felt compelled to apologize to a correspondent for not keeping those in America abreast of his activities."[401]

Garnet's speech so impressed a New Castle assemblage in 1850 that they resolved to condemn the White Church for its support of slavery and to support the Free Produce cause. The following is a partial reading of the Free Produce resolution:

> Seeing that the great design of the Fugitive Slave Act is to supply the markets of the world, and, above all, British markets with slave produce, in competition with free labour, this meeting would earnestly recommend to their friends the *Free Labor Movement,* as a legitimate and effectual method of putting down a system of wickedness such as can find no parallel on the face of the earth.[402]

---

and abolitionists, who put economic pressure on the United States for the repeal of slavery.

[401] Ibid., 64.

[402] Quoted in Ofari, 65. *Frederick Douglass Papers*, March 11, 1852.

Ofari reveals this observation of the consistency in the thinking of the New Castle assemblage and Garnet:

> The resolution showed that Garnet and the English free labor advocates were completely aware of the economic foundations of slavery. In their proposals was little of the moralistic sentimentality usually found in resolutions offered by American abolitionists. They were not far off in their estimate that if the cessation of trade between merchants and the planters eliminated a few markets, more damage would be done to slavery than had been accomplished by all the appeals and declarations put together.[403]

In covering Garnet's speech to a London assemblage in August 1850, a journalist for *The Antislavery Reporter* wrote that Garnet told the English their use of slave goods was inextricably tied to the evil of slavery:

> [Garnet] did not speak figuratively when he said, that the cotton which we used, the sugar with which we sweetened our tea, and the rice which we ate, were actually spread with the sweat of the slaves, sprinkled with their tears, and fanned by their signs, whilst the brutal driver goaded them to desperation, until an early grave relieved them from their misery. Could we then consent to give power to the arm that whirled the lash, and help to

---

[403] Ofari, 65.

drive the iron into the soul of the poor bondsmen [and women]?[404]

Garnet's speech proved powerfully persuasive and those assembled passed the following resolution that was fundamentally the same as Garnet's view:

Resolved, that this meeting holds with abhorrence the still existing institution of slavery, and concurs in the expression of the sentiments of our coloured friend, H.H. Garnet [sic], on the importance of the free-labour movement as a check to this barbarous system. Although this country has set the example of liberating the slave in her various colonies, yet in her large commercial connexions with the United States of America and Brazil she is virtually the upholder of slavery to a very considerable extent, and in this view of the case ought to exert herself to the utmost in its extinction. The recent oppressive law in the United States, and the high price of cotton in this country, have turned increasing attention to the loss of the slave, and an attempt to ameliorate his condition will perhaps at this time, above all others, be successful.[405]

Because the movement in the British Isles was relatively small, it was unable to achieve its goal "of

---

[404] Quoted in Schor, 117; *The Anti-Slavery Reporter*, January 16, 1851, 15.
[405] Schor, *The Anti-Slavery Reporter*.

rendering slavery unprofitable."[406] Garnet's efforts were a great help in keeping the Abolition and Free Produce Causes before the public, however.

Black Nationalism and Emigrationalism

In addition to advancing the Abolitionist and Free Produce Causes, Garnet took the British opportunity to condemn the American Colonization Society (ACS). Speaking to the British Foreign Anti-Slavery Society in 1851, Garnet made a harsh attack against the ACS:

> May we not judge people by the company they keep? May we estimate the American Colonization scheme by its president and officers? Slaveholders and their apologists. Who is its president and great supporter? A slaveholder (Henry Clay)! This society had encouraged outrage and oppression towards the coloured people, and in their affliction they deceitfully come up, [and] say, "Now had you not better go to Africa?" And when the coloured people reply that they would rather remain in their native country, they would urge the matter more persuasively, saying, "But don't you see that the laws are against you, and therefore you had better go?" Why, who had made these laws? The very people who would be first to transport them![407]

---

[406] Schor, 117-118; *The Anti-Slavery Reporter*, January 16, 1851, 9.
[407] Schor, 120-121; *The Anti-Slavery Reporter*, June 2, 1851, 86-87.

Early in his public career, Garnet opposed the efforts of the ACS believing it a scheme to remove free African-Americans and strengthen the slave-system.[408] In addition, Garnet saw little difference between African-American oppression and African colonization. In his "Address to the Slaves" in 1843, Garnet warned that prejudice against Blacks could be found on both sides on the Atlantic: "[I]t is impossible like the children of Israel to make a grand exodus from the land of bondage. The pharaohs are on both sides of the blooded waters."[409]

In his speech, "The Past and the Present Condition and the Destiny of the Colored Race Troy, 1848," Garnet reiterated his earlier colonization position emphasizing that America was the true home of African-Americans:

> Some people of color say that they have no home, no country. I am not among that number. It is empty declamation. . . . America is my home, my country, and I have no other. I love whatever of good there may be in her institutions. I hate her sins. I loathe her slavery, and I pray Heaven that ere long she may wash away her guilt in tears of repentance. . . . I love my country's flag, and I hope that soon it will be cleansed of its stains and be

---

[408] Ofari, 5.
[409] Ibid., 150.

hailed by all nations as the emblem of freedom and independence.[410]

For this reason and the reasons previously stated, Garnet was a vigorous opponent of colonization.[411]

Under the auspices of the United Presbyterian Church of Scotland, Garnet went to Jamaica as teacher-missionary. The Jamaican experience between 1853 and 1856 provided Garnet the opportunity to modify his anti-colonization views and to develop an idea of selective emigration. This was an idea to recruit skilled African-Americans for voluntary re-settlement to predominately Black cultures. Both parties benefited under the plan. The former benefited from the skills and motivation of the emigrants, while the latter were provided the chance to reach their potential, an opportunity denied to them in America.[412]

His first experience in a predominately Black country, Garnet was favorably impressed with Black land ownership and Black involvement in local governmental

---

[410] Ibid., 182.
[411] Ibid., 66-69.
[412] Ibid., 66-67.

affairs.[413]   He   soon   envisioned   African-American emigration to Jamaica to take advantage of the opportunities for   Black   self-advancement   that   were   unavailable   in America.[414]

While Garnet began a recruitment of African-Americans for re-settlement into Jamaica, he did not significantly alter his emigration policies. He was still of the major opinion that colonization was an evil idea promulgated by the ACS to rid the country of its entire Black population.   Garnet was thus consistent in his selective emigration strategy, seeking "an outlet for select individual who had skills."[415]

Garnet worked untiringly in Jamaica for the next three years teaching, performing ministries, studying, and analyzing the Black-Jamaican situation, and giving advice to Black intellectuals based upon his research.[416]   While satisfied with his work, Garnet felt too removed from the situation in America. In a letter to L.A. Chomeron, October 1854, Garnet expressed this worry: "But alas when I hear

---

[413] Jane Pease and William Pease, *Bound With Them in Chains* (Westport, CT: Greenwood Press, 1972), 182-184; Quarles, 216.
[414] Ofari, 66-70.
[415] Ibid., 68.
[416] Schor, 126-130.

the din of battle coming over from the shores of America my soul leaps up within me."[417] Garnet returned to Boston in February 1856.

The desire to seek a home abroad rejuvenated the Emigration Movement in the United States during the period between 1850 and 1861. By 1850 there was a feeling among African-Americans that they could not advance in America. Schor explains:

> The Fugitive Slave Law, mitigated by the passage of personal liberty laws, had placed the burden of proving one's freedom upon the accused. Then, too, the Dred Scott case of 1857 which declared the Negro to be property seemed to many [B]lacks a complete and categorical denial of [their] humanity. Although many Negroes looked to the Republican party to their political hope, and although the party grew at a phenomenal rate in the late 1850's, its commitment to Negro rights was limited to the territories.[418]

Several of the leading Black Nationalist thinkers began to devise various emigration projects.[419] In his article

---

[417] Quoted in Ofari, Garnet to L.A. Chomeron October 1754, Rhodes House Library.

[418] Schor, 151-152.

[419] For background information concerning the various emigration proposals during the nineteenth century, see Howard Bell, "Negro Nationalism: A Factor in Emigration Projects, 1858-19610," *The*

"The Rivalry between Frederick Douglass and Henry Highland Garnet" (1979), Joel Schor explains that Douglass did not favor emigration, labeling those African-Americans who left America as traitors.[420] Garnet countered with a compromise between the forced emigration idea of the ACS and Douglass' stay-at-home-no-matter-what philosophy.[421] As was previously stated, Garnet proposed a selective

---

Journal of Negro History XLVII I 47 (Jan 1962): 42-53; "Negro Nationalism in the 1850's," *The Journal of Negro Education* XXXV 1 35 (Jan 1966): 1-4; Richard Blackett, "Martin R. Delany and Robert Campbell: Black Americans in Search of an African Colony," *The Journal of Negro History* LXII 1 (Feb 1977): 1-25; and Floyd J. Miller, *The Search for Black Nationalist: Black Emigration and Colonization* (Urbana: University of Illinois Press, 1975).

[420] Schor, "The Rivalry between Frederick Douglass and Henry Highland Garnet," *The Journal of Negro History* LXIV 1 (Jan 1979): 33-36.

[421] From the introduction of the idea of colonization by the American Colonization Society in 1817 throughout the life of the idea, there has not been a monolithic emigration policy among Blacks. Frederick Douglass, for example, was adamant in his anti-colonization position. Writing in his newspaper, "The North Star," Douglass continued the condemnation of colonization:

> Upon one point we wish to be especially explicit and that is upon no consideration do we intend that our paper shall favor any schemes of colonization, or any measure the natural tendency of which will be to draw off the attention of the free colored people from the means of improvement and elevation here. Now, and always, we expect to insist upon it that we are Americans, that America is our native land; that we are American citizens; that it is the day of the American people so to recognize us.

See "Douglass' Month," January 1859, 2.

emigration policy. By 1848 the end of the Mexican-American War gave the South the opportunity to re-focus upon expanding slavery to the new territories. The growth of slavery, the political power of the South, and the general mood of disillusionment caused Garnet to announce the famous change in his colonization position: "I hesitate to say that my mind of late has greatly changed in regard to the American Colonization scheme. . . I would rather see a [person] free in Liberia than a slave in the United States.[422]

Garnet's emigration policy became the cornerstone for the philosophy of the African Civilization Society.[423] Founded in 1858 by Garnet and an integrated group, the aims of the Society were in "support of African settlements of Black missionaries to teach local natives to institute agricultural improvements and to educate them against the folly of participation in the slave-trade."[424] Garnet served as the Society's first president and one of its predominant spokespersons.

---

[422] "The Liberator," May 30, 1851.

[423] Richard MacMaster, "Henry Highland Garnet and the American Civilization Society," *Journal of Presbyterian History* 48 (January 1970): 95-112.

[424] Quoted in Schor, 115; "The Colored Citizen," February 27, 1841.

Garnet outlined the proposals for the Society in his "Speech Delivered at Coopers Institute New York City, 1860."[425] He began by making a brief statement about the status of African-Americans. He said that African-Americans were a people of talent, but because of prejudice against them their talents were not employed.[426] The African Civilization Society would "remove those barriers by discovering fields for the full and free exercise of their talents and energies either in our native land, in Central America, in Haiti, in any of the free West Indies Islands, or in Africa the land of our [foreparents]."[427] Garnet held that one of the basic keys to destroying the slave-trade was creating an alternative supply of cotton.[428] Garnet would have the Society's missionaries to teach the African leaders "better things to induce them to exterminate the slave-trade and engage in lawful commerce and in this way aid in destroying slavery in this and other lands."[429]

Several African-American leaders were suspicious of Garnet's proposals. They felt that the African

---

[425] For a complete text of the speech, see Ofari, 183-186.
[426] Ibid., 183.
[427] Ibid.
[428] Ibid., 183-184.
[429] Ibid.

Civilization Society was really the American Colonization Society in disguise.[430] This was a charge that Garnet vigorously denied. Garnet pointed to a major distinction between the two groups: the American Colonization Society advocated a forced mass colonization, while the African Civilization Society favored individual re-settlement through consent. Indeed, what Garnet desired to establish was a "grand center of Negro nationality from which shall flow streams of commercial, intellectual, and political power which shall make colored people respected everywhere."[431] Responding to a sarcastic question as to whether the center of nationality was to be built in Africa or America, Garnet articulated a clear statement of his pan-African ideal:

> I hope in the United States; especially if they reopen the African slave-trade. Then, if we do not establish a nationality in the South, I am mistaken in the spirit of my people. Let them bring a hundred thousand a year! We do not say it is not a great crime, but we know that from the wickedness of [humankind] God brings forth good; and if they

---

[430] Miller, "The Search for a Black Nationality: Martin R. Delany and the Emigrationist Alternative" (Ph.D. dissertation University of Minnesota, 1970), 63; Victor Ullman, *Martin R. Delany: The Beginnings of Black Nationalism* (Boston: Beacon Press, 1971), 214.
[431] Quoted in Ofari, 86; *Weekly Anglo-African*, September 10, 1859.

do it, before half a century shall pass over us we shall have a [N]egro nationality in the United States. In Jamaica there are forty [C]olored [persons] to one [W]hite; Haiti is ours; Cuba will be ours soon, and we shall have every island in the Caribbean Sea.[432]

Image Ownership: Public Domain
Martin Delany

---

[432] Quoted in ibid., 86-87.

Benefiting through the efforts of Martin Delany, a fellow Black Nationalist-emigrationist who negotiated an African land treaty, Garnet's emigration policy achieved moderate success.[433]   By 1861 the African Civilization Society's plans went into fatal decline. Prominent among the reasons for its failure were the "African Renunciation of Delany's land treaty, Yoruba warfare in the projected area of settlement, and endless bickering in the free Black community.[434]   Garnet's African Civilization Society's venture, however, was successful in laying the groundwork for future Pan-African ventures.

Black Nationalism in Relation to Theodicy

Closely related to Garnet's Black Nationalist thinking was his idea of theodicy. Garnet held a strong belief in an omnipotent, omniscient, and all-benevolent God.[435]   Garnet held an unwavering trust in this God and held God up to the Black race as the one, true God. How did Garnet reconcile his belief in both an omnipotent God

---

[433] Pease and Pease, 185-189; *Weekly Anglo-American*, October 1, 1859.
[434] Pease and Pease.
[435] For definitions of terms see the section of definitions on pages 4-10 of the study.

and a God who allowed the beginning of slavery? How did Garnet reconcile his belief in an all-benevolent God who allowed slavery to continue?

Garnet developed his Black Nationalist position in relation to his theodicy into an idea of Providence and African-American Resistance. Garnet traced the origins of slavery to European greed.[436] It was because of free will, according to Garnet, that men and women were provided the opportunity to choose between good and evil. The idea of free will holds that God created humankind with unrestricted minds of their own. Humans are therefore free to choose their courses of action.[437] Unfortunately, the Europeans abused free will and chose to create and maintain the slave-system. While this may answer the question of European opportunity and motive, it does not provide satisfactory answers for God's failure to balance God's injustice with humankind's wanton abuse of free will.

Garnet reasoned that it was not that God failed to act, but because of humankind's misuse of free will and

---

[436] Ofari, 134.

[437] Garnet based his idea of free will upon St. Augustine's theology of the human capacity for free will and personal responsibility. David Knowles, ed., and Henry Betterson (trans.), *The City of God* v. 9-11 (Penguin: New York, N.Y., 1972), 190-196.

other selfish interests that slavery took a life of its own. Because the slave-traders enjoyed the economic benefits and the slave-owners enjoyed the cheap labor force, slavery became an entrenched institution.[438] The White Church chose to accept slavery based on the idea of African inferiority or benign paternalism. Some White theologians went as far as to build theological and ethical systems to justify and support the institution. Explaining the institutionalization of slavery in his "Address to the Slaves," Garnet said:

> The voice of Freedom cried, "Emancipate your slaves." Humanity supplicated with tears for the deliverance of the children of Africa. Wisdom urged her solemn plea, the bleeding captive pleaded his innocence, and pointed to Christianity who stood weeping at the cross. Jehovah frowned upon the nefarious institution, and thunderbolts, red with vengeance, struggled to leap forth to blast the guilty wretches who maintained it. But all was vain. Slavery had stretched its dark wings of death over the land, the church stood silently by--the priests prophesied falsely, and the people loved to have it so. Its throne is established, and now it reigns triumphant.[439]

---

[438] Ofari, 146.
[439] Ibid.

While Garnet accepted the free will theory he did not view it as ultimate or final. At some point, God would break into history and abolish the slave-system.[440] Indeed, in his "Address to the Slaves" Garnet articulated a view of a "future judgment and the righteous retributions of an indignant God" for those who continued to support slavery.[441]

Because of God's future action for the oppressed, were they to sit idly and wait for God's liberation? Reasoning that Christianity made slaves docile and complacent, many African-Americans criticized Christianity precisely at this point. Believing that Christianity in its proper practice was decidedly liberating, Garnet was extremely hostile to the complacency view. Speaking of Garnet's view of the Black practice of religion, Ofari observed that:

> Garnet's actions were always determined by the needs of the Anti-Slavery Movement. His concern that [B]lacks have the benefit of religious training was based on his belief that it was a requisite for building character, strength, and discipline. Viewing religion as something that could serve [humankind], he meant to employ it as a vehicle for [B]lack self-expression and

---

[440] Ibid., 150.
[441] Ibid.

uplift. Garnet wanted to reconcile theory and practice in the church. One without the other was meaningless. His goal was to utilize the church in the liberation struggle. Devotion to God was equated with devotion to the struggle.[442]

Indeed, Garnet found that Whites took great pains to keep African-Americans from becoming Christians for the very reason that it had a liberation element. Huggins found that Garnet "thought Christianity the foundation of elevation and hope that makes tyrants quake at the thought of its spread."[443] Garnet incorporated the liberation element in his "Address to the Slaves," encouraging them to resist:

> If a band of heathen [persons] should attempt to enslave a race of Christians, and to place their children under the influence of some false religion, surely, Heaven would frown upon [those] who would not resist such aggression, even to death. If, on the other hand, a band of Christians should attempt to enslave a race of heathen [people], and to entail slavery upon them, and to keep them in heathenism in the midst of Christianity, the God of

---

[442] Ofari, 55. It is my position that Whites were more inclined to make African-Americans Christians than Garnet would have us believe. Garnet is right, however, in implying that Whites hid, or least made attempts to hide, the authentic liberating message of Christianity from the Black adherents.

[443] Huggins, 173.

heaven would smile upon every effort which the injured might make to disenthrall themselves.[444]

For those slaves who were in fact Christians, Garnet asked that they practice the authentic Christianity--that faith that inspired liberation. White Religion taught slaves to obey their owners and to submit to slavery; Garnet countered in teaching that voluntary slave submission was unchristian. Indeed, he made this position clear in his "Address to the Slaves" in saying that: "TO SUCH DEGRADATION IT IS SINFUL IN THE EXTREME FOR YOU TO MAKE VOLUNTARY SUBMISSION."[445]

Garnet reasoned that service to God required one to keep God's commandments. Slavery did not allow slaves to keep God's commandments because slaves were unable to enjoy the free exercise of their religion. It was extremely difficult for slaves to reach their God-given potential in an oppressed state. For example, slaves were denied opportunities for education, thus they were unable to study the scriptures. Indeed, those persons who had maximized their potential would be of greater service to God's glory. It

---

[444] Ofari, 148.
[445] Ibid., 147.

was, therefore, the slaves' Christian duty to resist slavery.

In his "Address to the Slaves," Garnet said:

> The [D]ivine commandments you are in duty bound to reverence and obey. If you do not obey them, you will surely meet with the displeasure of the Almighty. [God] requires you to love [God] supremely, and your neighbor as yourself, to keep the Sabbath day holy, to search the scriptures, and bring up your children with respect for the laws, and to worship no other God but [God]. But slavery sets all these at nought and hurls defiance in the face of Jehovah.[446]

In his article, *Henry Highland Garnet: Black Revolutionary in Sheep Vestments*, Arthur L. Smith makes the claim that Garnet justified violence to the religious community by putting the priority more on human suffering and the destruction of slavery, rather than the means to achieve the goals.[447] Thus, the idea of resistance to evil, especially when it served to block the authentic practice of Christianity, was an essential element in Garnet's Black Christian Nationalist thought.

---

[446] Ibid.
[447] Arthur L. Smith, "Henry Highland Garnet Black Revolutionary in Sheep Vestments," *The Central States Speech Journal* XXI 2 (Summer 1970): 93-98.

The idea of Providence is one of the essential concepts in Garnet's Black Nationalist position in relation to his theodicy. Garnet's idea of Providence refers to "God's purpose and goal for humanity. Providence concerns itself with the way in which God attempts to accomplish God's purpose in history."[448] Garnet believed that God's will leads to the vindication of the righteous. God's history leads to God's ultimate which are the ideals of liberation and justice.

One of the major sources of Garnet's belief in Providence was the idea of a moral order in the universe that good will ultimately triumph over evil. Expressing his indignation concerning General Seminary's discriminatory rejection of Crummell's application for admission, Garnet wrote: "God will see to it that the actions of those by whom the offense has come shall be weighed in the balance."[449] Incorporating the idea of the moral order into his "Address to the Slaves," the use of violence was secondary to moral suasion. Garnet made it clear that the slaves were to ". . .tell them (the slave-owners) in language which they would not

---

[448] Henry Young, "Black Theology: Providence and Evil," *Journal of the Interdenominational Theological Center* (Spring 1975): 87.
[449] Quoted in Schor, 24; *The Colored America*, September 28, 1839, 3.

misunderstand of the exceeding sinfulness of slavery and of the righteous retributions of an indignant God."[450]

An extremely important element in the moral order was the idea of an immutable, universal truth. In a speech to the Liberty Party in 1842, Garnet told the Libertarians that "the slaveholders count upon numbers; we upon truth, and it is powerful and will prevail."[451] One of the fundamental truths was Garnet's idea of God-given humanity and the sacredness of the human person. In his "Discourse Delivered in the House of Representatives Washington, D.C., 1865," Garnet warned those who made slaves, thus violating the sacredness of human persons, of God's future judgment:

> Our poor and forlorn brother whom thou has labelled "*slave,*" is also a man. He may be unfortunate, weak, helpless, and despised, and hated, nevertheless he is a man. His God and thine has stamped on his forehead his title to his inalienable rights in characters that can be read by every intelligent being. Pitiless storms of outrage may have beaten upon his defenceless head, and he may have descended through ages of oppression,

---

[450] Ofari, 150.

[451] Ibid., 143. The formal name of the speech: "Speech Delivered at the Liberty Party Convention Massachusetts, 1842." For a complete text see Ofari, 138-144.

yet he is a man. God made him such, and his brother cannot unmake him. Woe, woe to him who attempts to commit the accursed crime.[452]

Garnet's idea of Providence was also based upon his belief in God's plan to liberate the oppressed. In his "Speech Delivered at the Liberty Party Convention Massachusetts, 1842" Garnet told the Libertarians that:

All our success is of God, "who raiseth upon nation and putteth down another"; yes, that Almighty Being who said, "let there be light and there was light," has called into being the Spirit of this age, to bring out [God's] oppressed poor from under their task [persons]; and it is enough for us to be used as instruments in the hand of God, in accomplishing [God's] glorious purposes.[453]

This was also an element of the *zeitgeist*--the notion that the idea of liberation had come.

In his speech, "The Past and Present Condition and the Destiny of the Colored Race, Troy 1848," Garnet expressed a hope in the redemptive nature of Black suffering:

There are blessings in store for our patient, suffering race, there is light and glory. The star of

[452] Ibid., 191.
[453] Ibid., 139.

our hope is slowly and steadily rising above the horizon. As a land that has long been covered by storm and clouds, and shaken by the thunder, when the storms and clouds had passed away, and the thunder was succeeded by a calm, like that which cheered the first glad morning, and flower and shrub smiled as they looked up to God, and the mountains, plains and valleys rung with joy,--so shall this race come ;forth and re-occupy their station of renown.[454]

Another source of Garnet's belief in Providence was his hope in a liberated future. Central to any Liberation Movement is the idea of hope. Of several places that Garnet found hope, one was in America's religious life. While there were great national sins, there was piety as well. In his "Speech Delivered at the Seventh Anniversary of the American Anti-Slavery Society, 1840," Garnet said:

The truthfulness of the words of the British [statesperson}, that religion is the basis of civil society, is almost universally acknowledged. And the spirit of our institutions lays it down as a primary duty of Americans, to acknowledge the moral government of God in all our affairs. The greatest blessings which we have received as a nation, have been given unto us on account of the little piety that has been found among us. And no one will say that there has not been now and then

---

[454] Ibid., 182.

a pious soul among our people, although there is
enough sin among us to excite the tears of the
Christian world.[455]

Garnet hoped to impress Judeo-Christian values upon
American civil institutions. Such an infusion would ensure
the demise of slavery and hasten the day for universal
brotherhood and sisterhood.

By 1848, however, Garnet had come to a realization
that institutionalized religion, namely Christianity, brought
forth both good and evil. Christianity debased both Whites
and African-Americans, providing a double opportunity for
selfishness and theological mischief.[456] Yet Garnet clung to
the church as a foundation of hope for Black liberation.
Garnet expressed both his frustration and his hope in the
church in an 1848 article to the *North Star*:

> Much of the blame attached to this state of things
> (corruption among Blacks) lies at the door of what
> is called the church, and more rests upon our own
> heads. This church that has torn us must help to
> heal; who has scattered must help to gather; and
> both of these things we must do ourselves.[457]

---

[455] Ibid., 131.
[456] *North Star*, January 19, 1848; Ofari, 54-57.
[457] *North Star*.

While Garnet put the blame for a number of African-American problems at the doorsteps of the church, he was equally critical of the African-American community itself. A consistent advocate of self-reliance, Garnet articulated a view that held the African-American community responsible for their success and for a plan of elevation. Actually, Garnet had spoken about the means of elevation back in his 1843 "Address to the Slaves." There Garnet gave a brief answer to the question of how to achieve African-American elevation:

> By following after peace and temperance, industry and frugality, and love to God, and to all [people], and by resisting tyranny in the name of Eternal Justice. We must also become acquainted with the arts and sciences, and agricultural pursuits. These will elevate any people and sever any chain.[458]

Garnet, thus, did not speak eschatologically or in terms of a heavenly afterlife; he spoke in terms of an actualized physical hope.

Similarly, in a speech to the New York Negro State Convention in 1840, Garnet said: "African-American rights would be obtained only through the continued presentation

---

[458] Ofari, 182.

of the great truths pertaining to their specific wrongs accompanied by corresponding energy and activity on the part of the aggrieved."[459] While Garnet developed the truth into theories and strategies through which slavery and oppression would be combated, he also put the strategies into practice through his previously mentioned political-social-economic community-based programs. Garnet thus forged a connecting link between the idea of Providence, with its attending hope, and the idea of Resistance, with its call to African-Americans to challenge slavery and oppression.

Garnet's idea of Resistance complimented his idea of Providence in his Black Nationalist position in relation to his theodicy. Providence gave the hope, while Resistance provided the efforts to actualize the hope. While Garnet's idea of Resistance included violence, he did not mean an immediate resort to violence. By Resistance, Garnet meant that the slaves were to use "every means both moral, intellectual, and physical that promised success" in breaking the yoke of slavery.[460]

---

[459] *Minutes of the State Convention of Colored Citizens*, 21.
[460] Ofari, 148.

The fundamental source of Garnet's idea of Resistance was the Christian Religion. As previously stated, Garnet thought it a sin to submit to slavery. He found very little redeeming value in slave acquiescence. Indeed, Garnet felt it the slaves' Christian duty to revolt against slavery. Garnet emphasized these concerns in his "Address to the Slaves:"

> In every [person's] mind the good seeds of liberty are planted and [the person] who brings his [or her brother or sister] down so low, as to make him [or her] contented with a condition of slavery, commits the highest crime against God and [humanity]. [Brothers and sisters], your oppressors aim to do this. They endeavor to make you as much like brutes as possible. When they have blinded the eyes of your mind--when they have embittered the sweet waters of life--when they have shut out the light which shines from the word of God--then, and not till then has American slavery done its perfect work.[461]

Wanting to call more attention to the next idea Garnet published the sentence in bold capitals: "TO SUCH DEGRADATION IT IS SINFUL IN THE EXTREME FOR YOU TO MAKE VOLUNTARY SUBMISSION."[462]

---

[461] Ibid., 147.
[462] Ibid.

Further in the address, Garnet called attention to his thoughts by capitalizing another important sentence: "NEITHER GOD, NOR ANGELS, OR JUST MEN [AND WOMEN] COMMAND YOU TO SUFFER FOR A SINGLE MOMENT. THEREFORE IT IS YOUR SOLEMN AND IMPERATIVE DUTY TO USE EVERY MEANS, BOTH MORAL, INTELLECTUAL, AND PHYSICAL, THAT PROMISE SUCCESS."[463]

Perceiving the church as an integral part of the political, social, and economic community, Garnet put forth his idea of Resistance through his ministries. Garnet was an extremely dynamic, American social gospeler. He worked for the betterment of his community through a variety of social programs, including the African Civilization Society's emigration project and assistance to church and community members during emergencies. Jane and Williams Pease observed that Garnet "used the church as a means to elevate his people shaping his religion to sustain a practical social gospel rather than an intellectualized theology."[464] They characterized Garnet's pastorates as socially oriented:

---

[463] Ibid., 148.
[464] Pease and Pease, 165-166.

Not confined to religious worship, Garnet's churches were establishments designed to achieve social, economic, and political uplift among their parishioners. Moreover, Garnet's sermons, as much as ancillary church functions, served social needs rather than developing theology.[465]

Much like Richard Allen and the Free African Society, Garnet's ministry served a dual focus: "free and autonomous worship in the Afro-American tradition and the solidarity and the social welfare of the Black community."[466]

Other important sources of Garnet's ideas of Resistance were based upon his concepts of Black self-reliance and Black self-assertion. Because Whites did not experience the harshness of slavery and oppression, and because Whites were not as aggressive in combating oppression as Garnet thought they ought to have been, he reasoned that the best advocates for Black liberation were Blacks themselves. Writing about African-Americans in New York involved in a self-help project, Garnet said:

> Self-help--This principle is invincible. Regard it either in a moral, physical, or intellectual light, it is to an oppressed people what Moses was to the

---

[465] Ibid., 167.
[466] Wilmore, *Black Religion and Black Radicalism*, 82-83.

Hebrews--what Virginius was to Rome, and what Toussaint L'Ouverture was to his golden island of the ocean.

My heart leaps with joy as I behold my long-suffering and noble people laying aside their old garments of dependence, and entering upon their work.[467]

Garnet's ideas of Providence and Resistance and their corresponding sources served to develop a strong basis for Garnet's idea of Black Nationalism in relation to his theodicy.

Strengths and Weakness of Garnet's Theodicy

Garnet's theological world view envisioned a God both immanently involved in all of life and as life's ultimate sustainer.[468] There was a dynamic connection between God's omnipotence and a faith that provided guidance and power to sustain African-Americans through slavery and oppression. Closely related to the theological world view was the idea of Providence. Garnet believed that in God's

---

[467] *The North Star*, January 19, 1849.
[468] Edward Wimberly, *Pastoral Care in the Black Church* (Nashville: Abingdon, 1979), 25.

own time God would liberate the slaves and create a just social order.

Garnet's theodicy, Providence and African-American Resistance, was an attempt to provide his Black Nationalist thinking with theological answers to the problems of Black oppression. According to Garnet, because of their abuse of free will, the Europeans decided to create African slavery. Garnet believed that while God allowed the birth of those evils, God would not allow them to stand forever. To be sure, God would in a future time eradicate the slave-system and continue efforts to create a just social order. Yet at the same time, God commanded the slaves to work towards liberation. Because of God's idea that humans were the noblest of creation, God did not create humans for enslavement; nor did God intend for humans to submit to slavery. Garnet equated humble submission to slavery to participation in evil. Indeed, the refusal to allow slaves the free exercise of their religion denied the opportunities for the best services to God. Thus, Garnet's Black Nationalist position in relation to his theodicy combined God's Providence--the hope of a future liberation--with African-American Resistance--the idea of self-generative Black liberation activities.

One of the stronger dimensions in Garnet's idea of Providence and African-American Resistance was his emphasis upon a working-hope. Garnet impressed upon the slaves the idea that God worked God's purpose through history, sometimes transforming evil into God's good. Garnet stressed God's moral order in the universe and God's final judgment upon the wicked. In their book *Soul Theology: The Heart of American Black Culture*, Nicholas C. Cooper-Lewter and Henry M. Mitchel identified the *Providence of God* as one of the traditional core beliefs in African-American Religion.[469] They traced this belief from Traditional African Religion to present-day African-American Christianity.[470] Their analysis of the belief in the *Providence of God* is fundamentally the same as Garnet's idea of Providence:

> It is the deep and sweeping assertion that the whole universe is friendly or benevolent, and that its Creator is able and willing to turn into good ends whatever may occur. Within Black culture this is a given, but to minds shaped in other cultures, it may seem like wishful thinking--an imagined

---

[469] Nicholas C. Cooper-Lewter and Henry C. Mitchel, *Soul Theology: The Heart of American Black Culture* (San Francisco: Harper and Row Publishers 1986), 14.
[470] Ibid., 15-17.

comfort and escape from reality. However, among soul folk it is a foundational and fruitful insistence on which all life and effort depend. There can be no final disproof of it, because the doctrine always refers to ultimate ends; the disbelievers and challengers simply have not waited long enough. Oppressed people are supported by the conviction that the very Lord of the universe has guaranteed that their lives will always be worth living.[471]

This was an extremely powerful idea that gave the slaves a guarantee that their lives were worth living.

Not only did Garnet speak in terms of a spiritual-hope, but a working-hope as well. He felt that the oppressed could never dispense with their own efforts for liberation. If Garnet did not include the work ethic in his idea of hope, then many slaves and abolitionists who believed in his ideas may have taken a wait-on-God approach to liberation. The idea of direct action was a great contribution to the Abolition-Liberation Cause.

The idea of a working-hope inspired the concept of African-American self-reliance. Both were concepts that sprang from the belief that God sided with the oppressed. Garnet sized the idea of a liberating God and linked it to the

---

[471] Ibid.

reality of cross-generational suffering. The connection between the two provided a very powerful appeal for slave resistance. Garnet's ideas were one of the earliest expressions of a militant Black Theology. Its strength is contained in the idea of a God who is displeased with cross-generational suffering and a God who will support the activities of the oppressed to free themselves from their oppressors.

Closely related to the idea of a working-hope are the concepts of African-American self-reliance and self-assertiveness. These concepts are two of the pillars of a Liberation Movement and ensure that the issues of oppression are taken seriously and are always in the forefront. Because most oppressed communities are less empowered and have low self-esteem, self-reliance and self-assertiveness are enabling tools. They empower the oppressed with a sense of identity, community resourcefulness, and a certain aggressiveness.

Garnet's explanation for the beginning of slavery puts the blame where it belongs, upon the Europeans who began it. Yet, Garnet was never really able to explain God's failure to act during the three-hundred-year reign of slavery. The hope of a liberated future; the belief in God's ability, and indeed God's acts in transforming evil to good; and the belief in the idea that God sides with the oppressed, are not quite the same as an immediate, Godly intervention to abolish slavery and oppression.

Summary

This chapter gave a brief biographical sketch of Garnet, focusing on those life experiences that influenced his idea of Black Nationalism in relation to his theodicy. The chapter traced the development of Garnet's ideas of Black Nationalism and examined their sources; the chapter examined Garnet's ideas of Black Nationalism and economic democracy; and examined Garnet's ideas of Black Nationalism and emigration. The critical analysis of those Garnet ideas gave the essential basis for the next task--the analytical development of Garnet's theodicy: "Providence and African-American Resistance." Finally, the chapter critiqued Garnet's idea of Providence and African-American Resistance.

Chapter IV: **ALEXANDER CRUMMELL (8919-1821): PROVIDENCE AND DIVINE RETRIBUTION-RESTORATION**

This chapter provides a biographical sketch of Crummell, focusing on those life experiences that influence Crummell's theodicy. This chapter examines Crummell's concepts of Liberian Nationalism and African-American Uplift. There is a specific focus on Crummell's ideas of Emigration, Evangelism, Civilization, and African-American Uplift. Finally, the chapter critiques Crummell's theodicy, Providence and Divine Retribution-Restoration.

Biographical Sketch of Crummell

Alexander Crummell (1819-1898) was born in 1819 to free parents in New York City. Boston Crummell, Alexander's father, claims descent from the Timanee of West Africa.[472] According to Alexander, his father was stolen from Africa at about twelve or thirteen years old, between 1780 and 1781.[473] Never legally emancipated,

---

[472] George W. Forbes, "Alexander Crummell, "The Forbes Papers, Boston Public Library, 1-3.
[473] Henry L. Phillips, In Memoriam of the Late Rev. Alexander Crummell, D.D. of Washington, DE.C. (Philadelphia, 1899), 9.

Boston announced his liberation to his owner, Peter Schermerhorn of New York City, and left to begin a free life in another section of town.[474] Alexander took delight in being known as the "boy whose father could not be a slave."[475] Alexander's mother was Charity Hicks Crummell, a member of a New York family that had known freedom for several generations.[476]

Young Alexander benefited from the free African-American community in New York City. His adult concepts of Black Nationalism and theodicy were shaped by the ideas of Abolitionism, Black Nationalism, Ethiopianism, Civilization, and Black Religion that were popular during his boyhood days.[477] In addition, Alexander

---

[474] Wilson Moses, *Alexander Crummell: A Study of Civilization and Discontent* (New York, N.Y.: Oxford University Press, 1989), 12.
[475] Quoted in ibid., who cite *The Liberator*, September 5, 1835, in Forbes.
[476] Moses, 11.
[477] *Ethiopianism* symbolized Black African power. The term implies a view that Black Africans would reclaim their true identity and bolster their self-esteem. Becoming a major there in nineteenth century Black Nationalist thinking, Ethiopianism proposed the Black Africa would rise to its preordained position of glory and power. See St. Clair Drake, *The Redemption of Africa and Black Religion* (Chicago: Third World Press, 1970), 9-11.
　　Crummell used the term *civilization* throughout his speeches and writings. Unfortunately, he did not offer a precise definition. There are, however, certain implications for the term that are revealed from the research of this study: *civilization* refers to exalted action

received the best education available to free African-Americans of New York City during the Antebellum Period. In his article "Alexander Crummell: Black Nationalist and Apostle of Western Civilization" (1988), Alfred Moss discussed the socio-political and economic activities of African-Americans in New York and Crummell's direct benefits from their efforts:

> The [B]lacks of New York were actively involved in abolitionist activities, agitation for greater political rights, and efforts to arrest the pattern of social segregation that excluded them from public schools and places of public accommodation. . . . They attempted to secure greater respect from [W]hites and increased political, social, and economic opportunities for themselves. One of the most important expressions of this drive for betterment was the time, energy, and resources that went into the creation of social institutions to provide needed services for a segregated and disadvantaged community. Crummell was a direct beneficiary of these activities, both emotionally and practically. He grew up witnessing all around him [B]lacks—his family prominent among them—

---

both on the part of humankind and government—indeed all things Western. See Wilson Moses, "Civilizing Missionary: A Study of Alexander Crummell, "*Journal of Negro History* 60 (April 1975): 231-233.

individually and mutually promoting self-worth, independence, and community.[478]

The Crummell family seemed to enjoy an elite status in New York City. Closely associated with some of the best African-American minds in the city, the Crummell's had the distinction of *Freedom's Journal*, the first African-American newspapers, being found in their home.[479] Samuel Cornish and John Russwurm were co-editors and believed in the idea of African-American self-improvement. The two men dedicated the paper to "publicizing useful knowledge of every kind and everything that related to Africa and to proving that the natives of it were neither so ignorant nor stupid as they were generally. . .supposed to be."[480] Alexander was impressed by their philosophy of African-American Uplift and would incorporate it into his future thinking.

---

[478] Alfred Moss, "Alexander Crummell: Black Nationalist and Apostle of Western Civilization" in Leon Litwack and August Meier, *Black Leaders of the Nineteenth Century* (Urbana: University of Illinois Press, 1988), 238-239.

[479] I. Garland Penn, *The Afro-American Press and its Editors* (Springfield, Massachusetts: Wiley, 1891), 27.

[480] Quoted in Moses who cites *Freedom's Journal*, March 16, 1827.

The list of distinguished visitors to the Crummell home provided Alexander with exposure to the anti-colonization views of Samuel Cornish and the pro-colonization views of Peter Williams, the African-American Episcopal priest, and an apologist for Paul Cuffee and his colonization efforts.[481] While Boston Crummell held fond memories of Africa, he was nevertheless opposed to colonization.[482] Alexander, much like the visitors to his home, would have ambivalent feelings about colonization, first rejecting it and later modifying his view.[483]

Boston established himself as a leader in New York City's African-American community and nurtured in Alexander a profound sense of self-worth and self-reliance. Boston's success enabled him to provide a comfortable, secure life for his family. Closely related to Alexander's

---

[481] See H. Sheldon Harris, *Paul Cuffee*: *Black American and the African Return* (New York, N.Y.: Simon and Schuster, 1972); Floyd J. Miller, *The Search for Black Nationality: Black Emigration and Colonization, 1878-1863* (Urbana: University of Illinois Press, 1975).
[482] Moses, 11-12, who cites Nathaniel P. Rogers in *The Liberator*, July 25, 1835.
[483] Crummell's Emigrationist-Civilizationist thinking evolved through three major shifts: first, exclusive African-American emigration; second, inclusive emigration, especially Anglo-Christians; and finally, exclusively African-American indigenous agencies.

self-reliant philosophy was his idea of *Civilization*.[484] The latter view implied the superiority of Western Civilization and the need for the Black race to acquire it.

In addition to Boston's example of self-uplift and the traffic of self-reliant African-Americans that passed through the Crummell home, Alexander's quest for Civilization was further nurtured through his contact with White abolitionists. Alexander attended the African Free Schools, institutions that were supported by White abolitionists who espoused the idea of Civilization.[485] Unlike most African-American boys who worked menial jobs, Alexander worked in the American Anti-Slavery Society's New York office through an opportunity provided by White abolitionists.[486] Alexander's contact with upper-class Whites would lead him to identify with the upper

---

[484] Crummell revealed a basic definition for civilization in his pamphlet of 1898 *Civilization the Primal Need of Race*. "What African-Americans need is *civilization*. They need the increase of [their] higher wants of [their] mental and spiritual needs," quoted in Wilson Moses, "Civilizing Missionary: A Study of Alexander Crummell, "*Journal of Negro History* 60 (April 1975): 233, who cites Alexander Crummell, "The Attitude of the American Mind Toward the Negro Intellect" in *The American Negro Academy Occasional Papers* No. 3 Washington, D.C., 1898, 15.

[485] Moses, *Alexander Crummell: A Study of Civilization and Discontent*, 278.

[486] Ibid.

classes and to adopt elitist attitudes such as law, order, and tradition.[487]

Boston Crummell was also a stalwart abolitionist/equal rights activist and served on the Board of Directors of the Phoenix Society of New York.[488] Founded in 1833, the Phoenix Society's objectives were twofold: "to protect against discrimination in public places and to promote the improvement of the [C]olored people in morals, literature, and mechanical arts.[489] Wilson Moses, a Crummell biographer, reveals that "the society is believed to have had the widest influence and largest membership among organizations of Blacks in New York City.[490] Boston was also a member of the fundraising committee for the first National Negro Convention in Philadelphia in 1831 that opposed colonization. Young Alexander was an active participant in the activities of the Phoenix Society and benefited from their self-improvement philosophies. He most likely heard, and was impressed by, the conversations

---

[487] Ibid.

[488] Benjamen Quarles, *Black Abolitionists* (New York, N.Y.: Athenaeum, 1968), 602.

[489] Moses, 14.

[490] Ibid. See also Dorothy Porter, "The Organized Education Activities of Negro Literary Societies 1828-1846, "*Journal of Negro Education* V (October 1936): 556-566.

between his father and his father's friends concerning the business of the National Negro Conventions, and other national abolitionist news. Moses reveals further that Crummell's formative years were influenced by a rich blend of intellectual abolitionist-Black Nationalist thought:

> He knew Samuel Cornish and. . . .his bitter politics, his sense of outrage, and. . . .anticolonization sentiments. He was much closer. . . .to Peter Williams who had been an apologist for Paul Cuffee, John Russwurm, and other colonizationists. . . .Crummell heard at an early age the myth that God was on the side of Black people, who were destined to rule the world some day; Ethiopia would stretch forth her hands unto God. Since David Walker's supposed assassination was household rumor in Crummell's circles, he would have known of David Walker's *Appeal* just as he knew of Nat Turner's slave revolt. . . .Ethiopianism persisted in his rhetoric for the rest of his life and was the basis of his later homilies on Black Nationalism and his belief in the "destined superiority of the Negro."[491]

---

[491] Moses, 278; Carter G. Woodson, ed., *The Mind of the Negro as Reflected in Letters During the Crisis* 1800-1860 (Washington, D.C.: Association for the Study of Negro Life and History, 1926).

While studying in the African Free Schools Numbers One and Two, Crummell met Henry Highland Garnet, Thomas Sidney, and James McCune Smith, the four becoming life-long friends.[492] Crummell, Garnet, and Sidney continued to the Canal Street High School graduating in 1835. The three men enrolled in Noyes Academy in Canaan, New Hampshire, but because of the racist Canaanite attitudes, the students were forced to return to New York.[493]

Crummell enrolled in Oneida Institute, Whitesboro, New York, an institution founded by Beriah Green, a radical abolitionist and Presbyterian minister.[494] While at Oneida, Crummell experienced a religious conversion.[495] Early attracted to the Episcopal Church, Crummell decided to pursue the Episcopal priesthood.[496] Moss explains:

> His attraction to this largely [W]hite and
> socially conservative denomination can be
> traced directly to the examples and
> influence of his father, of Peter Williams,
> and of other members of the [B]lack elite

---

[492] Crummell, "Eulogium on Henry Highland Garnet D.D." (1882), in Crummell *African and America,* 275.

[493] Ibid., 280-281.

[494] Moses, "Civilizing Missionary," 239.

[495] Ibid.

[496] Ibid.

who were Episcopalians. The appeal was reinforced by a belief that the liturgy, theology, and history of the Episcopal Church had played a large role, throughout the English-speaking world, in creating and refining a class of pious, cultured, public-spirited, often wealthy individuals who were models of the best types of social leaders and reformers. . . .He also hoped, as an Episcopal priest, to stimulate greater missionary work among [B]lacks, not only for religious purposes, but in order to employ his church as a cultural agency capable of helping to expand the size, quality and material success of the [B]lack elite.[497]

Crummell moved to Philadelphia where he came under the jurisdiction of Bishop Henry Onderdonk. Refusing to submit to the Bishop's request that he "exclude himself from any bodies responsible for church governance," Crummell was dismissed from the Diocese.[498] Returning to a small parish in New York City, Crummell was further discouraged when his preaching was criticized as unintelligible and lacking emotion.[499] Broadening his

---

[497] Ibid.
[498] Moss, 240.
[499] Ibid.

ministry, Crummell joined the struggle for equal voting rights in New York State, participating in the Negro Conventions and working to improve African-American education.[500] Crummell drew heavily upon these experiences, for the fundamental basis of the future Black Nationalist thoughts. Moss explains:

> All these experiences stimulated Crummell to begin to systematize many ideas that later became important components of his Black Nationalist and Pan-African ideologies. Eventually the meagre return from an ungratifying ministry convinced him that it was part of his mission to find a solution to the major problems of Black people. These he conceived as moral weakness, self-hatred, and industrial primitiveness.[501]

Crummell decided to leave for England in 1847 to provide better financial security for his wife and four children and to pursue a more effective ministry.[502] Crummell referred to his English sojourn between 1848 and 1853 as "a period of grand opportunities, of the riches

---

[500] Ibid.
[501] Ibid., 340-341.
[502] Ibid., 341. Crummell's wife was Sarah who he married around 1841. Crummell, *The Greatness of Christ and Other Sermons* (New York: Thomas Whittaker, 1882), 243.

privileges, of cherished remembrances and of a golden light."[503] Crummell traveled throughout the British Isles soliciting funds and preaching and lecturing about the American Abolition Movement. He studies at Queens College, Cambridge graduating with a B. A. in 1853.

Late in 1853, Crummell went to Liberia as an Episcopal missionary. Believing that African-Americans held a special duty to reclaim Africa for Christ, Crummell focused on the regeneration and evangelization of Africa.[504] Crummell performed many duties in Liberia, including college teaching and the promotion of Liberian Nationalism. In addition, he promoted African-American Liberian emigration through American speaking tours, but always his priority was his church.[505]

Settling in Washington, D.C., Crummell founded the Saint Luke's Episcopal Church. In the later years of his life, Crummell became a highly respected elder statesperson

---

[503] Crummell, "Jubilate: The Shades and Lights of a Fifty Years Ministry" (1894), in Moses, *Destiny and Race: Selected Writings, 1840-1898* (Amherst: the University of Massachusetts Press, 1992), 39.

[504] Crummell, "Emigration an Aid to the Evangelization of Africa" (1863), in Crummell, *Africa and America*, 421.

[505] Kathleen O'Mara Whale, "Alexander Crummell: Black Evangelist and Pan-Negro Nationalist," *Phylon* (1966), 388-395.

among the African-American Episcopalians. In addition to his pastorate, Crummell taught at Howard University between 1895 and 1897. One year prior to his death in 1898, Crummell organized the American Negro Academy to stimulate African-American intellectual excellence and to counter the stereotype against African-American inferiority.[506] Through this organization, Crummell left one of his lasting legacies: the need for an educated class of African-Americans to lead and redeem the race. Crummell died in 1897 and his remains were shipped to New York City for his funeral in St. Phillips Episcopal Church. An impressive crowd of the African-American leadership were in attendance.

Liberian Nationalism and African-American Uplift

As previously stated, Crummell went to Liberia as a missionary for the Episcopal Church. He gives loyalty to the parentland and medicinal purposes as the motivating factors for relocating to African: "[M]y heart, from youth, was consecrated to my race and its interests, and I was ordered to a tropical climate, and I chose the land of my

---

[506] Crummell, "Civilization the Primal Need of the Race" (1898) in Moses, 285-286.

[foreparents]."[507] Crummell's plan for the regeneration of Liberia focused on his concepts of Emigration, Christian Evangelism, Civilization, and Liberian Nationalism. The following sections will examine these four ideas and his concept of African-American Uplift, an idea developed during Crummell's final stay in America.

Emigration

Crummell revealed the fundamental basis for his Emigration theory in his sermon, "Emigration and Aid to the Civilization in Africa" (1863).[508] Crummell posits that Jewish slavery in Egypt was an essential feature of God's Providential Design to colonize the Jews and relocate them in Canaan.[509] Crummell maintained that Emigration was among the commonest movements of humankind:

> All along the tracks of time we see traces of such movements on every soil on earth. Indeed the fact of [E]migration is almost coeval with humanity itself among the earliest of human records. It seems to have been a spontaneous instinctive tendency of human nature.[510]

---

[507] Moses, 40.
[508] Crummell, *Africa and America*, 405-430.
[509] Ibid., 407-409.
[510] Ibid., 410-411.

Indeed, Emigration was as old as the Bible, because from the earliest scriptures Noah and his descendants were forced to move to different parts of the world.[511] History was characterized by the events of Noah's dispersion scattering different races of the world to every corner of the earth.[512] Thus, Crummell did not find Emigration an anomaly, but on the contrary, a traditional historical event and one that affected Africa:

> And thus you may see that [E]migration is a marked feature of the world's history and that the transplantation of fragments of the children of Africa to this western coast is not an exceptional fact; is not an isolated event. Colonization is history promoting whole faces of men [and women], and determining the destiny of nations and continents.[513]

Crummell reasoned that Emigration was both an integral part of history and originated from and was directed by God. Indeed, Crummell believed all history was directed by God for God's purpose: "[a]ll human events have their place in that grand moral economy of God in which [God] is an ever present ever active agent, they are all elements

---

[511] Ibid.
[512] Ibid., 411-412.
[513] Ibid., 412.

and instruments in [God's] hand for the accomplishment of the august objects of [God's] will."[514]

Crummell reasoned that God's plan would come into reality through humankind's efforts. Through influenced by God's Providence, men and women were nonetheless free willed:

> not that people are every mere machines,
> even in God's hands; but when righteous
> deeds are wrought, God either gives the
> large suggestion, or adjusts the fit position,
> or directs the concurring events, or orders
> the happy [P]rovidence; so that while
> [people] act on their own personal
> responsibility, they nevertheless act either
> consciously or unconsciously as the agents
> of God.[515]

Hence, throughout the history of Emigration, God has been an essential spirit of the movement, authorizing it when it originated for good and turning it away from evil when it originated for selfish or other ill-conceived motives. (Because of its importance, Crummell's reconciliation of

---

[514] Ibid., 413.
[515] Ibid., 413-414.

the conflict between God's predestination and humanity's free will, bill be examined later in this chapter.)

Thus, Crummell found nothing inherently wrong with the idea of Emigration, the question was how best to use Emigration for God's purposes? Crummell reasoned that Emigration was a useful tool for the work of Evangelism and that God ordained African-Americans for the special task of reclaiming Africa for Christ. He wrote:

> This continent (Africa) is to be reclaimed
> for Christ. The faith of Jesus is to supercede
> all the abounding desolation of heathenism.
> And the church of Christ is to enter in, in
> His name and to subdue by the spirit its
> crowded populations to His yoke, and to
> claim the whole continent for her Lord. . .
> .In this work the colored people of America
> are largely to participate.[516]

Answering those who criticized his Emigration policies, Crummell wrote letters from his Liberian post to America in Support of his position.[517] By the mid-nineteenth century many African-Americans were born on American soil and knew very little about African culture, and for that single reason did not care to be repatriated to

---

[516] Ibid., 421.
[517] Wahle, 389.

the parentland. On the contrary, Crummell argued that African-Americans held a special kinship and duty to their African brothers and sisters.

> But believing that [children] held some relation to the land and their [parents], I wish to call the attention of the children of Africa in America to their relations and duty to the land of their [parents]. And even on such theme I know I must prepare myself for the rebuff from many who will ask why talk to us for [parentland]![518]

Extolling their record of unremunerated labor, military service, and birthright, there was a strong sense among African-Americans that America was their true home. While Crummell did not refute their claims, he was opposed to the stay-in-America-no-matter-what philosophy. Indeed, Crummell found many opposed to Emigration for purely selfish reasons: "some of my friends say can't spare [Black people]. . .need them in the [United States]. . .[i]t is really this we need to use them for our

---

[518] Crummell, Letter, High School, Mount Vaughan, Cape Palmas, Liberia, September 1, 1860, Schomburg Collection, New York Public Library, quoted in Riggins Earl, "Toward a Black Christian Ethic: A Study of Alexander Crummell and Albert Cleage" (doctoral dissertation Vanderbilt University 1978), 148.

purposes."[519] For those who were unable to reach their potential in America, and for those who tired of oppression, Crummell believed Africa to be a land of opportunity. More importantly, Africa was also a place in which they could restore their human dignity.[520]

While Africa offered African-Americans restorative opportunities, African-Americans offered redeeming qualities for Africans. Africa provided a place where African-Americans could restore their dignity; while African-Americans provided Africans with knowledge of Christianity and Western Civilization. The two peoples were thus able to provide for their mutual needs. Crummell made an appeal for African-American emigrants who would thus provide a civilizing and Christianizing element:

> The civilizing Black [persons] should be
> zealous to rescue the [parentland] from
> beneath the accretions of civil and moral
> miseries from the heterogeneous idolatries.
> All her [children] who haply have ability to
> aid in her restoration should show their love
> toward their [parentland] performing a

---

[519] Crummell, "A Plea to Americans for the Successful Growth of Liberia," Crummell Manuscript Collection, MS No. 317 (1863), New York Public Library, quoted in Wahle, 391.
[520] Earl, 147.

particular love that which was theirs by providential commission.[521]

In addition to an appeal for emigrants, Crummell espoused the doctrine of self-love. He opposed the idea of *Agape* that loved the oppressor unconditionally. According to Gayraud Wilmore, Crummell was one of the first African-American theologians to question the *Agape* doctrine of Christianity. He proposed self-love as a Christian principle that the oppressed Black race was to espouse if it were to cast off oppression and rise to equality with the White nations of the world.[522] Crummell used the principle of self-love to support his African Emigration policy. He reasoned that African-Americans should go to Africa "not merely for philanthropic reasons but for reasons of the natural desires of people who have regard for themselves and for the acquisition of power accomplished something worthy of a great people."[523] Explaining the self-love principle, Crummell wrote:

---

[521] Crummell, Letter to High School Mount Vaughan, 10, quoted in Earl, 147-148.

[522] Gayraud Wilmore, *Black Religion and Black Radicalism: An Interpretation of the Religious History of Afro-American People* (Maryknoll, N.Y.: Orbis 1983), 34.

[523] Earl, 148.

I am aiming at the principle of [s]elf-love
which spurs men [sic] on to self-advantage
and self-aggrandizement; a principle which,
in its normal state and its due degree, to use
the words of Butler, "is as just and morally
good as any affection whatever." In fine, I
address myself to all that class of
sentiments in the human heart which creates
a thirst for wealth, position, honor; and
power.[524]

Crummell thus opposed the meek and subservient ideas of Christianity taught to the slaves by White missionaries. Crummell proposed an idea of self-love that enabled the slaves to provide for their own needs first, in order to prepare to fulfill their Godly commissions to serve others.

In summary, Emigration was a natural historical event. Indeed, God initiated the Emigration idea and directed it through God's will. Such a Godly institution was thus a Divine tool and could be used effectively for God's purposes. Because Africa was in an heathen, uncivilized condition, there was a great need for civilizing Christian missionaries. African-Americans were tailor-made for this assignment. They offered kinship and indigeneity, whose

---

[524] Crummell, ibid., quotes in Earl, 148-149.

qualities would enhance contact with the natives and lend permanency to the missionary efforts. Crummell introduced a new principle to the idea of Emigration: Black self-love that proposed love of self in order to reach the person's highest human potential; and love of Blacks by Blacks in order to elevate the race. Thus Crummell set forth several fundamental reasons for his African Emigration policies.

Christian Evangelism

Another important dimension of Crummell's plan for the redemption of Africa was his focus upon Evangelism. The primary basis for Crummell's evangelical efforts was the New Testament commission to: "[g]o ye therefore and teach all nations baptizing them in the name of the [Creator] and of the Son and of the Holy Ghost."[525] Crummell endeavored to fulfill the commission through a comprehensive plan to evangelize Liberia.

In his discourse, "the Regeneration of Africa," delivered before the Pennsylvania Colonization Society in 1865, Crummell set forth the basic plan for his Liberian

---

[525] Matthew 28:10. Quoted in Crummell, "The Regeneration of Africa" (1965), in *Africa and America*, 431.

Evangelical Campaign.[526] Crummell's research of the history of Christian Missions revealed that by middle of the fifteenth century, Christianity had spread to the Americans and to parts of Asia, but was still relatively unknown in the majority of Africa. "Two thousand years have passed away," said Crummell, and "yet Africa with her hundreds of millions of souls is still heathen! The abominations of paganism still prevail through all her domains."[527] Crummell thus took the New Testament commission as both prophecy and a mandate to evangelize Africa.[528]

How was Crummell to effect the evangelization of Africa? He sought help through a superior people, a people superior in terms of Christian knowledge and Civilization. He reasoned that: [in] every instance that we know of where [people] have been morally elevated, they have always had the missions from superior people of either letters or grace as the origination of such elevation."[529] Once selecting the superior group, the Gospel was to be carried into Africa by

---

[526] Ibid., 431-454.
[527] Ibid., 434.
[528] Ibid.
[529] Ibid., 435.

foreign missionaries, but the permanent work was to be performed by indigenous people.[530]

Indigeniatey offered a sense of ethnic pride and a means of providing an understanding of African myths, folklore, and religiosity. Crummell sought to provide Western missionaries the African perspective through African religious persons who would take into account the African world view. They would also provide African theology with a frame work of traditional African ideas. Crummell reasoned that:

> for the evangelization of any country the main instrumentality to be set to work was that of persons of like sentiments, feeling, blood, and ancestry with the people whose evangelization is desired. The faith so to speak must. . . .become incorporated with a people's mental, moral, and even physical constitution-vitalize their being and run along the channels of their blood.[531]

Providence provided the perfect group—African-Americans—to perform African Evangelism. African-Americans fulfilled both of Crummell's African

---

[530] Ibid., 436.
[531] Ibid., 438.

prerequisites: superiority and indigenous qualities. African-Americans suffered the evils of a people stolen from their native Africa and forcibly transplanted to America, yet they were blessed with conversion to Christianity and exposure to Western Civilization. African-Americans thus held a distinct advantage over non-African-related emigrants.[532] Crummell explained:

> Black Christian emigrants. . .are indigenous, in blood, constitution, and adaptability. Two centuries of absence from the continent Africa have not destroyed their physical adaptation to the land of their ancestors. There is a tropical fitness which inheres in our constitution, whereby we are enabled, when we leave this country, to sit down under an African sun; and soon, and with comparative ease, feel ourselves at home, and move about in the land as though we had always lived there. Children, too, are born to us in our adopted country, who have as much strength and vitality as native children, and soon we find ourselves establishing families right beside those of our heathen kinsfolk.[533]

---

[532] By 1895 Crummell would change this position. He would hold that the indigenous Africans were the ultimate missionary agency for the evangelization of Africa.

[533] Crummell, 442.

Fundamentally, and closely related to Crummell's beliefs in the redemption of Africa and God's Providential Design, was Crummell's basic belief in Evangelical Protestantism.[534] His Evangelical Theology was shaped by his American teacher, Beriah Green, and the Evangelicals in England.[535] While this study cannot draw a perfect line to the influence of the two, the research reveals a well-ordered, well-developed, Evangelical faith. Crummell held a personal faith that was characterized by a belief in his helplessness to sin; a belief in Christ as his savior; an insistence upon a high spiritual life, with a devotion to spread the Gospel; and an equal insistence upon the role of scripture as the rule of life.[536]

The problem of humankind's moral depravity was an essential element in Crummell's Evangelical thinking. He wrote in 1874 that "all persons are naturally alien from God, all persons have given their allegiance to Satan."[537] The sole means of redemption was the atoning grace of

---

[534] James R. Oldfield, *Alexander Crummell (1819-1898) and the Creation of an African American Church in Liberia* (Lewiston, N.Y.: Mellen Press, 1990), 47-49.
[535] Ibid., 48.
[536] Ibid., 45-46.
[537] Ibid., 45.

Christ. Crummell emphasized the atonement throughout his sermons and addresses:

> The world in which we live, alive in all other respects is prostrate under the stupefaction of spiritual death. . .The grand remedy for [humankind's] restoration is the cross of Calvary. . .If you are wretched and heartbroken on account of sin, your sorrow, your penitences cannot save you, you need the blood of Christ to wash it clean from all impurities.[538]

In addition, Crummell emphasized social holiness that combined faith with action. Like the Methodist evangelist John Wesley (1703-1791), Crummell stressed that "Christianity was essentially a social religion and to turn it into a solitary religion was to destroy it."[539] Crummell wrote in 1871:

> To be Christian means that persons believe in the Lord Jesus Christ as their saviour and their God and this same saviour is their example and pattern of their lives. But [these persons] who merely believe in Jesus but refuse to let their beliefs shape and

---

[538] *The Crummell Papers*, The Schomburg Collection MSS C107 C86, The New York Public Library, Quoted in Orfield, 45.

[539] Thomas Jackson, ed., *The Works of John Wesley A.M.* Third Edition (London: John Mason, 1829), V, 296.

color their lives are not in reality Christians.[540]

The Christian life is thus a set of beliefs and a life to be lived.

Indeed, Crummell was extremely critical of the other-worldly preaching of the accommodating stream of Black Religion.[541] He complained that: "[t]he single aim of the Black Religious teaching has been to get their [parishioners] to Heaven thus substituting rhapsody and at times hallucination for spiritual service and moral obligation in the relations of Life."[542]

Another important aspect of Crummell's Evangelical Protestantism was his idea of optimism. The Evangelicals gave the spiritual base, while Francois Guizot, the French historian, gave the intellectual base.[543] Crummell believed that all discussion of time past, present,

---

[540] *Crummell Papers* MS C163, Quoted in Orfield, 47.
[541] Crummell alludes to what Joseph R. Washington identified as the White stream of Negro Folk Religion. Here the Black preacher extolled the virtues of the next world as opposed to the Black stream that provided cover for the Black preacher to lead insurrections and escapes. Joseph R. Washington, *Black Religion: The Negro and Christianity in the United States* (Boston: Beacon Press, 1964), 33-34. See also Chapter Two of this dissertation.
[542] Orfield, 48-49.
[543] Moses, "Civilizing Missionary," 229-232; Orfield, 48-51.

and future are filled with God's presence in human affairs. Like most Evangelical Protestants of the mid-nineteenth century, a source of his optimism was the idea of Millennialism or Post-Millennialism, the belief that God would usher in an era of peace and good will among humankind before the second coming. All progress, according to Millenialist thinking, worked toward the end.[544] Intellectually, Crummell found support in Guizot who held it be self-evident that ". . .[C]ivilization is an ongoing process the great end towards which world history moves presumably under [P]rovidential aegis."[545] Crummell recognized both the ideas of progress and Providence in his efforts to elevate the Black race. In his sermon, "The Destined Superiority of the Negro" (1877), Crummell wrote:

> You need not entertain the shadow of a
> doubt that the work which God has begun
> and is now carrying on, is for the elevation
> and success of the Negro. This is the
> significance and the worth of all effort and
> all achievement of every signal
> [P]rovidence, in this cause; or otherwise all
> the labors of [humankind] and all the

---

[544] Orfield, 48-49.
[545] Moses, 230; Francois Guizot, *General History of Civilization* (New York: 1842), 27-28.

mightiness of God is vanity! Nothing,
believe me, on earth, nothing brought from
perdition, can keep back this destined
advance of the Negro race. No conspiracies
of [persons] or devils! The slave trade
could not crush them out. . .The Negro
[B]lack, curly-headed, despised, repulsed,
sneered at—is nevertheless, a vital being,
and irrepressible. Everywhere on earth has
been given to [them] by the Almighty
assurance, self-assertion, and influence.[546]

In summary, Crummell believed in a well-rounded
Gospel that took seriously fruitful living, social
consciousness, belief in a human progress and destiny
hereafter. Fundamentally, he was an Evangelical Protestant
with a burning zeal to offer humanity the one solution to
their sinful condition: the atoning grace of Jesus Christ.
Crummell's historical research revealed that Africa was the
least evangelized and perhaps the most uncivilized of all the
continents. He believed that African-Americans were
predestined to carry the Gospel and Civilization back to the
parentland. Because of their kinship to Africans, African-
Americans held a special duty to elevate their kinspeople

---

[546] Crummell, "The Destined Superiority of the Negro" (1877), in
Wilson Moses, 204.

through the spread of the Gospel and Western Civilization. African-American indigeneity gave them a distinct advantage over non-Africans to perform Evangelism with power and permanency. Crummell thus responded in obedience to the mandate of the great commission to spread the Gospel throughout the world.

Civilization

Closely related to Crummell's Evangelical mission were his efforts to bring Civilization to Liberia as well. Crummell reasoned that conversion of itself was only half the effort; missionaries had the additional duty to elevate their new converts' external circumstances. Crummell wrote:

> But what is to be done with [those] converts as to all the external circumstances of [their lives] and being? Are they to be left in the rude crude half animal conditions in which the missionary first found [them]? Surely not, for Christianity is, in all ways of life a new creation. This man child [sic] is to be reconstructed. All the childishness of inheritance is gradually to be taken out of his [sic] brain and all the barbarism of the

ages to be eliminated form his [sic] constitution.[547]

Crummell thus reasoned that civilizing efforts were a correlative duty to conversion.

Crummell's idea of Civilization is based largely upon Francois Guizot's use of the term. Unfortunately, Guizot did not leave a concise definition. At best, we have a definition by Charles Henry who wrote what he believed Guizot meant: "Civilization may be taken to signify merely the multiplication of artificial wants, and of the means and requirements of physical enjoyment. It may also be taken to imply a state of physical wellbeing and a state of superior intellectual and moral culture."[548] Crummell's best clarification of what he meant by Civilization is revealed in his address, "Civilization as a Collateral and Indispensable Instrumentality in Planting the Christian Churches in Africa" (1895), where he defined Civilization as:

> [The clarity of the mind from the dominion
> of false heathen ideas. . .the conscious
> impress of individualism and personal
> responsibility. I mean the recognition of
> the *body*, with its desires and appetites and
> passions as a sacred gift, and as under the
> law of divine obligation. . .the honor and
> freedom of womanhood, allied with the
> duty of family development. I mean the
> sense of social progress in society. . . the
> entrance of new impulses in the actions of
> policy of the tribe or nation. I mean an

---

[547] Crummell, "Civilization as a Collateral and Indispensable Instrumentality in Planting the Christian Church in Africa" (1895), in Moses, 270.

[548] Guizot, 18; Quoted in Moses, "Civilizing Missionary," 231.

elevated use of material things and higher
range of common industrial activities. . .the
earliest possible introduction of letters, and
books, and reading, and intelligence to
[persons, their families, and their social
circles].[549]

Crummell's initial conception of Africa was a dark
continent, uncivilized and predominately pagan. Indeed,
this was a consistent theme throughout his African
sojourn.[550] By 1860 his perception of the African continent
revealed one of the lowest levels of heathenism:

> Darkness covers the land, and gross
> darkness the people. Great evils universally
> prevail, confidence and security are
> destroyed. Licentiousness abounds
> everywhere. Moloch rules and reigns
> throughout the whole continent, and by the
> ordeal of Sassywood, Fetiches, human
> sacrifices, and the devil-worship is
> devouring men, women, and little
> children.[551]

---

[549] Moses, "The Destined Superiority of the Negro" in Moses, *Destiny and Race*, 272.
[550] Moses, "Civilizing Missionary," 239.
[551] Crummell, "The Relations and Duty of Free Colored Men in America to Africa (1860), in Crummell, *The Future of Africa: Being Addresses Sermons, Etc., Etc., Delivered in the Republic of Liberia* (New York, N.Y.: Scribners 1862), 220.

Observing the economic and political powers of the Christian West, Crummell saw a fundamental relation between belief in the true, Christian God and the human progress. He reasoned that "a nation's progress towards [C]ivilization could be measured in proportion to the clearness of its idea of God."[552] Indeed, it was because Africa foreparents refused to worship the true Christian God that God allowed them to become enslaved (because of their importance to Crummell's Black Nationalist theodicy, these ideas will be examined in the next sections.)[553]

Indeed, Crummell had little tolerance for the materialism of Traditional African Religious practices.[554] He saw those practices as some of the fundamental stumbling blocks to Liberia's Civilization. Crummell followed the Platonic school of thought that placed the priority on ideas rather than materialism.[555] Crummell reasoned that the ideological aspects of Christianity would

---

[552] Ibid., 274.
[553] Crummell, *African and America*, 418.
[554] Crummell, "God and the Nation" (1854), in *The Future of Africa*, 153.
[555] Forbes, 10-13. Moses, "Cambridge Platonism in West Africa: Alexander Crummell's Theory of Development and Culture Transfer," *New England Journal of Black Studies* No. 3 (1983): 60-77.

serve to stimulate the growth and development of Liberian Civilization. He wrote:

> If the people think that God is a spirit, that idea raises or will raise them among the first of nations. If on the other hand, they think that God is a stone, or a carved image, or a reptile, they will assuredly be low and rude. A nation that worships rocks or ugly idols can never while maintaining such a style of worship become a great nation.[556]

While seeing the constant need for the uplifting and Civilization of African peoples, Crummell's faith in them was nevertheless great.[557] He envisioned the building of a great African nation that would serve as an international model. Crummell's experiences with discrimination in the West allowed him to gain a deep understanding of the immoral and dehumanizing practices of Anglo-Saxons. Crummell sought to appropriate this understanding in building a nation where he could "actualize the ideals of personal freedom, intellectual advancement, social comfort, domestic bliss, and religious growth."[558]   Rhetorically

---

[556] Ronald K. Bucket, "A Profile of Black Episcopal Clergymen in Antebellum America." Working paper presented in the Academy of Religion, November 9, 1980, Dallas, Texan, Quoted in Moses, "Civilizing Missionary," 239.
[557] Ibid.
[558] Earl, 169.

explaining his idea of the ideal African government, Crummell asked the citizens of Monrovia:

> Will you inaugurate in this country a free
> enabling enlightening governmental system,
> a system capable of elevating the degraded
> and civilizing the heathen; a system which
> will enlarge the souls of men [and women]
> give them manhood [and womanhood] and
> superiority and without going beyond the
> proper sphere of government serve as an
> auxiliary agent to evangelize the continent
> and to raise the souls of men [and women]
> in heaven.[559]

Crummell's concept of the ideal government would thus guarantee legal equality and respect for human rights.

In summary, Evangelism and Civilization were correlative concepts for Crummell, the one by necessity followed the other. If Africa were to be lifted from its heathen condition, then worship of the true God and its attending Civilization were imperative. Once acquiring the appropriate level of Civilization and morality, Africa could thus build noble and productive nations based upon Crummell's universal ideals.

---

[559] Crummell, "The Responsibility of the First Fathers of a Country for their Future Life and Destiny" (1963), in Crummell, *Africa and America*, 139.

Liberian Nationalism

Crummell's original purposes in emigrating to Liberia were missional and educational. He was prepared to spread the Gospel in the parentland and to train young Africans for the ministry. His earliest contacts with the Liberians who exhibited and extraordinary sense of racial pride turned him, however, towards civil and national interests. Crummell wrote:

> When I went to Liberia my views and purposes were almost entirely missionary in their character, and very much alien from anything civil or national; but I had not been in the country three days when such was the manliness [sic] I saw exhibited, so great was the capacity I saw developed, and so many were the signs of thrift, energy, and national life which showed themselves, that all my governmental indifference at once vanished, aspirations after citizenship and nationality rose in my bosom, and I was impelled to go to a magistrate, take the oath of allegiance and thus become a citizen of Liberia.[560]

---

[560] Crummell, "The Progress and Prospects of the Republic of Liberia" (1961), in Moses, *Destiny and Race*, 165-166.

From thenceforth Crummell became an ardent Emigrationist, vigorously calling African-Americans to return and redeem Africa.

Crummell held a high regard for African Nationality. Manifested through twenty years of his Liberian efforts, there were two major elements in Crummell's Liberian Nationalism: faith in God's Providential Design to redeem Africa, and an enormous sense of racial pride.[561]

Crummell believed that it was a part of God's Providential Design that Africans would be separated from the parentland. They would experience severe hardships, including discrimination and slavery. Eventually, the captives would be freed to return and build Africa to one of the superior continents.[562] Crummell recognized several events that revealed "that the day of the regeneration of Africa and [its] children is fast drawing nigh," the liberation of Haiti, the abolition of the English slave-trade, and White support of African missionary efforts.[563]

---

[561] Wahle, 390.

[562] Crummell, *Africa and America*, 405-430.

[563] Crummell, "Sermon on Job," Crummell Manuscript Collection, MS No. 341 (1853) New York Public Library, quoted in Wahle, 389-390.

Crummell was a stalwart Black Nationalist. He took great pride in his stark African features and felt that all African peoples were "members of a but rising race whose greatness was yet to be achieved."[564] When Crummell arrived in Liberia in 1853, it was a struggling country of 335,000 with 225,000 natives and 10,000 American-Liberians.[565] While struggling to industrialize, achieve Civilization, and gain diplomatic relations from the West, Crummell saw a prosperous Liberian future. If Liberia was to attain its greatness, then it had to reject the materialist worship of idol Gods, achieve Civilization, and offer a spirit of Liberian Nationalism.

Central to Crummell's theology were the concepts of idealism, anti-materialism, and true Godly worship. The great Civilizations of North America and Europe held idealistic persons who worshipped a spiritual God. Wherever Crummell found a great Civilization he found true worship. He wrote: [w]here on earth can you find a nation that worships birds, beasts and creeping things that is great and powerful, and free."[566] Indeed the concept of a

---

[564] Crummell, "God and the Nation" (1854), in Crummell, *The Future of Africa*, 167.
[565] Moses, *Alexander Crummell*, 92.
[566] Crummell, *The Future of Africa*, 154-159.

spiritual-type God inspired images of a God "so infinite that the depts. Of the earth are not deep enough for [God's] penetrating gaze; and the boundless seas not grand and majestic enough for [God's] swelling thought; nor the illimitable spheres above vast and extensive enough for excursive reason."[567] These mysterious and tremendous images would inspire the worshipper to seek satisfaction in the Infinite and the Eternal. Similarly, Crummell reasoned that a nation of spiritualed worshippers would progress towards greatness and immorality.[568]

Crummell sought to build Liberian spirituality and inspire his sister and brother Liberians towards national greatness. Liberian progress, like all African progress, would be based on a Black manifestation of Christian truths. Crummell would assimilate the cultural and religious values of the West, thereby building upon their scientific, technological, and moral advancements. This was not a complete sellout, according to Wilson Moses, because Crummell reasoned that scientific, moral, and cultural truths

---

[567] Ibid.
[568] Ibid.

were universal and belonged to all.[569]   Crummell thus sought to borrow from the West and improve their ideas.

Hence Liberian Nationalism was a complex of racial pride, right-minded worship, belief in the true, Christian God, and scientific, educational, and cultural advancements. Liberia was thus to give hope to other African nations for greatness and superiority.

Disappointed and frustrated in his lack of progress in Liberia, Crummell decided to return to America in 1873. Failing to achieve his goals of large-scaled African-American Emigration and Liberian regeneration, Crummell assailed the American-Liberian ruling elite who neglected the indigenous people. He reasoned that the American-Liberians' refusal to educate and train the indigenous people was based upon a pseudo-sense of superiority and indigenous disdain. Because the indigenous people were left untrained, Liberia was unable to develop a basic infrastructure that ultimately served to impede Liberian progress and limit its stability. In addition, Crummell criticized African-Americans who mostly showed little interest in Liberia. While Crummell was unsuccessful in

---

[569] Moses, 92-98.

many of his goals, he was nevertheless a pioneering African missiologist and a Pan-Africanist who instilled pride in Liberia's past and hope for the future.[570]

African-American Uplift

Upon his return to America in 1873, Crummell accepted the call to become rector of Saint Luke's Episcopal Church in Washington, D.C.[571] He immediately began to work for African-American Uplift, a complex of ideas that included civil rights, racial solidarity, educational advancement, and economics. The idea of African-American Uplift "was based upon the assumption that by the acquisition of wealth and morality attained largely by their own efforts Negroes would gain the respect of White men [and women] and thus be accorded their rights as citizens."[572]

There was a close relation between Crummell's idea of Liberian Nationalism and his advocacy of African-American Uplift. The affinity between the two concepts

---

[570] Wahle, 394-395.

[571] Moses, 196-221.

[572] August Meier, *Negro Thought in America 1880-1915: Racial Ideologies in the Age of Booker T. Washington* (Ann Arbor, Michigan: University of Michigan Press, 1969), 42-43.

was superbly illustrated in his sermon, "The Social Principle among a People and its Bearing on their Progress and Development" (1875).[573] By social principle Crummell meant, "the disposition which leads [humankind] to associate and join together for specific purposes; the principle which makes families and societies, and which binds [humankind] in unity and brotherhood [and sisterhood], in races, churches, and nations."[574] Crummell advocated the social principle in Liberia, proposing that American-Liberians build roads to the interior, train the indigenous people, and establish government farms. He reasoned that mutual respect would open roads and enhance intrastate travel and trade.[575]

Speaking of African-American Uplift, Crummell reasoned that the persistence and pervasiveness of racism blocked African-Americans from becoming members of mainstreams society. African-Americans thus formed their own institutions that performed basically the same functions

---

[573] Crummell, "The Social Principle among People and its Bearing on their Progress and Development" (1875), in Moses, *Destiny and Race*, 254-268.
[574] Ibid., 256.
[575] Crummell, "Our Nation Mistakes and the Remedy for Them," (1870), in *Africa and America,* 169-177.

as white institutions except for the name. Prefiguring E. Franklin Frazier, Crummell reasoned that the African-American community was in reality a nation within a nation.[576] He wrote:

> We are living in this country a part of its
> population and yet in diverse respects, we
> are as foreign to its inhabitants as though
> we are living in the Sandwich Islands. It is
> this our actual separation from the real life
> of the nation, which constitutes us a "nation
> within a nation": thrown very considerably
> upon ourselves for many of the largest
> interests of life, and for nearly all our social
> and religious advantages.[577]

Because of such a state, African-Americans were to work in unity, but they were disunited and untrusting. Crummell continued:

> As a consequence on this state of things, all
> the stimulants of ambition and self-love
> should lead this people to united effort for
> personal superiority and the uplifting of the
> race; but, instead thereof, overshadowed by
> a more powerful race of people; wanting in
> the cohesion which comes from racial
> enthusiasm; lacking in the confidence

---

[576] Moses, 257; E. Franklin Frazier and C. Eric Lincoln, *The Negro Church in American/The Black Church Since Frazier* (New York, N.Y.: Schocken Boos, 1978), 35-50.
[577] Moses.

which is the root of a peoples' stability;
disintegration, doubt, and distrust almost
universally prevai81 and distract all their
businesses and policies.[578]

Crummell reasoned that there were two fundamental ideas that caused disunity among African-Americans: the beliefs "that the colored people of this country should forget as soon as possible that they are colored people. . .and. . . that colored [people] should give up all distinctive effort as colored [people] in schools, churches, associations, and friendly societies."[579] Crummell argued that as long as racism existed, African-Americans could never forget that they were Black.[580] For the first belief, denied access into the broader society's institutions, discrimination was obviously correlative to skin color. For the second belief, it would be disastrous to relinquish African-American institutions in hopes of becoming accepted into White institutions. It was therefore a must, according to Crummell's reasoning, for African-Americans "to strive for footing and for superiority in this land on the line of race as a temporary but needed expedient for the ultimate extinction

---

[578] Ibid.
[579] Ibid., 260-261.
[580] Ibid., 261-262.

of caste and all race distinctions."[581] It was the duty of African-Americans to look after their own interests, for if they did not, no other people would.

While living in America and concerned about African-American Uplift, Crummell remained equally concerned about African Civilization, Pan-Africanism, and Emigration.[582] Because of his experiences in Africa, Crummell was invited to speak at the Congress in Africa during the fall of 1895 at the Atlanta and Cotton States Exposition.[583] Crummell's Emigrationist thinking had evolved through three major shifts during this career. During his Liberian Missionary Period, Crummell advocated African-American Emigration in order to

---

[581] Ibid., 263.

[582] Pan-Africanism refers to "the unification of all Africans and people of African descent." Specifically it refers to "racial solidarity among Black people and native Africans." Gregory U. Rigsby, *Alexander Crummell: Pioneer in Nineteenth Century Pan African Thought* (Westport, CT.: Greenwood Press, 1987). Crummell's idea of Pan-Africanism went beyond the goal of racial solidarity. He viewed Pan-Africanism as an evolutionary step towards the unity of humankind. Ibid. See Bracey, Meier, and Rudwich *Black Nationalism in America,* xxvi-xxx.

[583] The Atlanta and Cotton States Exposition, a national conference organized by Booker T. Washington, was the occasion for a Congress on Africa and the first colored women's conference. The exposition is best known for the site where Booker T. Washington gave his famous speech promoting the segregation of the races.

evangelize and civilize the country.[584]   After a number of failures and frustrations, Crummell called upon England, the United States, and Belgium to assume a major missionary role.[585] By 1895 Crummell had come full circle in terms of his idea of outside help.   He believed the indigenous Africans the best agency for African Evangelism.[586]

Crummell delivered two addresses to the Congress of Africa.   In his first address, "the Absolute Need of an Indigenous Missionary Agency for the Evangelized of Africa" (1895), Crummell argued that indigenous Africans were the best agency to redeem the continent. He wrote: "It seems evident. . .that. . .the native man [sic], as far as possible is to be used for conveying the truths to his fellows [sic]."[587]   Indeed, Crummell implied that indigenous people were the only agency capable of reaching their kinspeople because foreign missionaries encountered three formidable hindrances.   "First, the bar of settled custom and the prejudice which follows; second, the formidable barrier of

---

[584] Crummell, *Africa and America,* 421.
[585] Wahle, 393-394.
[586] Moses, 277-283.
[587] Ibid., 278.

language; and third, the natural repugnance to [D]ivine truth and opposition it always breeds.[588]

Crummell's newly developed Emigration position came into conflict with the ideas of Henry McNeal Turner (1834-1915), a Bishop of the AME Church.[589] Ironically, Turner came to accept the philosophy of African Emigration through a speech delivered by Crummell 1862.[590] While Crummell had changed his original ideas about Emigration, Turner found them just as compelling in 1895. (Because of the centrality of Turner to this study, he will be examined in detail in Chapter Five and two men's ideas will be compared in Chapter Six.)

In his second address to the Congress, "Civilization as a Collateral and Indispensable Instrumentality in Planting the Christian Church in Africa" (1895), Crummell argued that missionaries owed a duty to their converts to work equally as hard for their material success as they did for their spirituality.[591] Crummell wrote:

---

[588] Ibid.
[589] Moses, *Alexander Crummell*, 253.
[590] Ibid.; Redkey, Respect Black, 13.
[591] Crummell, "Civilization as a Collateral and Indispensable Instrumentality in Planting the Christian Church in Africa" (1895); Quoted in Moses, *Destiny and Race*, 269-276.

The heathen convert, convert though he
[sic] be, is a disorganized being, and needs
reconstruction in every segment of his [sic]
outer being and in every relation of his [sic]
life. . . The Gospel of our Lord Jesus Christ
is a grand and majestic economy, which
while taking in, indeed the individual, and
his [or her] interests, stretches out, with
[D]ivine and saving intents to the largest,
widest circles of human interests below the
skies. . . While the salvation of individual
souls is the primary duty of the missionary,
the obligation is manifest to lift up as far
and as fast as possible, the whole level of
society into order, rectitude, and excellence
for the honor and glory of God and the
progress of [humankind].[592]

Actually, this was a consistent theme in Crummell's
thinking because he long held that material progress would
accompany the acceptance of the Gospel in Africa.[593] Yet
civilized societies had separated spiritual and material
forces. Moreover, he had maintained that all great
Civilizations had put the priority on spiritual forces.
Expanding his thinking, Crummell now believed the idea of
Civilization included both material and spiritual forces, with

[592] Ibid., 271-271.
[593] Moses, *Alexander Crummell*, 252.

emphasis on the latter. Wilson Moses explained the restatement of Crummell's position and his enlarged use of the term *Civilization*:

> [Crummell] had long held that progress and material development would accompany the arrival of the Christian message in Africa. He had asserted that the personality of Jesus Christ was the major historical force for promoting progress and reform. Now, however, he seemed to be stating a more materialistic ideology. Civilization must be seen as "a collateral and indispensable instrumentality in planting the Christian Church in Africa." He did not say that [C]ivilization must precede Christianity, but even to describe it as "indispensable and collateral" was to make a very strong statement. It was in no way a contradiction of anything he had ever believed about practical Christianity, nor was it surprising given the practical concerns he had demonstrated during his own missionary venture.[594]

In summary, Crummell returned to America and immediately began to work for African-American U0plift, and idea that the acquisition of wealth and morality secured through African-American self-efforts that would gain

---

[594] Ibid., 253.

White respect and full citizenship privileges.[595] Crummell came full circle on his idea of Evangelism. He first reasoned that African-Americans were the ultimate African evangelical assistance.[596]He next solicited European and American evangelical assistance.[597] He finally came to the conclusion that if Liberia was to be redeemed, redemption would have to be performed by the indigenous people.[598]

Crummell's Theodicy

Crummell's theological explanation for African slavery is revealed in his sermon, "Emigration an Aid to the Evangelization of Africa" (1863).[599] Crummell reasoned that God allowed African-American enslavement because of sins committed by prior African generations. While fully aware of the person of God, God's jealous nature, and what God required, African foreparents, nevertheless, refused to worship and obey God. They went so far as to reject God completely and to push the knowledge of God further away

---

[595] Meier, 42-43.

[596] Crummell, *Africa and America*, 421.

[597] Wahle, 393-394.

[598] Crummell, "The Absolute Need of an Indigenous Missionary for the Evangelization of Africa" (1895), in Moses, *Destiny and Race*, 277-283.

[599] Crummell, *Africa and America*, 405-430.

with every succeeding generation. Because of their gross disloyalties, God withdrew God's support. Crummell wrote:

> For, first of all, our [foreparents] in remote generations "when they knew God, glorified [God] not as God," and "did not retain [God] in their knowledge," and from age to age their [children] *our* ancestors wandered off further and further from the true God, and kept heaping abominations through long centuries, until the Divine patience was exhausted, and God withdrew from sires and their habitations, and extinguished "the forbearance and long-suffering" of which is the direst wrath![600]

Without God's protection Africa was thus vulnerable to the ravages of the slave-trade. Crummell wrote: "And then the Almighty permitted the most cruel of all marauders to devastate the coast and to carry off its people into foreign slavery and the most terrible was all this contribution upon Africa and her sons [sic]."[601]

In his dissertation, "Toward a Black Christian Ethic: A Study of Alexander Crummell and Albert Cleage,"

---

[600] Ibid., 418.
[601] Ibid.

Riggins Earl posits that Crummell's theodicy of slavery was part of his larger theology and the fall of humankind.[602] Earl's research reveals that Crummell viewed the historical development of humankind and their nations from an evolutionary perspective. Reasoning that humankind both in their individual and corporate identities would eventually suffer for the sins of their ancestors,[603] Crummell explained the theology of evolutionary spiral in his sermon, "Building Men," in 1882. He wrote:

> But [humankind] fell from their high estate
> into woe and ruin; and then God began
> again the refashioning of humanity out of
> the ruins of the fall. And ever since [God]
> has been building up [humankind] by all the
> operations of the kingdom of grace by the
> working of the spirit. In this work angels
> and [humankind] too, are workers together
> with God to the same gracious end.[604]

Thus Africans and African-Americans were not to believe that they were singled out for punishment because of

---

[602] Riggins Earl, "Toward a Black Christian Ethic: A Study of Alexander Crummell and Albert Cleage" (Ph.D. diss., Vanderbilt University, 1978), 153-154.
[603] Earl.
[604] Crummell, *The Greatness of Christ*, 260-262.

inferiority. Rather they were to realize that this was God's way of reshaping them for greatness.

Crummell reasoned further that the benefits of slavery outweighed the losses.[605] Indeed, one of the distinctive benefits of slavery was the gift of the English language.[606] It was very obvious that Crummell found native African languages inferior to the English language. Crummell believed the gift of the English language providential:

> Among the other providential events, the fact that the exile of our parents [sic] from their African homes to America had given us, their children, at least this one item of compensation, namely the possession of the Anglo-Saxon tongue. . .and that was impossible to estimate too highly the prerogatives and the elevation the Almighty has bestowed upon us in our having our own the speech of Chaucer and Shakespeare.[607]

---

[605] Crummell, "The English Language" (1860), in *The Future of Africa*, 18.
[606] Ibid.
[607] Ibid.

Crummell found the native African languages "harsh, abrupt, energetic, indistinct in enunciation, meager in point of words, abounding with inarticulate nasal and guttural sounds, and passing but a few inflections and grammatical forms."[608] In terms of their moral character, Crummell said: "They are characterized by lowness of ideas; and are marked by brutal and vindictive sentiments, and principles which show a predominance of animal propensities. . .absence of clear ideas of justice, law, human rights and governmental order."[609] He believed native African languages void of "those supernatural truths of a personal, present Deity, of the moral government of God, of [humankind's] immortality, of the judgment and of Everlasting Blessedness which regulate the lives of Christians, are entirely absent or else exist and are expressed in an obscure and distorted manner."[610]

The English language, on the other hand, was superior for Crummell because it was "baptized in the spirit of the Christian faith."[611] Thus those who acquired the language benefited from its unusual force and power and its

---

[608] Ibid.
[609] Ibid.
[610] Ibid., 19-20
[611] Ibid.

peculiar identity with religion (Christianity). In addition, those who acquired the language were able to identify with the democratic and free governments of the west.[612]

In addition to the English language, the slaves achieved a high degree of Civilization and were restored to their relationship with the true, Christian God. Crummell reasoned that God allowed a defeated people to compensate for their losses by taking the best that the captors have to offer so as to elevate to a higher level.[613] Crummell wrote: "when the Israelites left Egypt they were instructed by the Almighty to borrow every man of his neighbor and every woman of her neighbor jewels of silver and jewels of gold."[614] Indeed, the slavery experience provided African-Americans the opportunity to appropriate democratic principles and English and religious literature. Crummell wrote:

> The invaluables gained have been a "Bill of Rights," "the right of trial by jury," or "an act of Habeas Corpus." The theory of free speech of free press "or constitutional government and the English Bible." And all the vast wealth, both religious and

---

[612] Ibid., 18.
[613] Ibid., 419-420.
[614] Ibid., 27.

political, of the literature of England and
America.[615]

The restoration of the slaves' relationship to the true,
Christian God was perhaps the cornerstone of Crummell's
theory of Providential Design. While yet slaves, later
African generations were exposed to Christianity.
Crummell explained:

> At the close of nigh three centuries,
> millions of the children of Africa on the
> isles and the continent of America have
> been turned from the paganism of their
> [parents]; the people that sat in the darkness
> have seen a great light," God has redeemed
> this injured people and fearfully scourged
> their oppressors; tens of thousands of them,
> in all the lands of their thralldom, have
> received the enlightenment which comes
> from books and seminaries from the Bible
> and churches.[616]

The final stage in Crummell's grand scheme of
Providence and Divine Retribution-Restoration was the
commencement of the work to reclaim Africa for Christ.
Armed with the English language, exposure to Western
Civilization, and the knowledge of the true, Christian God,

---

[615] Ibid., 27-28.
[616] Crummell, *Africa and America.*

African-Americans were well-equipped for the task. Indeed, Crummell reasoned that it was the "duty and spiritual obligation" for African-Americans to evangelize and civilize the African continent.[617]

Strengths and Weaknesses of Crummell

There are immediate and obvious problems attendant to Crummell's theory of Providence and Divine Retribution-Restoration. First, to claim that the Christian God is the true God and one that was rejected by West Africans during the slave-trade is highly ethnocentric and historically inaccurate.[618] Influenced by his Cambridge education and his Christian beliefs, Crummell sought to impose the idea of the Christian God upon West Africa. Henry Young criticized Crummell's position in saying:

> [Crummell] considers only the Christian conception of God as the real God; for him the God of Traditional African Religions was not real but was the God of paganism (Crummell, *Africa and America*, 414). He did not realize however that the God of Traditional Africa Religions predates the emergence of Christianity in Africa. In

---

[617] Ibid., 421.
[618] John Hope Franklin, *From Slavery to Freedom: A History of Negro Americans*, 2nd ed. (New York, N.Y.: Alfred A. Knopf, 1956), 34.

West Africa, where the bulk of the slaves
came from and the portion of Africa to
which Crummell referred, the Christian
notion of God was almost unknown until
the Portuguese and Spaniards started
missions in the area during the sixteenth
century.[619]

Secondly, if God willed the slave-system and are not

men and women mere puppets? Does this not absolve

Whites from their responsibility for slavery? Riggins Earl

found Crummell's answers in Crummell's focus on his

theory of the God-humankind relationship.[620] He reasoned

that because God governed the wicked, God exercised

masterful authority over their evil ways.[621] Indeed, God

took what humankind willed for evil and used it for God's

good. This from Crummell was God's historical pattern

since creation: "Wherever [God] sees wrong [God] steps in

and interferes to turn it to some way into good even as when

Adam sinned [Goid] began at once a scheme to counteract

the malignant scheme of Satan."[622] Earl found Crummell's

---

[619] Henry Young, *Major Black Religious Leaders: 1775-1940*
(Nashville: Abingdon, 1977), 116.
[620] Earl, 156-158.
[621] Crummell, 414-415
[622] Ibid., 415.

perception of all human events as having their place in the Divine economy of things, even slavery.[623]   Young, however, is unimpressed with Crummell's reasoning and rejects his analysis:

> Certainly his theory of [P]rovidence is
> inadequate in that it totally frees the
> oppressors and slave holders from all
> feeling of guilt and responsibility for the
> enslavement of Black Americans.
> Following Crummell's thinking God used
> the slave holders as instruments for
> punishment for [God's] people. This not
> only condones slavery but makes it an evil
> that Black Americans brought upon
> themselves.[624]

Two of the fundamental ideas of Crummell's theory of Providence in relation to his idea of theodicy and Black Nationalism are the concepts of Divine Retribution and Restoration. The concept of Retribution drew heavily upon biblical analysis and historical illustrations. Crummell equated the Israelite captivity in Egypt and Babylon with African-American slavery.[625]   Young criticizes Crummell

---

[623] Earl, 157.
[624] Young.
[625] Crummell, 416.

for his lack of the proper method of historical criticism in regard to comparing the experience of the Israelites and the existential situation of African-Americans. There is no historical evidence for God's allowing the enslavement of Africa-Americans in the same manner as God punished Israel for forsaking God.[626]

The concept of Restoration focuses on the regeneration and evangelization of Africa. Crummell proposed that African-Americans emigrate to Africa so as to evangelize and civilize the continent. In addition to rejecting Traditional African Religions in favor of Christianity, Crummell worked for an imposition of Victorian Civilization. Indeed, most of the sermons published by Crummell during his Liberian years reveals what Wilson Moses found as "an inability to question the values of Victorian Civilization."[627] This attitude is consistent with Crummell's Western ethnocentrism that refused to recognize the value of African Civilizations.

Central to Crummell's Restorative concept was the idea that God predestined African-American slavery. If

---

[626] Young, 117.
[627] Moses, "Civilizing Missionary," 236.

slaves believed this it would have been extremely difficult to motivate them for self-liberative efforts. While some slaves believed their bondage the will of God, most did not. Henry Young explains:

> Believing that they were created in the image of God the slaves felt that they were God's children. . .although some succumbed to the owner's indoctrination that slavery was ordained by God, the dominant belief was to the contrary. This contrary belief was that God made [humankind] of one blood and that it is not God's will that any [person] should keep another in bondage and captivity. This belief was grounded in the view that God's desire is that all [persons] should be free. The same Bible which the [slave-owners] used to validate slavery once in the hands of the slaves, was used to condone their fight for freedom. They understood Christianity in light of this sense of freedom and liberty. With this new freedom consciousness the slaves felt that willfully to submit to slavery meant to go against God's will, which was analogous to being non-Christian.[628]

Notwithstanding the vigorous criticism leveled against Crummell's theory of Providence and Divine

---

[628] Young, "Black Theology: Providence and Evil, "*Journal of the Interdenominational Theological Center* 40 (Spring 1975): 89.

Retribution-Restoration, in this regard, the writer reveals certain strengths. While believing the Black race predestined for slavery, Crummell did not believe the Black race was singled out for slavery.[629] Crummell perceived slavery in societal and theological terms. He saw slavery as a part of a great social evil and believed the Black race predestined to suffer greatly for a noble end.[630] Crummell reasoned further that because the Black race endured slavery it was evidence of their superiority and their choice for a great purpose.[631]

Crummell's idea of Providence and Divine Retribution-Restoration gave a sense of racial pride and hope to people of African descent. His theory of African-American self-love was the first to challenge the *Agape* doctrine of traditional Christianity. He believed that the meek philosophy of orthodox Christianity served to perpetuate slavery. If African-Americans were to be liberated, then they had to have a love for themselves that would inspire them to seek freedom. In addition, Crummell's theory motivated a small contingent of African-

[629] Crummell, "The Negro Not Under Curse" (1860), in *The Future of Africa*, 327-354.
[630] Crummell, "The English Language" in Ibid., 18.
[631] Crummell, "Hope for Africa" (1860), in Ibid., 319-320.

Americans to return to Liberia to help regenerate the country.

Summary

This chapter we gave a biographical sketch of Crummell with particular attention to those life experiences that influenced his ideas of theodicy. The chapter examined Crummell's concept of Liberian Nationalism and African-American Uplift, specifically focusing on his ideas of Emigration, Evangelism, Civilization, and Liberian Nationalism and African-American Uplift. Having critically examined those concepts, the chapter provided the biblical, historical, and philosophical background for Crummell's theodicy. The chapter then extrapolated Crummell's idea of Providence and Divine Retribution-Restoration, the essence of his theodicy, from the various sources. Finally, the chapter critiqued Crummell's idea of Providence and Divine Retribution-Restoration, which illuminated its strengths and weaknesses.

Chapter V: **Henry McNeal Turner (1834-1915): Black Theology**

Image Ownership: Public Domain
Henry McNeal Turner

This chapter provides a brief biographical sketch of Turner, focusing on those life experiences that influenced his fundamental ideas of Black Nationalism and Black Theology. The chapter traces the development of Turner's specific ideas of Black Nationalism and African-American Uplift,

Emigrationism, Black Theology, and theodicy. In addition, the chapter examines the sources of Turner's specific ideas. Finally, the chapter critiques Turner's idea of Black Theology (which is the essence of his theodicy) by illuminating its strengths and weaknesses.

The son of free parents, Hardy and Sarah Greer Turner, Henry was born near Newberry, South Carolina on February 1, 1834. [632] His maternal grandfather was the son of an African prince captured when a boy and sold into American slavery. [633] According to a Turner biographer, he attributed his interest in Africa to that story. [634] Because of English law that forbade the enslavement of royal blood, the grandfather and his descendants were declared free. [635] While

---

[632] Henry McNeal Turner Papers, box 106-1, folders 1 and 2, Moorland-Spingam Research Center, Howard University; Mungo M. Ponton, *Life and Times of Henry M. Turner* (Atlanta: A.B. Caldwell Publishing Company, 1917), 33; John T. Jenifer, *Centennial Retrospect History of the African Methodist Episcopal Church* (Nashville: AME Sunday School Union, 1916), 390.

[633] Ponton, 25.

[634] 3Stephen Angell, *Bishop Henry McNeal Turner and African-American Religion in the South*(Knoxville: University of Tennessee Press, 1972), 7

[635] Ponton, -36; Jenifer, 392; William J. Simmons, *Men of Mark,* 805-806.

free, young Turner's life was in some sense not unlike that of the slaves he was compelled to work in the field alongside of his slave brothers and sisters "under the meanest sort of cruel overseers. .[but] he generally whipped all the overseers that tried to whip him, knowing that he was freeborn and could never be legally reduced to slavery."[636] The field-work experience provided Turner with an indelible impression of the harshness and cruelty of slavery.[637]

In *Bishop Henry McNeal Turner and African American Religion in the South,* Stephen Angell revealed that Turner early expressed his intentions to be a leader of his people. The young Turner found the basis for his decision in a dream that saw him on top of a mountain instructing people. Turner reasoned that God had ordained him for something great. Angell wrote that Benjamin Tanner, one of Turner's later friends, observed that this dream was the guiding star for Turner's entire life.[638]

---

[636] Ibid., 806-807.
[637] Jenifer.
[638] Angell, 9.

Image Ownership: Public Domain
Denmark Vesey

Because of the Denmark Vesey conspiracy in 1822, South Carolina forbade the education of African-Americans.[639] Notwithstanding the proscription, Turner learned to read and write through the clandestine teachings of a kind White lady.[640]   Turner's ideas of

---

[639] Ibid.

309

Black Nationalism, Black Theology and the theodicy are revealed in his speeches and writing. The following sections will extrapolate those ideas from his major speeches and writings during the last quarter of the century after Emancipation.

Turner's Black Nationalism was fundamentally a reaction against the disrespect shown to African-American men and women. He consistently agitated Black Nationalist ideologies for the personhood rights of African-Americans. By personhood rights Josephus Coan explained that Turner

———————————————

meant: "giving Black people their inalienable rights to life, liberty, and the pursuit of happiness as any other American. It called for the elimination of injustice, oppression, disfranchisement, and other forms of inhuman treatment."[641]

As early as his boyhood in South Carolina, Turner stood for his personhood rights. Knowing that he was free, Turner refused to be whipped. Understanding the value of an education, Turner refused to allow the White system of repression to deprive him of the opportunity to feed his mind and develop his potential. Turner received secret lessons in violation of state law and continued private study once the authorities enforced the rules. Licensed to preach by the White Methodist Church, Turner became a traveling evangelist, preaching to both African-American and White congregations throughout the South. As a free African-American, he resented the restrictions placed upon his travels and the obstacles to the effective performance of his

---

[641] Josephus Coan, *Bishop Henry McNeal Turner Speaks to His Generation*, Heritage lecture Series No. 2 Delivered at the 88th Convocation Celebration Turner Theological Seminary, Interdenominational Theological Center, February 1, 1982 (Atlanta: AME Church, 1982), 18. Dr. Coan directed me to the Special Collections Department of the Interdenominational Theological Center, Atlanta, Georgia, where I found this valuable pamphlet.

ministry. Coming into contact with the AME Church for the first time in 1858, Turner was thoroughly impressed with its message of liberation and human wholeness. He immediately decided to transfer to the AME connection. The AME Church provided Turner his first opportunity to advocate his philosophy of Black Nationalism. About this great turning point in Turner's life, Redkey wrote:

> His nascent nationalism found its first outlet in New Orleans where in 1858 he discovered something new to his experience—a church governed solely by Blacks, the AME Church. Without hesitation he joined it, partly as an act of defiance against Whites and partly from attraction to an autonomous Black organization in which he could realize his ambition for status and power.[642]

Having taken the assignment to work in the Freedpersons Bureau after the Civil War, Turner resigned the lucrative position because of the disrespect shown him because of his color. He returned to the AME Church, the only institution he felt that would allow him "the freedom to lead and the people to direct."[643] The Georgia Republican

---

[642] Redkey, *Black Exodus: Black Nationalist and Back to Africa Movements, 1890-1910* (New Haven, Conn.: Yale University Press, 1969), 25.

[643] Ibid., 26.

Party, however, provided Turner an additional opportunity to develop his leadership and uplift his people through elective politics. Because of the unfair treatment of African-Americans by the Republican Party and the White Georgia officials, Turner retreated from politics bitter and disillusioned. Redkey describes Turner's state of mind and his new strategy for the African-American situation:

> As he entered the prime of life, Turner was a bitter, disillusioned man. He had tasted the things he wanted most in life--political power and prestige--only to have had them snatched away by the prejudice of White America. Most [B]lacks reacted to the loss of their rights and privileges either by protesting through the Republican Party or by acquiescing to their situation--by trying to get along with the least amount of agitation.... Turner, however...was too energetic and ambitious to follow the path of least resistance...he found himself a [B]lack [N]ationalist with a burning desire to see his people do well. If White American would not let [B]lacks perform their highest abilities in the United States, Turner reasoned then [B]lack people must establish their own nation.... Turner proceeded on his nationalistic career working within his all-

[B]lack [C]hurch and urging his people to emigrate.[644]

Turner advocated emigration to Africa as a place where African-Americans could govern themselves, reach their potential, restore their dignity, and as the future sections of this book will reveal, fulfill God's providential plan to Christianize the African continent. Thus, Turner's "life of Black Nationalist agitation," writes Redkey, "was founded on the frustrations of great energy and talent by the prejudice of White America."[645]

As the previous section revealed, Turner was not at first the militant Black Nationalist. On the anniversary of Emancipation, Turner exhibited a great faith in White America. In his 1866 Address, "On the Anniversary of Emancipation," Turner articulated a hope that White Americans and the former slaves would become brothers and sisters.[646] He asked for reconciliation hoping that the freedpersons would forgive their former owners for the ordeal of slavery. Turner wrote: "[L]et us love the Whites and let by-gones be by-gones, neither taunt nor insult them for past grievances. Respect them, honor them, work for

---

[644] Ibid., 29.
[645] Ibid., 24.
[646] Redkey, *Respect Black*, 5-12.

them, but still let us be men and women."[647] Turner concluded the address with an admonition to the freedpersons that revealed his faith in White America: "Let us show them (the Whites) we can be a people, respectable, virtuous, honest, and industrious and soon their prejudice will melt away and with God...we will all be a family."[648]

Another of Turner's early speeches reveals his faith in the viability of politics. Continuing his theme of reconciliation and liberation, Turner envisioned the gradual equalization of African-American rights and assimilation into mainstream American society. Deeply involved in politics during the early years of Reconstruction, Turner felt compelled to advocate African-American participation. He wrote in 1866:

> For [Negroes] to stay out of politics is to level themselves with a horse or a cow. ...If [Negroes] are to be men [and women] full and complete they must take part in everything that belongs to [personhood]. If he [or she] omits a single duty, responsibility, or privilege, to that extent he [or she] is limited and incomplete.[649]

---

[647] Ibid., 11-12.
[648] Ibid., 12.
[649] Ibid.

Turner reasoned that the national government had a duty to protect the rights of its citizens.[650] The Emancipation Proclamation, the Thirteenth, Fourteenth, and Fifteenth Amendments to the United States Constitution, were strong evidence that the government would take its duty seriously. Indeed, Emancipation marked the beginning of a new age of American equality. A rapid succession of African-American setbacks followed that were inconsistent with Turner's thinking, and however. The federal troops were removed from the South. The Supreme Court declared the Civil Rights Act of 1875 unconstitutional wrote the infamous *Plessy vs. Ferguson (1896)* opinion that gave legality to the "separate but equal." doctrine.[651] In addition, lynchings, unsolved murders, voter intimidation, and peonage increased.[652] It was from this background of disillusionment that Turner's Black Nationalism developed.

In their efforts to stifle African-American political participation, the predominately White, Georgia

---

[650] Ibid., 5-12.

[651] Rayford W. Logan, *The Negro in the United States* (London: Van Nostrad Reinhold Company, 1970), 37-50

[652] According to John Dittmer, Turner was one "first to make effective use of the term *peonage*." Turner offered relief from the practice of peonage through a bill he sponsored in the Georgia legislature to protect share croppers and to establish an eight hour work day. See Litwack and Meier, 258.

Reconstruction General Assembly refused to permit the seating of the African-American representatives. Turner made an impassioned address before the legislature protesting the injustice. In his speech "On the Eligibility of Colored members to Seats in the Georgia Legislature" in 1868, Turner said:

> I hope that I am a member of this body.... I shall neither fawn nor cringe before nay party nor stoop to beg them for my rights. Some of my colored fellow members in the course of their remarks took occasion to appeal to the sympathies of members on the opposite side and to eulogize their character for magnanimity. Reminds me very much...of slaves begging under the lash. I am here to demand my rights and to hurl thunderbolts at the men [and women] who would dare to cross the threshold of my [personhood]. There is an old aphorism which says, "Fight the Devil with fire and if I should observe the rule in this instance I wish...to understand that it is but fighting them with their own weapon."[653]

The deteriorating status of African-Americans during the 1880's embittered Turner against the United

---

[653] Redkey, 15.

States. Leaving politics after the Georgia Assembly refused to seat him in 1868, Turner was quite apathetic about the Presidential Election of 1880. Writing in the *Christian Recorder* on March 25, 1980, Turner said the following about politics and his feelings towards the United States:

> I have thought it prudent to keep out of the Presidential agitation for the reason that I am down upon the whole nation. I think my race has been treated by it with the kindness that a hungry snake treats a helpless frog. I am as near a rebel to this Government as any Negro ever got to be. My race has been treated with so much treachery, vile contempt, and diabolical meanness, that I have but little in the country anyway.... I have been made sick a thousand times-- wished I had never been born, so that I might not have been a witness to the deviltry perpetrated upon my people by a so-called civilized country.[654]

There was thus a mutual feeling of disrespect between Turner and the United States.

The national government through the judicial branch continued to abandon its support of African-American rights. The Civil Rights Act of 1875 had prohibited discrimination in public businesses such as restaurant,

---

[654] Ibid; "The Presidential Election of 1880" (1880), 49.

ballparks, and railroads. Yet many railroad companies continued to operate segregated cars reasoning that the federal government had overstepped its authority in trying to regulate private businesses. The railroad companies argued that Congress had no such power and rules purporting to regulate such businesses were unconstitutional. In 1883 the majority of the court sided with the railroad company. Redress for public discrimination was thus left to the states.[655] The court's decision was a farce, for Turner, and it effectively renounced the civil rights of African-Americans. Turner wrote a stinging criticism of the court's decision and concluded that the court's thinking:

> Absolves the Negro's allegiance to the general government, makes the American flag to the Negro race a rag of contempt instead of a symbol of liberty. It reduces the majesty of the nation to an aggregation of ruffianism opens all issues of the late war, sets the country to wrangling again, puts the Negro back into politics, revives the Ku-Klux Klan and the White leaders, resurrects the bludgeons, sets [people] to cursing and

---

[655] Angell, 163-168.

blaspheming God and [humankind] and literally unties the Devil.[656]

By 1884 Grover Cleveland, a Democrat, had captured the White House. There was a great fear among African-Americans that the Democrats would return them to slavery. In his speech, "The Democratic Victory," in 1884, Turner chastised those African-Americans who spoke against their color and personhood rights. Turner said:

> White is God in this country and Black is the Devil. White is perfection, greatness, wisdom, industry, and all that is high and holy. Black is ignorance, degradation, indolence, and all that is low and vile, and three fourths of the colored people of the land do nothing day and night but cry: Glory, honor, dominion, and greatness to White. Many of our so-called leading men [and women] are contaminated with this accursed disease, or folly as well as the thoughtless masses; and as long as such a sentiment pervades the colored race, the powers of heaven cannot elevate them. No race of people can rise and manufacture better conditions while they hate and ignore themselves. A [person] must believe that he

---

[656] Redkey, "The Barbarous Decision of the Supreme Court" (1883), 60.

[or she] is somebody before he [or she] is acknowledged to be somebody.[657]

Turner was extremely critical of African-Americans who were ashamed of their Blackness. He reasoned that Black was just as good as White and insisted that African-Americans respect Black.

The status of African-Americans from past, present, to future has been the focus of ongoing discussions. It was no less an important subject during the quarter century after Emancipation. Turner shared his view on African-Americans and social intercourse with Whites in an editorial that appeared in the *Christian Recorder* in 1884.[658] He reasoned that if African-Americans were to claim America as their true home, then social intercourse with Whites on an equal basis was a necessary element. Subordinate African-American roles would bring about social inferiority and ultimate social extermination. Turner wrote:

> If Negroes do not intend to emigrate to Africa and build up a nation and establish themselves on that line before the world…then they must have social contract with Whites if they remain here or go to the

---

[657] Ibid., 71-72.
[658] Ibid., 73-75

wall. Tell them in the lights of history and philosophy that whoever this [W]hite race does not consort with, they will crust out; that social equality is as necessary to our existence in this land as [your people] if we expect to remain in this country, and the sooner we commence the work, the better for our children.[659]

Turner thus equated social intercourse with social equality and social equality with mutual respect for personhood rights.

Because of a severe economic depression in 1893, Congress proposed to substitute silver for gold as the national monetary base. Opposed to the idea, President Grover Cleaveland pushed for a repeal of the Sherman Act, the legislation that empowered Congress to purchase generous amounts of silver. With the aid of the Northeastern Republicans, President Cleaveland prevailed, but he incurred the bitter anger of the Southerners and Westerners. They opposed President Cleaveland's policies on the grounds that his efforts to maintain the gold reserves adversely affected the value of the currency. Basically farmers, the Southerners and Westerners put the responsibility for their declining farm prices on the

---

[659] *Christian Recorder*, June 4, 1884

inadequate currency supply. They reasoned that the coinage of more silver would supply the monetary needs of the nation.[660]

Turner, with as much militancy as ever, opposed both ideologies, reasoning that they were of little use of African-Americans who were forgotten, oppressed, or killed. Giving his advice to the African-American community in an article in the Voice of Missions, Turner wrote:

> All the advice we have to give to our people, or the Negro, is vote for the gold standard, if you think it will help to kill this rotten old sham of a nation,; vote for the silver platform, or 16 to 1, if you think that will assist in its destruction. What time has the fool Negro to bother with the gold or silver side either, while he is lynched, burnt, flated, imprisoned, etc., two-thirds of the time for nothing. Vote any way in your power to overthrow, destroy, ruin, blot out, divide, crush, dissolve, wreck, consume, demolish, disorganize, suppress, subvert, smash, shipwreck, crumble, nullify, upset, uproot, expunge, and fragmentize this nation, until it learns to deal justly with the [B]lack man. This is all the advice we have to give.[661]

[660] John Krout, *United State Since 1865* (New York, N.Y.: Barnes and Noble, 1960), 74-76.
[661] Redkey, 175.

There was a great debate concerning the military role of African-Americans during the conflict between Spain and the United States during the closing years of the nineteenth century. Were African-Americans to participate in the military campaign abroad while they were not yet accorded full citizenship rights at home?

Those African-Americans who favored Black participation saw the war as a golden opportunity to prove their loyalty and to ameliorate their status. William Gatewood reveals several of the pro-war arguments:

> Pro-war elements within the Black community found a military confrontation with Spain desirable because, in their view, it would bestow substantial benefits upon Negro Americans. A few emphasized that a war over Cuba would diminish the color prejudice of White Americans by bringing them into direct contact with a predominantly colored culture. Others maintained that freedom of the colored people of Cuba would have a healthy influence in bringing better conditions for our race in general.[662]

---

[662] William Gatewood, *Black Americans and the White Man's Burden* 1898-1903 (Chicago: University of Illinois Press, 1975), 24.

On the other hand, there was vocal African-American anti-war element. They strongly believed that "a solution to the race problem in the United States took precedence over any involvement in the Cuban crisis."[663] Gatewood revealed several of the anti-war arguments:

> Anti-war [spokespersons] denied emphatically that Black citizens had any obligations to prove themselves by responding to a call to arms. They contended that the valor and loyalty of Negroes had been amply demonstrated in every war in which the United States had been involved from the American Revolution on. To counteract the notion that Negroes would promote the progress of the race by flocking to the colors in case of a conflict with Spain, the anti-war elements called attention to the barren results of their participation in previous wars.[664]

Turner was an outspoken critic of African-American participation in the war. For him, for African-Americans to die for a country that continued to oppress and lynch them was utterly absurd. Thus Turner wrote:

---

[663] Ibid., 31.
[664] Ibid., 34.

The colored man would far better be
employed in remaining at home, marrying
wives and giving the race sons and
daughters and perpetuating our existence,
than rushing into a death struggle for a
country that cares nothing for their rights
or [personhood], and wait 'til they are
wanted, and then the nation will feel and
know [their] worth and concede [them]
the respect due the defenders of a nation.[665]

The representative focus upon Turner's speeches and writings of the quarter century after Emancipation has revealed several important implications about Turner's liberation thinking. There was an early Turner faith in White America's commitment to African-American equality. The commitment gave way to White insincerity and African-American setbacks. Turner's Black Nationalism was thus his response to the frustrations of White prejudice against the African-American race. Turner then became one of the most prominent advocates of Black Nationalism during the last quarter of the nineteenth century.

---

[665] Redkey, "The Quarrel with Spain" (1898), 173-174

Turner's Emigrationism

In his extreme disappointment with the deteriorating situation of African-Americans, Turner developed a far-reaching Black Nationalism that absolved African-Americans from allegiance to the United States and demanded emigration to Africa. There were several factors that accounted for Turner's advocacy of African emigration: (1) the declining status of African-Americans during the last quarter of the nineteenth century; (2) his theory of Providential Design; and (3) the European partition of Africa.

First, it ought to be clear that Turner never considered himself a colonist, but an emigrationist. The idea of emigration may be distinguished from the idea of colonization in that the former was a Black Nationalist response to White oppression, while the latter was the White plant to eliminate African-Americans from the United States.[666] Prior to the Post-Reconstruction Period, Turner had a casual relationship with the American Colonization Society (ACS) and had sporadically supported

---

[666] Ibid., "Early Emigration Ideas" (1866), 13; "The American Colonization Society" (1876), 43.

emigration[667]. The deteriorating situation for African-Americans during the Post-Reconstruction Period prompted Turner to reassess his emigrationist position. His matured thoughts brought him to the inescapable conclusion that:

> There is no more doubt in my mind that we have ultimately to return to Africa than there is of the existence of a God; and the sooner we begin to recognize that fact and prepare for it, the better will be for us as a people. We there have a country unsurpassed in productive and mineral resources, and we have some two hundred millions of our kindred there in moral and spiritual blindness. The four millions of us in this country are at school, learning the doctrines of Christianity and the elements of civil government. And as soon as we are educated sufficiently to assume control of our vast ancestral domain, we will hear the voice of a mysterious Providence, saying "Return to the land of your [parents].[668]

Turner's emigration embroiled him in a long controversy with his AME colleagues and contemporaries. Frederick Douglass, Henry Tanner, and the Reverend H.G.

---

[667] It was an 1862 speech by Alexander Crummell, an agent for the American Colonization Society , that converted Turner to Emigrationism. Redkey, Black Exodus, 28; Angell, 120-121.

[668] Redkey, Respect Black, "The American Colonization Society" (1875), 42.

Offley were Turner's chief contemporary opponents. He called them elitist persons who had achieved some success and hoped to further their status.[669] Turner claimed that while the three men were out of touch with the poor Black masses, it was his message of emigration that touched the lives of the lower classes.[670]

It was from Turner's vigorous defense of emigration that he got the reputation of having a biting tongue and a pungent vocabulary.[671] Answering a charge by Offley to which Turner vehemently objected, he said, "If all the riff-raff White [people] worshippers, aimless, objectless, selfish, little-souled and would-be White Negroes of this country were to go to Africa, I fear it would take a chiliad of years to get them to understand that a Black man or woman could be somebody without the dictation of the White [race].[672] In his article, "The Rhetoric of Bishop Henry McNeal Turner," Melbourne Cummings argues that

---

[669] Melbourne Cummings, "The Rhetoric of Bishop Henry McNeal Turner" Journal of Black Studies 12 (June 1982): 460-461; Frederick Douglass, Christian Recorder, February 1, 1883; Redkey, "Emigration to Africa" (1883), 57-58.

[670] Redkey.

[671] Cummings, 461.

[672] Redkey, 57.

is the language of biting sarcasm that Turner employed against his opposition that:

> greeted the opponents of Turner's emigration scheme. This is the kind of language that made him so appealing to the masses. The language, his style, his purpose did little to win Turner friends from among the group that opposed his emigration views, but his followers enjoyed this blunt, open manner, his colorful, sometimes coarse language, and his ability and willingness to attack radical oppression and the evasive, ambiguous prattle of both Black and White [spokespersons].[673]

Cummings claims further that Turner's Emigration Movement was one of the first significant rhetorical movements designed and spearheaded by African-Americans.[674]

The AME Church was sharply divided on emigration. Payne was a sharp critic, while Turner was an ardent defender. Thus two of the church's most forceful personalities were on opposite sides of the controversy.[675]

---

[673] Cummings, 462

[674] Ibid., 457. Frederick Douglass immediately comes to mind as a rhetorician but he is distinguished for his speeches and writings and not as a founder of a movement on a massive scale like Turner's Emigration.

[675] Angell, 136.

Payne reasoned that the goals of emigration were unrealistic.[676]   Indeed, the use of the Exodus by the emigrationists falsely equated the Emigration Movement with the liberation of the Hebrews in the Old Testament. While both African-Americans and the Hebrews were victims of oppression, it did not necessarily follow that African-Americans would be liberated in the same way as were the Hebrews. The Old Testament Exodus offered an essential salvation and enlightenment for the oppressed, while the contemporary Emigration Movement offered no such qualities. Stephen Angell further explained Payne's reasoning:

> In other words, the experience of the ancient Hebrews was necessarily unique Black Americans' perceptions that they suffered from a similar oppression did not justify their expectations that the Exodus could be repeated at will. The Exodus was a unique historical instance of God's liberating action not a paradigm of such liberation.[677]

Payne opposed Turner's idea of an AME mission to Africa. Payne did so on pragmatic grounds, reasoning that

---

[676] Ibid.., 136-137.
[677] Ibid.

the AME Church did not have the adequate financial resources to support a comprehensive overseas mission. Moreover, White missionaries were already performing an admirable work.[678]

Turner's advocacy of African missions was based upon his strong conviction that God had liberative and redemptive purposes for African-Americans. In 1889, Turner wrote:

> Let men and women see and recognize the hand of God in the institution of slavery, and dispose of its remains as God directs, and endless blessings flow alike to White and Black. The Christianized Negro will be a blessing to the missions of Africa and the wealth of that giant continent will be a blessing to the White race. Slavery has been a dark providence humanly speaking but behind it God hides a smiling face if men and women will only see their duty and adjust themselves to it.[679]

In a letter to William Coppinger, Secretary of the ACS, Turner's concluding paragraphs underscored the belief in God's plan to use African-Americans to redeem Africa. Writing in 1866 he said: "God is, and will [continue to

---

[678] Ibid., 136.
[679] Ibid., 93.

withhold] political rights from us, for the purpose of turning our attention to our [parentland] that we are destined to be missionaries to the millions of African."[680]

Turner reasoned that God permitted the enslavement of African-Americans in order to bring Africa into contact with Western Civilization and Christianity 9because of its importance to Turner's Black Nationalist theodicy this idea will be examined in the next sections). Turner wrote in 1888 that "God intends that God's degraded race, which has been dwarfed through ages of heathenism, shall imbibe your Civilization with its religion and when sufficiently sobered through generations of self-possession, return to African and bring its millions to Christ and Heaven."[681] Continuing the same theme, Turner wrote in 1895: "[t]he heathen Africans eagerly yearn for that Civilization which they believe will elevate them and make them potential for good."[682] In this view, Turner followed the idea of Alexander Crummell; but, unlike Crummell, Turner made it clear that American Whites had been disobedient to God's command by not receiving Black as brothers and sisters.

---

[680] Ibid., "The Question of Race" (1884), 73.

[681] Ibid., 74.

[682] Ibid., "The American Negroes and their Parentland" (1895), 167.

Whites refused to share with Blacks the riches of the nation and help them return to Africa with the education and resources necessary for their mission--the creation of a Black nation free from imperialistic exploitation by the nations of Europe (the distinctions in the thinking between Crummell and Turner will be examined in Chapter Six of this book).[683]

The creation of an African nation would provide opportunities for both African-American leadership and responsible Black nationhood. In Turner's view, "there was no personhood future for African-Americans in the United States.... The only thing left for the [Negroes] to do is to build themselves a country of [their] own to make and give evidence of their personhood by successfully doing such things as other people have done."[684]

In Turner's view, without a successful country founded and operated by African people, they could never expect to be respected in the international community. Turner asked in an 1883 editorial:

Do you know of any instance in the world's history where a people shut out from all

---

[683] Wilmore, *Black Religion and Black Radicalism*, 124.
[684] Redkey, "Planning a Trip to African" (1891), 84

honorable positions from being kings and queens, lords, and dukes, presidents, governors, mayors, generals, and all positions of honor and trust by reasons of their race ever amounted to anything? No, I will answer for you. There is no instance on record, except where preceded by revolution.... And until we have Black [people] in the seat of power respected honored, beloved, feared, hated, and reverenced, our young [people] will never rise for the reason they will never look up.[685]

Contrary to the idea portrayed by his critics, Turner was not an advocate of wholesale emigration. He supported those who chose to remain in America. He firmly believed that "[African-Americans] were American citizens insomuch as [they] had watered the land with [their] sweat, purchased it with their blood, and were made of its dust."[686] Thus Turner maintained upward mobility for African-Americans on both continents.[687]

Of those who desired to emigrate to Africa, "five or ten thousand" per year was the desired number.[688] Not interested in the undesirables, Turner courted "the better

---

[685] Ibid., "emigration to Africa" (1883), 53.
[686] Quoted in Angell, 265, *Christian Recorder*, April 4, 1878
[687] Angell, 265.
[688] Ibid., 56.

class of men and women to go and build up a majority nation" in Africa.[689]

In addition to relief for African-Americans and elevation for Africans, Turner's advocacy of emigration would become a symbol of African competence and person hood. Redkey explained:

> Turner saw the [parentland] as a great symbol for the entire race, and he   saw it primarily as a political symbol, for he was essentially a political [person]. In a time when Blacks were being divested of political power in the United States, and when some Black leaders were settling for subordinate patronage offices and personal economic gain rather than true political power, Turner still linked the fate of the African-American with politics.[690]

Turner was also concerned about the European partition of Africa. He felt that African-Americans should emigrate to Africa to secure a part of the continent exclusively for the Black race. [691]

Turner sought to tap the federal government, the ACS, and the African-American capital to finance his plan of emigration. He reasoned that the federal

---

[689]Ibid., "The Question of Race" (1884), 73.

[690] Redkey, *Black Exodus*, 34.

[691] Ibid., *Respect Black*, 55.

government ought to appropriate emigration money for those who wished to resettle in Africa. He calculated that the government owed the former slaves "forty billions of dollars for actual services rendered, estimating one hundred dollars a year for two million of us for two hundred years."[692]

Although Turner's advocacy of emigration was solidly opposed by many African-American leaders, thousands of poor African-American Southerners shared his vision of returning to the parentland to live free of White tyranny. The final assessment of Turner's African dream reveals that it failed for lack of finances. John Dittmer, however, lauded Turner in saying "more than any other public figure of his day, he encouraged identification with the African homeland instilling confidence and pride among African-Americans inferiorited." [693]

---

[692] Ibid.
[693] Litwack and Meier, 253. See also Jane Herndon, "Henry McNeal Turner's African Dream: A Re-evaluation" *Mississippi Quarterly* 22 (Fall 1969): 327-336.

Turner's Black Theology was a religious expression of his Black Nationalism. Translating the message of the Gospel into Black liberation, Turner's Black Theology manifested itself in the struggle for African-American justice and equality.

Fundamentally, Turner believed in the Parenthood of God, the redeeming grace of Christ, and the brotherhood and sisterhood of the human family.[694] Believing in the absolute sovereignty and omnipotence of God, Turner expressed this view on numerous occasions. In his speech to the Georgia legislature protesting his ouster in 1868, Turner equated the denial of his seat to a denial of both his dignity and self-worth, and ultimately his humanity.[695] Because those qualities were God-given, to deny them to a member of the human family was contrary to the will of God. Following this line of reasoning Turner asked "[i]s the created greater than the Creator? [Are men and women] greater than God?"[696]

---

[694] Coan, *Turner Speaks to This Generation*, 6.
[695] Redkey, 16-17.
[696] Ibid., 18

In discussing the Negro problem in an article in the *Christian Recorder* in 1889, Turner expressed the following views about God:

> There is a God that runs this universe; nor are nations and people any exception. True, an infinite number of laws may harness up the mighty machinery, and serve as so many potencies in its mysterious and marvelous revolutions; but there is a God in the background nevertheless, and God rules in the armies of Heaven and among the inhabitant of Earth.[697]

Continuing the theme of God's omnipotence, Turner made the claim in the next sentences that some institutions, like slavery, were temporary; while other institutions, like those attributed to the Godhead," were eternal. [698] The temporary institutions were made by human beings while the eternal institutions were created by God.[699]

Addressing the Congress on Africa in 1896, Turner said: "God who is spirit made the world and controls it and the Supreme Being [can] be sought and found by exercising

---

[697] Ibid., 74.
[698] Ibid.
[699] Ibid.

faith in God's Only Begotten Son."[700] Turner thus revealed who created the universe, who controls it, and through whom reunification with the Creator-Controller is mediated.

Turner reasoned that reunification with God is the ultimate goal for the human family. This required a loving relationship not only with God but with other members of the human family as well, known through the person of Jesus Christ. This was indeed the crux of the Gospel: one was to love God and one was to love the human family. Josephus Coan further explained Turner's theology:

> Turner reasoned that Christians have the duty to respond in faith and obedience to the Gospel which is God's whole continuous redemptive action toward human beings known especially in Jesus Christ. That response called for right relationship with God. It also demanded the right relationship with all of God's human creatures regardless of their racial or ethnic origins, in spite of their differing cultural and social status. For Turner, right relationship with God is impossible without right human relationship. Religion and ethics belong together.[701]

---

[700] Coan, 8.
[701] Ibid., 5-6

Focusing upon the existential situation of African-Americans during the last quarter of the nineteenth century, Turner found them lacking in justice and equality and oppressed by White America. Turner's theology therefore was a theology of liberation that endeavored to remove barriers to holistic relationships between members of the human family and members of the human family and God.

During the last decade of the nineteenth century, a spate of prejudicial literate developed. Southern White theologians developed literature that alleged the inferiority of African-Americans and predicted that inferiority would be their future status as well. In addition, the White racists popularized a belief that White was Godly and Black was satanic.[702]

Turner was compelled to rebut those arguments in order to uplift his people who were already under the strain of worsening economic, political, and social conditions. Turner's rebuttals were based upon affirmation of the equality of humankind and the ideal of colorblind society.[703] Turner reasoned that God diversified God's creation. While there was diversity, there was equality in God's diversity

---

[702] Angell, 260-261.
[703] Ibid., 115

and Whites had no right to challenge or re-order God's creation. Turner wrote in 1868:

> God saw fit to vary everything in nature. There are no two [persons] alike--no two voices alike--no two trees alike. God has weaved and tissued variety and versatility throughout the boundless space of [God's] creation. Because God saw fit to make some Red, and some White, and some Black, and some Brown, are we to sit here in judgment upon what God has seen fit to do? As well might one play with the thunderbolts of Heaven as with that creature that bears God's image--God's photograph.[704]

Turner reasoned that African-Americans like Frederick Douglass, Daniel Payne, and Henry Highland Garnet, who labored under severe handicaps, had demonstrated their ability to contribute positively to society.[705] Turner further reasoned that "greatness has no color; learning is neither White nor Black. There is no such thing as [C]olored intelligence, White intelligence, or Black intelligence."[706]

---

[704] Redkey, 16.

[705] Angell, 259

[706] Quoted in Angell; Turner, *Introduction to the Black Side* by Earl R. Carter (Atlanta, 1894), vii.

Turner turned from a defensive strategy of affirming human equality and the ideal of a colorblind society to a more aggressive strategy in promoting the greatness of African-American personhood. He chose this strategy because of the White racists' insistence that the present status of African-Americans was unalterable due to their inherent inferiority.[707] Turner wanted to restore the hope of African-Americans in themselves and in their future. He thus predicted a great future for African-Americans in articulating the belief that the White race would fail and the Black race would become preeminent.[708] He wrote in 1884: We are not dying out, as predicted. The Negro is the junior race of the world with the possible exception of the Australians, we have a great and grand future. Our race will be waxing for centuries after the White race will have commenced to wane. The Negro is a [child], the White is an [adult]. When the [adult] shall have reached old age and in the same kind of dotage that characterizes the American Indian, the [Negroes] will be in their prime and glory and ruling the world.[709]

---

[707] Angell, 260-261.
[708] Redkey.
[709] Ibid.

Turner know the power of symbols in a symbol-oriented society. He reasoned that the negative connotations associated with Blackness were extremely dangerous conceptions. Not only had White theologians popularized the belief that Black was satanic while White was Godly, the idea had crept into the thinking of African-Americans. Turner met the challenge of anti-Black rhetoric with a Black rhetoric of his own. He made a bold pronouncement that "[t]he Devil was White and was never Black."[710]

So strong was the idolatry of Whiteness in the African-American community that it "reduced them to obsequious believers in their own spiritual inferiority."[711] Closely related to the belief in African-American spiritual inferiority was a belief in a White God who favored White over Black. Because religion was the "prime expression of African-American personhood and their will both to exist and to improve their spiritual situation,"[712] Turner thus had to fashion a strong response to White idolatry. While addressing an African-American Baptist Convention in 1895, Turner proclaimed that God was a Negro. [713] The

---

[710] Angell, 261; Redkey, 73.
[711] Wilmore, 125.
[712] Ibid., 221; Litwack and Meier, 260.
[713] Voice of Missions, November 3, 1895.

White press immediately condemned Turner for what they considered "demented language."[714] Turner replied in saying:

> We have as much right biblically and otherwise to believe that God is a [N]egro, as you buckra or [W]hite people have to believe that God is a fine looking, symmetrical, and ornamented [W]hite [person].... Every race of people since time began who have attempted to describe their God by words, or by paintings or by carvings...have conveyed the idea that the God who made them and shaped their destinies was symbolized in themselves.... Yet we are no stickler as to God's color, anyway, but if [God] has any we would prefer to believe that is it nearer symbolized in the blue sky above us and the blue water of the seas...but we certainly protest against God being a [W]hite [person] or against God being [W]hite at all.[715]

Turner's belief in an African-Americanized God must be understood from within the context of the African-American experience. Turner's pronouncement was an attempt to destroy the negative connotations associated with

---

[714] Ibid., February 1898.
[715] Redkey, 176-177.

Blackness and to give African-Americans hope through a God who identified with their struggles for liberation.

Turner's Theodicy of Slavery

If God is omnipotent and the absolute sovereign of the universe, and if God is Black and identifies with the struggles of the African-American race, then how did Turner account for slavery? Turner's speeches and writings reveal that he viewed slavery as a White duty to Africans as a trust from God and as a part of God's Providential Design.

Turner revealed the idea that slavery was a White duty to Africa as a trust from God in his address "On the Anniversary of the Emancipation" in 1866. He said:

> God seeing the African stand in need of civilization, sanctioned for a while the slave trade--not that it was in harmony with [God's} fundamental laws for one [person] to rule another, nor did God ever contemplate that the Negro would be reduced to the status of a vassal, but as a subject for moral and intellectual culture. So God winked, or lidded [God's] eyeballs, at the institution of slavery as a test of the White [Race's] obedience, and the elevation of the Negro. The African was,

I have no doubt, committed to the care of the
White [Race] as a trust from God....[716]

Turner hastened to make the point, however, that the
slave-owners abused God's trust. In return for
unremunerated labor, the slave-owners were to educate and
civilize the slaves. The White clergy was to inform the
slave-owners of the personhood rights of the slaves and the
White Church was to ensure that the rights were upheld.
Turner continued this line of thought in saying:

> But that the [W]hite [Race]
> barred...improvements for the Black Race
> was the crime which offended Heaven. We
> have given the White Race our labor...in
> return they should have educated us...and to
> have seen that Africa was well supplied with
> missionaries. ...Had the ministers exhausted
> half their learning...in showing [W]hite
> people their duty to the Negro as a trust from
> God, than trying to prove the [D]ivine right of
> slavery, Africa would have been two thirds
> civilized...twice as wealthy, and the bones of
> [our people should not lie over every]
> Southern state....[717] Had the White people
> treated slavery as a trust from God...it would

[716] Ibid., 7.
[717] Ibid.

have gone on until it became a social burden...and it would have passed away.[718]

Closely related to Turner's idea of slavery as a trust from God was Turner's idea that slavery was a part of God's Providential Design. Revealing this idea in an article in the *Christian Recorder* in 1888, Turner said:

Slavery was a Providential institution, not a Divine institution; for had it been, it would have been as eternal as any attribute belonging to the Godhead. One is temporary and contingent, the other is immutable and eternal. God was not asleep or oblivious or passing events. When the [Negro] was being captured, and brought to this country and subjected to a state of unrequited servitude...[they] knew the horrors of their past and present condition, and foresaw the grand sequel which awaited the termination of their slave ordeal. {God] knew the slave regime, although exceedingly protechnical at times, was the most rapid transit from barbarism to Christian [C]ivilized for the [Negro]. Negro, as I am, and being thoroughly acquainted with the characteristics of my race, I am frank to make

---

this declaration, odd as it may seem to many.[719]

Turner followed Crummell in this response articulating the general idea that slavery was a part of God's Providential Design.[720] (The difference in the two men's specific use of Providence will be examined in the next chapter.)

Turner's idea of theodicy reasoned that it was God's intention to use slavery for God's good purposes. Indeed, God used the slave-system to civilize the Africans and to convert them to Christianity. The slave-system provided the best opportunity to facilitate the rapid transition from the slaves' state of barbarism to Christian Civilization.[721]

An important element in Turner's theodicy of slavery was the fact that Whites abused God's trust in developing and maintaining a barbaric slave-system that did not provide for the means of African-American elevation. Not pleased with these abuses, God in God's absolute sovereignty abolished the slave-trade. Unlike Eternal institutions that were created by God and lasted forever,

---

[719] Ibid., "The Question of Race" (1888), 74.
[720] Crummell, *Africa and America*, 418. See Chapter Three of this study.
[721] Redkey, 74.

slavery was a Providential institution made by human beings and only temporary.[722]

It was Turner's belief that God would use the misuse of God's trust by Whites to lift the Black race to greatness. Their greatness would include the qualities of liberation and redemption. The freed African-Americans had the choice to return to Africa or stay in America. The former group was to take the best of what they learned of American civilization (while it was not the best of what Whites could have given, it was superior to African civilization) back to the parentland and elevate Africa to preeminence.[723] The latter group was to work diligently for African-American Uplift in order to achieve standing and influence in American society.[724] The misuses of God's trust by Whites

---

[722] Ibid.

[723] For all of Turner's talk about Black Nationalism he seems to have been stricken with a bit of Anglophilism. For him, the qualities of the ideal society were Western, civilized, and Christian. Turner would accept neither indigenous African royalty nor Traditional African Religious practices as substitutes for Western Civilization or Christianity.

[724] Henry Young takes the position that Turner proposed full-scale emigration to Africa as a place where African-Americans could achieve success in developing livelihoods, but not in becoming men and women. Young, 147-149. The research of this study does not agree with Young's analysis of Turner's thinking. This research reveals that Turner took a two-pronged approach advocating emigration on the one hand, and African-American Uplift on the other hand, for those who

was thus another instance in world history where God took evil and used it for God's good. Turner's theodicy of broken trust, Providential Design, and redemption thus offered hope and encouragement that God was with African-American in their struggles for justice and equality.

Strengths and Weaknesses of Turner's Black Theology

The strengths of Turner's idea of Black Theology lies in his attempt to make God relevant to the African-American existential situation. Turner's Black Theology articulated the belief if an omnipotent God. Turner appropriated this idea in creating a worldview that envisioned a God immanently involved in all of life, in control of the universe, and a God who would set things right in God's own time.[725] There was thus a powerful belief that there could be certainty that God was in control. Thus having addressed Divine existence, Turner made the claim that God was with African-Americans in their struggles for liberation.

---

wished to remain in America. See pages 199-206 of this section and notes 103 and 105.

[725] Wimberly, 25.

In accounting for slavery, Turner reasoned that God allowed it so that African-Americans would encounter Western Christianity and thus be equipped for a missionary crusade to Africa. Turner took great pains to show, however, that Whites abused God's trust in developing and maintaining a barbaric system of slavery that denied both African-American personhood and the means of elevation. Turner thus located the cause of African-Americans suffering in the White abuse of God's trust.

Interpreting the biblical message, Turner found both the philosophical base and historical evidence of a just God. In his famous speech to the Georgia Assembly in 1868, Turner said:

> Justice is the great doctrine taught in the Bible. God's eternal justice is founded upon truth. And the [person] who steps from justice steps from truth and the [person] cannot make his [or her] principles prevail. You may expel us…by your vote today but while you do it remember there is just God in Heaven whose all seeing eye beholds alike the acts of the oppressor and the oppressed and who despite the machinations of the wicked never fails to vindicate the cause of

justice and the sanctity of [God's] own handiwork.[726]

Continuing in the same speech, Turner alluded to the historical destruction of the oppressor nations: "Go on with your oppression. Babylon fell. Where is Greece? Where is Ninevah? And where is Rome the great empire of the world? Why is it that Rome stands today, in the broken fragments throughout Europe? Because oppression killed her."[727]

Furthering his attempt to make his religion relate to the African-American situation, Turner articulated the view that God is a Negro. This idea provided the African-American community with a God who identified with their struggles for liberation. The idea was powerful for its symbolism as well, because it gave ultimate power to a Black being and allowed a despised and dejected race to view the Ultimate Sovereign of the universe in terms of themselves.

Turner's Black theology was consistent in its demand for African-America personhood rights. He advocated full and complete African-American personhood rights. He advocated full and complete African-American

---

[726] Redkey.
[727] Ibid.

participation in American society.[728] For Turner, personhood was a God-given identity and a quality that could not be denied. He asked that all African-Americans demand "their inalienable rights to life, liberty, and the pursuit of happiness as any other American."[729] He believed that in demanding their personhood rights, both African-American self-respect and self-uplift would emerge.

Turner's advocacy of emigration helped to set the tone for Marcus Garvey's "Back to Africa Movement" of the next century.[730] Turner assisted several thousand politically disenfranchised and economically deprived African-Americans to relocate to Africa and enjoy a liberated life.

Turner's idea of Black Theology gave hope to the African-American community that God would ultimately free them from their oppressors. Turner emphasized a hope for the here and now rather than a futuristic eschatological hope. Henry Young explains:

---

[728] Coan, 12.
[729] Ibid., 8.
[730] Robert Weisbord, "The Back To Africa Idea," History Today (Great Britain) 18(1): 30-37; Young, 152-162.

Turner's theology did not gear itself toward a fixation with Heaven and when he did used the word Heaven it was in comparison with this world. He believed that [men and women] should live in Heavenly places in this world. This is why he gave his life to the eradication of injustice, humankind's inhumanity to humankind, oppression, unrighteousness, and all sorts of social evils. He did not do this in the attempt to better prepare [men and women] for Heaven. He did it so that [men and women] could become what God wants them to be here on earth.[731]

There were thus several powerful ideas and beliefs that formed the fundamental basis for Turner's efforts to make sense out the African-American experience of suffering and oppression.

The ideas that slavery was a White duty to Africa as a trust from God and a part of God's Providential Design were weak aspects of Turner's Black Theology. Turner's theodicy makes God responsible for slavery through God's Providential Design. Is there a difference between barbaric slavery and a purported human slavery? If so, does this mean that a purported humane slavery is acceptable to God?

---

[731] Ibid., 149.

In Turner's thinking the qualities of Christianity and a degree of Civilization were positive benefits of a barbaric slave-system that could be used to redeem Africa. Because God allowed the good of redeeming Africa to come from the evil of Whites, does this mean that slavery has redemptive qualities? Why were Africans chosen to be sufferers? Could not God have accomplished the task of redeeming Africa without African suffering? Turner's Black theology does not satisfactory resolve these difficult issues.

Turner's bold claim that God is a Negro and identifies with African-American liberation seems to refute the claim by the twentieth century theologian, William Jones, that God may be a White racist. Jones argues that either God is identified with the oppressed to the point that their experience becomes God's or God is a God of racism. Jones argues that prime refutation of Go's White racism is to point to a definitive exaltation -liberation event for Blacks which will clearly disclose God's favor towards Blacks.[732] Turner, however, was unable to point to such an event. The fact is that massive African-American suffering continued.

---

[732] William Jones, *Is God a White Racist?* (Garden City, N.: Anchor Press Doubleday), 116-120.

The prominent weakness in Turner's thinking are therefore Black Theology's inability to give a satisfactory account of slavery; Black Theology's unfair emphasis on African-American redemptive suffering; and Black Theology's ability to point to a definitive liberation-exodus event for African-Americans.

Summary

This chapter provided a biographical sketch of Turner focusing upon those life experiences that influenced his ideas of Black Nationalism in relation to his theodicy. We also provided the historical background for Turner's fundamental ideas about Black Nationalism and Black Theology. Having provided this background, the chapter examined the sources of Turner's Black Nationalism and Black Theology. The chapter then extrapolated Turner's specific ideas of Black Nationalism, African-American Uplift, Emigrationism, Black Theology, and theodicy from his major speeches and writings during the last quarter of the nineteenth century. The chapter We then examined the specific Turner ideas. Finally, the chapter critiqued Turner's ideas of Black Theology, which is his theodicy, to illuminate its strengths and weaknesses.

Chapter VI: **COMPARISON OF THE THEODICIES OF GARNET, CRUMMELL, AND TURNER**

Image Ownership: Public Domain
Alexander Crummell

This chapter compares the theodicies of Garnet, Crummell, and Turner. The first section provides a discussion of the classical theodicies of Augustine, Aquinas, and Ireaneus. The second section focuses on three contemporary theodicies in relation to the African-American perspective. Having set a classical background and having discussed three contrasting contemporary theodicies, the next three sections focus on the thoughts of Garnet, Crummell, and Turner in relation to their theodicies and their thoughts on the Black race. The fifth section provides a comparison of the theodicies of the three men. Finally, the last section provides an analytical summary of the previous discussions. Specifically, the views of the three men in relation to their ideas concerning God and evil, the nature and destiny of the Black race, and theodicy, are analytically summarized.

Classical Theodicy: Augustine, Aquinas, and Ireaneus

The questions that surround theodicy are as old as human awareness. What accounts for evil in the world? What is God doing in evil times? What of the moral character of God? Does God create both good and evil?

Every culture and every religion wrestles with the questions posed by theodicy.

Fundamentally, the question of theodicy begins with the problem of evil. If God is God, why then evil? If God is all good, omnipotent, and omniscient, why does God not exclude evil? What is the definitive answer for the why of evil?

In general, the experience of evil has two basic distinctions: natural and moral. Natural evil refers to the experience of pain and despair which takes place beyond the reach of human freedom. For example, earthquakes and floods which bring about pain and death. Moral evil refers to pain and deprivation that flows from human choice. For example, the deliberate choice to cause harm. Because the dissertation focuses on the experience of African-American oppression and African-American slavery, the following sections are concerned only with moral evil.

Historically, Christian thought concerning theodicy has moved between two polar positions: Monism and Dualism. Monism claims that the universe forms an ultimate harmonious unity. This view suggests the theodicy that evil is partial and it works toward the good. Dualism, on the other hand, claims that the world process is involved in a constant struggle between two equally opposing forces, good and evil. There is an insistence that good and evil are irreconcilably opposed to one another and that their duality can be overcome only be one destroying the other. The ideas of Monism and Dualism will figure prominently in the future discussions about theodicy in this chapter.

Two of the fathers of Western Christianity, Saint Aurelius Augustine (A.D. 354-430) and Saint Thomas Aquinas (A.D. 1226?-1274), provide the classical Christian response to the problem of evil. The thought of Augustine is developed in response to the Manichean belief system. Synthesizing various Gnostic belief systems, Manichees (A.D. 215-276), a Persian prophet, offered a clear dualistic explanation. Reality, according to Manichees, is a cosmic struggle between co-equal and dialectic powers: the good manifested in spirit and light and the evil, embodied in matter and darkness. Sin takes place when the soul escapes from the kingdom of darkness (the body) into the kingdom of light (the spirit). There is an insistence that all matter is evil.

During the younger stages of his life, Augustine embraced the philosophy of Manicheanism. He found his dual explanation for the problem of evil simple and satisfying. Converting to Christianity, both his belief in the one God concept and the idea of an absolutely good, omnipotent, and omniscient God came into conflict with his former belief system. He thus rejected Manicheanism as too simplistic a perspective for the grave problem of evil.

Yet, it was his new belief system that brought the moral character of God into question. If the One Sovereign God is absolutely good and omnipotent, why does God allow evil to exist? If God does allow evil to exist, is God really good? From where does evil come? When the experience of evil and suffering are juxtaposed with two of the fundamental beliefs traditionally associated with Ethical Monotheism, the problem of theodicy comes into focus.

In the view of Augustine, God is completely and eternally good. Indeed all natures are good. Writing in the Confessions, Augustine argued, "Here is God, and here is what [God] created. God is good, utterly and entirely better than things which God has made. But, since [God] is good, the things that God has made are also good. This is how [God] contains them all in [God] and fills them all with [God's] presence."

Holding the belief in an absolute good God and the belief that all natures are good, Augustine wrestled with the origin of evil. Writing in the Confessions, Augustine asked: Where then does Evil come from if God made all things and because [God] is good, made them good too? It is true that

[God] is the supreme good, that [God] is a greater good than these lesser goods which God created. But the creator and all [God's] creation are both good. Where then does evil come from?

Augustine offers an explanation of evil as a privation of being. For him, to the extent everything is positive, it is good. It becomes evil only when it ceases to be what it ought to be. Evil is a negative being, an absence of a positive good that ought to be present. Evil thus has no ontological being, it exists as the privation of a perfect being. Developing the privation theory, Augustine wrote:

What is that which we call evil but the absence of good? In the bodies of animals, disease. . .means nothing but the absence of health; for when a cure is effected, that does not mean. . .the evils which were present-. . .the diseases and wounds. . .go away from the body and dwell elsewhere: they altogether cease to exist; for the wound or disease is not a substance, but a defect in the fleshy substance--the flesh itself being a substance and therefore something good, of which those evils--that is privations of the good which we call health--are accidents. Just in the same way, what are called vices in the soul are nothing but privations of a natural good. And when they are cured, they are not transferred elsewhere: when they cease to exit in the healthy soul, they cannot exist anywhere else.

It was the work of Saint Thomas Aquinas that enabled Augustine's view to prevail in Western Christianity. Except for the Aristotelian model of act and potency, the main elements of the thought of Augustine are embodied in the theology of Aquinas. Using Aristotle's metaphysical model of act and potency, Aquinas provides an understanding of the structure of reality. In the view of Aquinas, "Every nature is either act or potency or a composite of the two. Whatever is act, is a perfection and is good in its very concept. And what is potency has a natural appetite for all the reception of act; but what all beings desire is good." Aquinas implies that nature or being, whether fully realized or in potential towards realization, is basically good. He repeats from a slightly different perspective what Augustine had said earlier: evil is simply the privation of a perfect being and therefore has no ontological status. Evil can exist only in something good because as a lack of being or privation it needs a host or a foundation which is a being and hence good.

Another important element in the view of Augustine and Aquinas is the doctrine of free will. The free will proponents argue that human beings have the capacity for good or for evil. God created humankind in this way so as to have genuine response. Obviously, there are those whose failings provide the opportunity for evil. Moral evil for Augustine and Aquinas thus takes place in the will.

Irenaeus (c 120-200), Bishop of present-day Lyons, offers an alternative to the Augustinian type of theodicy. There are significant areas of agreement between the two thinkers, however. Both reject a dualistic solution and look to God as the ultimate source of reality. Irenaeus, however, has an understanding of creation and the role of men and women that gives his theology a developmental rather than a static context.

In the view of Augustine, men and women were created perfect but fell from grace because of a free act of rebellion against God. The disobedience disrupted the Divine plan and introduced evil into the world. Humankind inherits Adam's guilt and their sufferings are Divine punishment for sin.

In contrast to the Augustinian point of view, Irenaeus maintains that men and women were created in an early stage of developmental awareness with the capacity and the call to grow toward ultimate perfection. While not completely perfect, or totally evil, humankind began in a childlike condition open to growth. Irenaeus wrote:

If. . .anyone say. . .could not God have exhibited [humankind] as perfect from the beginning? Let the [person] know that all things are possible to God. But created things must be inferior to [God] who created them. . But inasmuch as they are not uncreated. . .they come short of the perfect. Because, as these things are of later date, so are they infantile; so are they unaccustomed to, and unexercised in, perfect discipline. For as it certainly is in the power of a mother to give strong food to her infant, [but she does not do so], as the child is not yet able to receive more substantial nourishment; so also it was possible for God to have made [humankind] perfect from the first, but [humankind] could not receive this [perfection], being as yet an infant.

Within this evolutionary perspective, Irenaeus works out a "theology of development." That is to say, while human beings are created in the image of God, they still have to grow through free choice into the likeness of God. In this view the fall of Adam is understood as an occurrence in the childhood stage--a lapse that can be attributed to human immaturity. Irenaeus explains:

> By this arrangement, a created and organized being is rendered after the image of the uncreated God. It was necessary that humankind in the first instance be created; and having been created, should receive

growth; and having received growth, should be strengthened; and having been strengthened, should abound; and having abounded, should recover [from the disease of sin]; and having recovered, should be glorified; and being glorified, should see his [or her] Lord.

Irenaeus reasons that the encounter with good and evil enhances human growth. Only by experiencing the tension between good and evil was humankind to learn the better choice:

> [For] how, if we had no knowledge of the contrary, could we have had instruction in that which is good? . . . For just as the tongue receives experience of sweet and bitter by means of tasting, and the eye discriminates between black and white by means of vision, and the ear recognises the distinctions of sounds by hearing; so also does the mind, receiving through the experience of both the knowledge of what is good, become more tenacious of its preservation, by acting in obedience to God. But if any one do shun the knowledge of both kinds of things, and the two-fold perception of knowledge, [one] unawares divests [oneself] of the character of a human being.
>
> Thus, the Irenaeusian approach to the problem of evil stands in contrast to the Augustinian type of theodicy. John Hick sums up the two contrasting points of view:
>
> First, instead of the fall of humankind being presented as in the Augustinian tradition as an

utterly catastrophic event completely disrupting God's plan, it pictures it as something that occurred in the childhood of the race, an understandable lapse to weakness and immaturity, rather than an adult crime full of malice and pregnant with perpetual guilt. Second, instead of the Augustinian view of life's trials as divine punishment for Adam's sin, Irenaeus sees our world of a mixed good and evil as a divinely appointed environment for [humankind's] development towards the perfection that represents the fulfillment of God's good purpose for [humankind].

This section has briefly examined classical theodicy in the thinking of Augustine and Aquinas. In addition, the section has focused on the theodicy of Irenaeus, another classical thinker, who offers a contrasting point of view to the Augustinian type of theodicy.

Three Contemporary Theodicies and the African-American Perspective:
the Finite-Infinite God, the Absolute God, and the Limited God

In this dissertation, theodicy is not the general question. Theodicy is a group issue. It refers to a suffering of a people--Black people. Thus, while the previous section focused on classical theodicy from the Western Christian perspective, this section is concerned with contemporary theodicy from the African-American perspective.

While there are numerous contemporary types of theodicies, this section focuses on three: (1) the Infinite-Finite God theodicy of Professor Edgar Sheffield Brightman; (2) the Absolute God theodicy proposed by four contemporary African-American theologians: Benjamin E. Mays, J. Deotis Roberts, Nicholas Cooper-Lewter, and Henry Mitchell, and (3) the Limited God theodicy of William Jones. The three types of theodicies are valuable for this section because they provide the clear polar and middle-of-the-road contrast of beliefs that are found in the African-American community.

Professor Edgar Sheffield Brightman, a prominent Theistic Personalist, offered the idea of a Finite-Infinite God. According to Brightman, radical evil could not be reconciled with Divine omnipotence. For Brightman, "God is limited by external, uncreated, unchosen factors within [God's] own nature and ontological being." While [God] is the source and ground of all creation, [God], nevertheless, is limited in power.

The idea of a limited God is developed through the alien facet to the "given." The given are the elements within the nature of God, while the alien facets are those elements outside of God's will. God is able to control those elements within God's nature, but God is unable to control those elements outside of God's will. God is thus the finite-infinite controller of the given. Major Jones provides an excellent commentary on Professor Brightman's idea:

> There is an alien facet to the "given," an element not within the scope of God's will; and yet, the "given" is eternal within the will of God. This combination of the uncreated laws of reason and of the equally uncreated disorderliness, pain, and suffering are, existentially speaking, a "surd." The given includes both the rational and nonrational aspects within God's ontological being [Paul Schilling, God and Human Anguish (New York, N.Y.: Abingdon Press, 1977)]. The former consists of the norms of reason and other orderly values; the latter are processes in the divine consciouness that exhibit, by analogy with human experience, "all the ultimate qualities of sense objects (qualia), disorderly impulses and desires. . .and whatever in God is the source of surd evil." [Edgar Sheffield Brightman, The Problem of God (New York , N.Y.: Abingdon Press, 1930), 113]. The nonrational "given" is thus the retarded factor that resists the efforts of God's perfectly good will to order reality according to [God's] rational and positive intent.

The will of God is thus affected by locating evil within God's ontological being. Jones further explains Professor Brightman's view:

By locating evil within the ontological being of God, Brightman concedes that God's will cannot, as of now, overcome all of the recalcitrant elements in the nonrational "given." That is, God does not have absolute control over all those processes within [God] that might be compared to the sensory, affective, and emotional life of human beings. The hampering effects of those elements within God's personality are due to excess or non-disciplinary evil.

Commenting further on the view of Professor Brightman, Jones writes:

Brightman concludes that within God's ontological self there must be a "resistant given" that blocks and limits God's own immediate and full realization of all the good that God wills. The cause of evil, the world's imperfections, and evil's persistence, are expressions of God's limited powers, and seemingly lack of the absolute ability to act.
Professor Brightman leaves a hope, however, While God has limits, God has the will to seek the ultimate good. Indeed, Professor Brightman describes God as the "cosmic person whose will is controlled or governed by creative patient will." Humankind is to join in partnership with God to advance creation towards the ultimate good. "The personality of God conceived as a supreme person, together with the sacredness of human personality, expresses," for Brightman, "the true genius of the Christian religion."

The view of Brightman is generally unacceptable for the African-American community because of a good-evil dualism within the ontology of God. The concept of a limited God is mostly rejected in the African-American community in favor of an all-powerful God who rules all of creation and in God's own time will set things right. This is an extremely important faith claim for Black Christians, and it guarantees that their lives are worth living.

Opposed to Professor Brightman's view of God are several Black theologians, Benjamin E. Mays, J. Deotis Roberts, Nicholas Lewter-Cooper, and Henry Mitchell, who conceive of God in terms of omnipotence and the traditional African-American God ideas.

The seminal research concerning the African-American concept of God is The Negro's God as Reflected in his Literature, a 1938 book by Benjamin E. Mays. Treating two basic types of African-American literature, "mass" and "classical," his research reveals the "popular" and "intellectual" ideas of God, respectively. Dividing his research into several time periods, Mays' first segment is limited to the years between 1760 and 1865. Having researched numerous prayers, sermons, spirituals, and other "mass" type of literature of the first period, Mays found a general God-concept among the masses:

God is the ultimate sovereign of the universe. God is all-wise. God is all-good. God is all-powerful. God answers the prayers of the righteous. God rewards the righteous, while God punishes the wicked. Everything works for the good of those who love God and seek to obey God's will. God is both here in the world and "up yonder" in heaven. From time to time, God steps down and actively involves the [God-self] in human affairs.

Thus, the masses had a strong, clear, and simple view of God: God is all-good and all-powerful. These ideas suggest a theodicy of a God who is too wise to make mistakes, too just for evil conduct, and powerful enough to realize God's will.

J. Deotis Roberts, writing some fifty-three years after the publication of Mays, identifies the God idea among Blacks in general. In addition, he provides theological discussions that both explain their ideas and suggest their theodicies.

Roberts believes that Christianity is a revealed religion. Revelation is about the way that the truth about Christianity is acquired. Revelation is a constant unveiling process. While there is no universal agreement as to the source, authority, and knowledge of revelation, revelation as such is fundamental to the Christian faith claim. Speaking of the Judeo-Christian God, Roberts says this:

The Judeo Christian God, the God of the Bible, unveils [the God-self] through an "I-thou" encounter with the patriarchs, prophets, and the people of promise in the Old Testament. God fulfills this same revelation in and through Jesus as the Christ. God continues to make God known through the apostles and the Christ. Through the agency of the Spirit, God within, the self-disclosure and the unveiling of the mind and will of God is an experience of Christians in their personal lives.

The understanding of God is thus for Roberts related to the dignity and destiny of humankind. God speaks to humankind in a particular historical and cultural setting. The revelation for oppressed African-Americans must be that God is their strength and salvation. In summarizing the meaning of revelation in the Christian faith, Roberts makes the point that:

Theology, as reflection upon experience, must relate what God is saying and doing to the human condition. God is a God who acts and [God] takes action upon what [God] speaks. In this way revelation is related not only to creation and redemption but also to providence as well. Humankind is addressed by God as they are and where they are, even if they are called forth to change their condition. . . . A worthy theological enterprise brings the revelation and the human situation together in order that a man [or woman] may be able to find themselves or ethnic understanding and thereafter liberation or fulfillment. This is the nature, medium, and message of God's revelation to [humankind] which is here applied in Christian theological perspective to Black consciousness in a White racist society.

According to Roberts, African-Americans are not generally concerned about the question of God's existence. Agreeing with Dubois, Roberts maintains that it was the African religious element that survived acculturation into the White oriented culture. Roberts therefore takes the position that:

The problem of God presents itself to Blacks in terms not of the existence of God but rather in terms of the moral attributes of God. Reflection upon the Black person's God must deal with creation, providence, power, love, justice, evil, and the like. The Christian understanding of God must develop out of the Black presence in a White racist society and out of an experience of oppression endured for almost four centuries.

Much like Augustine who believed in the goodness of nature, Roberts affirms the belief in the goodness of creation. For him, both the creation of nature and human life are good. There is a correlative belief for oppressed persons: the affirmation of a good creation affirms the personhood of creatures including African-Americans.

For Blacks to maintain a belief in the goodness of creation, where they are oppressed and powerless, Roberts claims that it is extremely important that they conceive of God as all-good and all-powerful. This is true because an all-good God without power is weak, anemic, and unable to realize God's will. An all-powerful God without justice may be unconcerned about a rejected and abused people. So the omnipotence of God and the justice of God are correlative. Roberts wrote explaining the importance of the twin attributes:

> All-power is a precious attribute of God for Black people; for them impotent goodness has little appeal. Faith has to appeal, as Pascal has taught us, to "the reasons of the heart" as well as to "the reasons of the head." I submit that a God who is absolute in both power and goodness makes sense to Black [people]. Absolute goodness is important as well as absolute power. Absolute power ensures the ultimate triumph of the good; but absolute goodness assures us that absolute power will not be abused. While goodness is an intrinsic value, power is an instrumental value. God is manifest in what H. H. Farmer calls the "goodness" of God. Power is the means whereby this goodness at its best is manifest in human life and history.

How does Roberts reconcile the idea of the goodness of nature with sin and evil? Roberts argues for the finiteness of humankind and the human dependency on God. There is a falleness of humankind that has caused a broken relationship between God and humanity and among the human family.

What is the answer to the race problem? The fall of humankind caused disharmony in creation. Evil, which includes the elements of racism and oppression, is a direct result of the fall. Roberts argues for a liberation--a movement to free all Blacks from the forces of oppression. The Liberation Movement involves Blacks and Whites acting through vigorous protest, speaking and moving through both the Black and White churches.

In addition to liberation, Roberts calls for reconciliation--the movement to bring the races together on an equal basis. It is a post-revolutionary situation that seeks to make the elements of universality in the Christian faith inclusive and colorless. Whites do not have to become Black to be reconciled with Blacks, but they must accept Blacks as equal. The humanity of both Blacks and Whites is thus protected. Men and women, through the help of God, are to work for reunion with God and reunion among themselves.

Another important contribution to the body of literature concerning Black religious beliefs and the conception of God in particular is Soul Theology: The Heart of American Black Culture by Nicholas C. Cooper-Lewter and Henry H. Mitchell. The authors identify and examine ten basic African-American religious beliefs. Their conceptions of God are revealed through their basic beliefs in the providence, justice, and omnipotence of God.

The providence of God is the most essential and inclusive of Black religious beliefs. It is a sense in which God is in control and therefore guarantees that life is worth living. Cooper-Lewter and Mitchell explain: "The Bible passage that expresses it best is Paul's famous word to the Romans 'and we know that God works in everything for the good of those who love [God] and are called according to [God's] plan....'" Explaining it in everyday terms, Cooper-Lewter and Mitchell claim that:

> Providence is the deep and sweeping assertion that the whole universe is friendly or benevolent, and that its Creator is able and willing to turn into good ends whatever may occur. Within Black culture this is a given, but to minds shaped in other cultures, it may seem like wishful thinking--an imagined comfort and escape from reality. However, among Soul folk it is a foundational and fruitful insistence on which all life and effort depend. There can be no final disproof of it, because the doctrine always refers to ultimate ends; the disbelievers and challengers simply have not waited long enough.

Oppressed people are supported by the conviction that the very Lord of the universe has guaranteed that their lives will always be worth living.

The second of the basic Black beliefs is the idea that God is just. Cooper-Lewter and Mitchell explain this doctrine as it touches both the privileged and the underclasses in Western culture:

> In the culture of the privileged classes and the power elite, enthusiasm for this doctrine results from a vision of God as enforcer or guarantor of the status quo. God threatens with justice those who break the social contract, raining retribution on those who dare to contradict the common code, which favors the class on top. However, the same divine quality is the hope of the have-nots. Justice is the limit placed on exploitation; it is the vengeance and vindication without which their lowly lives would have little meaning. God's holiness and righteousness synonyms for justice are the basis for all guilty conscience whatever the sin and among whatever sector of the population. It is hard to visualize any ethical decision where this doctrine has no relevance.

A third basic Black belief is the idea of the omnipotent God. This is the view that gives God the ultimate power over the universe. Because of God's Sovereignty there can be the Divine guarantee of the goodness and meaningfulness of life. Cooper-Lewter and Mitchell explain:

> If indeed God be God, there can be no outer limit to divine power and no entity capable of opposing it. Nothing can exist that is free of the ultimate control of the Creator and Lord of the universe. Human freedom, of course, amounts to a kind of exception, but it is ordained by God and constitutes a divine self-limitation. Omnipotence means all-powerful; if any strength were capable of resisting the direct edict of the Creator, that strength would itself be the real God. Life is good and Providence is certain, because there can be no ultimately contrary influence.

Indeed, omnipotence works to provide God with the power to realize God's attributes such as justice and love. Without such power God's attributes are essentially meaningless. Cooper-Lewter and Mitchell further explain:

Omnipotence is essential to the divine guarantee of the goodness and meaningfulness of life. Without it God could not squeeze blessings out of the abuses of human freedom that so often hurt believers. . . . No benevolent plan or kindly attribute of God is worth the mention if God does not have the power to do whatever is involved in making it happen in the real world.

Like Roberts, Cooper-Lewter and Mitchell provide answers for moral evil through the free will doctrine. They argue that men and women have the capacity for good and for evil. While the goal of God is a choice towards good, without free choice humans are mere puppets incapable of uncoerced devotion to God. But in those times when life seems unfair to those who are victims of suffering caused by moral evil, Cooper-Lewter and Mitchell found an extremely popular theodicy that provides in God, who is ultimately the final judge:

> In the end, one must know that no oppression goes unpunished and no sacrificial suffering goes unnoticed and unrewarded. The just God who is no respecter of persons gives none the power to trample the rights of others with impunity. Thus, the final judgement day feared by some becomes cause for the celebration of vindication and victory for the victims of history's most glaring injustices. One dare not suggest that this meaning and comfort conferred through God's justice are the unique possession of any special group or class, since all persons see themselves as oppressed one way or another.

Finally, William Jones proposes the idea of a limited God type theodicy. Jones' humanotheistic model of theodicy focuses on a religion of reason that evaluates the African-American experience of suffering and oppression.

He poses two fundamental questions: "What is the cause of Black suffering and who is responsible for it?"

Jones employs a theodicy based on a model of Divine Racism as the normative criterion for evaluating Black theodicy. His theodicy of Divine Racism reasons that God sanctions the division of humankind into an in-group and an out-group. The partiality towards the in-group alleviates their suffering and places a disproportionate share of the suffering on the out-group. Because God is responsible for the imbalance of suffering, it expresses God's will and purpose. God's partiality toward the in-group reveals God's ethnic identity with that group. In the American context God favors the White group and therefore is a White racist.

Fundamentally, Jones proposes the doctrine of a limited God, focusing on the contradiction between God's intrinsic goodness and the reality of Black oppression. Henry Young brings the contradictions by Jones clearer into focus in saying:

> If God is omnipotent why does [God] permit Black suffering to exist in the world? If God is unable to eliminate Black suffering in the world, then God is not omnipotent. And if God is able to eliminate Black suffering in the world and doesn't, [God] is partial or [God] is not intrinsically good.

In the view of Jones, the Black theologian has one of four choices: (1) "deny the reality of evil, (2) postulate a God who is beyond good and evil, (3) accept a God who somehow reconciles and harmonizes the two," or (4) accept the concept of a limited God. Having accepted the concept of a limited God, Jones' humanocentric theism enhances the importance of humankind by elevating them to a co-laboring relationship with God to achieve the right.

In the view of James Cone, another Black theologian, the humanist tradition offers a rational calculating approach to oppression. Indeed, where the odds are too great the humanists are pushed to the logical conclusion that the oppressed cannot win. This kind of thinking diminishes strength, stifles imagination, and blurs vision; and, indeed, where there is not vision the people perish. Cone concludes that the humanist tradition runs the risk of leading the oppressed to a level of hopelessness and despair.

Until Jones and the humanist are able to provide the oppressed with an ideology that allows the oppressed to struggle against oppression with a deeper level than that of Black Religion, Cone finds Jones' proposals unacceptable.

This section has discussed three contemporary theodicies in relation to the Black experience of slavery and oppression. Both the ideas of an infinite-finite God and an unlimited God are generally unacceptable for the Black community. The idea of an absolute God is the most attractive for the Black community.

Analysis and Comparison of the Idea of God and Evil

Having discussed classical theodicy and several contemporary theodicies in relation to the African-American perspective, this section specifically focuses on the view of God and evil from the points of view of Garnet, Crummell, and Turner.

The idea of a just and all-powerful God are consistent concepts in the thinking of Garnet, Crummell, and Turner. In demanding the liberation of the slaves, Garnet reminded the slave-holders of God's ultimate power and God's eternal justice: "I would beseech them to remember that the great day of God's final reckoning is just before us, remember God's eternal justice and then remember the outcast [bondpersons] and let [them] go forth free in the presence of God." Moreover, Garnet used the success of the Abolition Movement to focus on God's absolute power and God's ultimate retribution:

But sir, far be it from us to ascribe
the glory to ourselves. All our success
is of God "who raiseth up one nation
and putteth down another," yes, that
Almighty Being who said, "let there
be light" and there was light, has
called into being the spirit of this age,
to bring out [God's] oppressed poor
from under their [task-persons] and
is enough for us to be used as instruments
 in the hand of God in accomplishing
[God's] glorious purposes.

One of the fundamental problems posed by the attributes of an all-good and omnipotent God is the account of evil. While Garnet did not articulate a view concerning the origin of evil, he was decidedly a proponent of the free will doctrine. He reasoned that men and women are provided the opportunity to choose between good and evil. Indeed, it was the European abuse of free will that created and maintained the slave system. While Garnet accepted the free will theory he did not view it as ultimate or final. Using the slave system, for example, Garnet reasoned that God would at some point break into history and abolish it. Indeed, in his "Address to the Slaves" Garnet articulated a view of a "future judgement and the righteous retributions of an indignant God" for those who continued to support slavery. Garnet further reasoned that evil may be used for

God's goals and purposes. As a result of slavery, for example, the Western world was thus diversified with the arrival of the Africans. In addition, African-Americans benefited from the advances of Western Civilization. Moreover, they were equipped to return to Africa to elevate their people.

Using a redemptive suffering motif, Garnet reasoned that the slaves would be restored to their position of renowned for their unfortunate plight: "There are blessings in store for our patient, suffering race--there is light and glory. The star of our hope is slowly and steadily rising above the horizon." Reasoning that the suffering has redemptive value, Garnet equated Hebrew captivity in Egypt with Black slavery in America. Throughout the speeches and writings of Garnet are the twin themes of a just God with the corresponding power to support God's will.

Like Garnet, Crummell conceived of God as omnipotent and actively involved in human affairs. While Garnet arrived at this position through an immediate faith claim, Crummell developed his belief through a refutation of the philosophy of Manicheanism. As was previously stated in the opening section of this chapter, the Manichees divided the cosmology into two independent, competing forces: good and evil; the good led by God and the evil led by Satan. Crummell questioned the truth of this position: "But what is this, I ask, but a profane and damning Manicheanism, which sets a god of evil upon the throne of the universe right beside the One, Everlasting God, whom we own and reverence; dividing with [God] the empire of creation and with [God] determining its moral destinies?" Answering his own question, Crummell made this claim:

> We allow no such partnership in
> the moral government of God.
> We yield to no such heresies. . . .
> Dark and intricate as are many
> of the problems of life and history,
> we have learned to leave their
> solution to the providence of that
> one, sovereign, over-ruling Being,
> who "governeth all things in heaven
> and earth," and "ordereth the course
> of this world by [God's] own
> governance."

It is clear from Crummell's analysis that he believed in One God, Sovereign and Ruler over the cosmos.

In addition to the sovereignty of God, Crummell saw God both as immanent and transcendent. In God's immanence, "God is a dynamic, active, ever-present, moving force in the world." In God's transcendence, there is "nothing in the world removed from God's domain and control." Crummell reasoned that "God's omnipotent hand interpenetrated the totality of history and that the animating spirit of history was the very breath of God."

Crummell's idea of an omnipotent God directing the totality of history is closely related to Crummell's account for evil. Because Crummell rejected the bi-polar world-view of Manicheanism, he was unable to explain evil in terms of Dualism. Crummell thus accounted for evil as an element under God's control. Crummell took great care to explain that he did not conceive of God as the originator of evil, but as the power that controls it. Crummell wrote:

> We see everywhere God's hand in history.
> We feel that its animating spirit is the breath
> of God. In all the movements of society. .
> .we see the clear, distinct, "finger of God;"
>
> ordering, controlling, directing the
> footsteps of [humankind], of families,
> and of races. We apply his principle
> as well to those dark and disastrous
> histories, which. . .pain our hearts,

as to those grand and gracious ones,
which stir our liveliest sensibilities.
For while indeed God is not, and
cannot be "the author of evil," still
[God] is the Governor of the wicked,
and exercises a masterful authority
over their works and ways. And
this is the great principle in
God's moral government.

While God allows evil, Crummell reasons that: "God never allows evil to run unchecked, its own wild and uncontrolled career, and to have its own way. God always checks and thwarts sin in its workings and in its intended mischief." Indeed, God steps into history and turns evil towards good.

Crummell's idea of providential restoration is an example of God turning evil towards good. The concept of restoration focused on the regeneration and evangelization of Africa. African-American slaves, having reunited with the true God, were being prepared to redeem the continent for Christ. The African-American slaves were "turned from the paganism of their [parents]; the people that were in darkness have seen a great light."

Neither Garnet nor Crummell accounts for the origin of evil. They seem to accept evil as a given. Having accepted the unexplained origin of evil, Garnet developed the human response to it. He reasoned that men and women are free to choose between good and evil. Crummell refused to provide a rational explanation regarding the origin of evil. He chose to focus on what God does to control and define it. Crummell makes the claim, however, that the evil of slavery may be traced to the will of God. There is no inconsistency, for Crummell, because in his view, God designed slavery to uplift the Black race.

While Garnet and Crummell focused on the concept of God in God's objective essence, Turner conceived of God in terms of God's relation to Black liberation. The attributes of God were not as important as what God meant for humanity. For Turner and his community this meant understanding God in the context of slavery and oppression. Turner thus argued that God must both identify with African-Americans and represent a powerful Black symbol. Actually, it was an inclusive concept because Turner argued that all ethnic groups should perceive God in light of their own ethnicity. Turner wrote: "Every race of people since time began who have attempted to describe their God. . .have conveyed the idea that the God who made them and shaped their destinies was symbolized in themselves." Turner went to the extent to declare God a Negro. This was an extremely important declaration because it helped to negate the idea that Black symbolized evil and White symbolized good.

While what God meant for Black people in the context of slavery and oppression was extremely important for Turner, the attributes of God's justice and omnipotence were important as well. In his impassioned speech on the "Eligibility of Colored Members to Seats in the Georgia Legislature" in 1868, Turner condemned the White legislators for refusing to seat its Black members. In addition, he made references to God's wrath and justice:

> Justice is the great doctrine taught in the Bible. God's eternal justice is founded upon truth. And the [person] who steps from justice steps from truth and he [or she] cannot make his [or her] principles prevail. You may expel us, gentleman, by your vote today; but while you do it, remember there is a just God in Heaven, whose all-seeking eye beholds alike the acts of the oppressor and the oppressed, and who, despite the machinations of the wicked, never fails to vindicate the cause of justice and the sanctity of [God's] own handiwork.

Again in the same speech, Turner warned the legislators about their oppressive behavior and God's consequential punishment: "Go on with your oppression. Babylon fell. Where is Greece? Where is Nineveh? And where is Rome, the mistress Empire of the world? Why is it that she stands, today, in broken fragments throughout Europe? Because oppression killed her."

The relationship between God's justice and God's omnipotence provided Turner with the faith in a God who is totally in control of the universe. In an 1889 article discussing the Negro problem, Turner wrote:

> There is a God that runs this universe. And nations and people are no exception. True, an infinite number of laws may harness up the mighty machinery and serve as so many potencies in its mysterious and marvelous revolutions. But there is a God in the background, nevertheless, and [God] rules in the armies of Heaven and among the inhabitants of the earth.

Turner thus interpreted all events as being a part of God's providential plan for the world.

How then does Turner account for the origin of evil? How does Turner account for slavery and oppression in light of the justice and omnipotence of God?

Turner, like Garnet and Crummell, refused to offer a rational explanation regarding the origin of evil. Turner, like his colleagues, seems to accept evil as a given. Having accepted the existence of evil, Turner distinguished between "providential institutions" and "divine institutions." The former are temporary while the latter are eternal. Based on this theory Turner reasoned that "slavery was a [temporary], providential institution, not a divine institution, for had it been it would have been as eternal as any attribute belonging to the Godhead." Turner thus realized the temporary status of slavery.

Because of the omnipotence of God, Turner knew that God could have prevented slavery. Yet, God's refusal to prevent slavery did not make God responsible for it. Turner believed that Whites were solely responsible for slavery. Slavery was not willed upon Blacks by the creator. Indeed, at some point, God would eradicate the evil institution. Turner wrote: "When the Negro was being captured, and brought to this country and subjected to a state of unrequited servitude, [God] knew the horrors of their past and present condition and foresaw. . .the termination of their slave ordeal."

There are thus different views among the three men as to whether Africans, Whites, or God have the responsibility for slavery. Crummell put the responsibility for slavery, in part, on the refusal of the African foreparents to worship the Christian God. In the account of Turner, slavery is a White trust ordained of God. In the systematic thinking of both men, Whites are absolved from the liability of slavery. Garnet is vigorously opposed to both ideas and puts the blame for slavery on the Whites who began it for selfish purposes. Garnet thus made an attempt to absolve

God from the liability of slavery and to keep the justice of God intact.

Analysis and Comparison of the Nature and Destiny of the Black Race from the Points of View of Garnet, Crummell, and Turner

This section focuses on the differences and similarities among Garnet, Crummell, and Turner concerning their positions on the nature, thought, and destiny of the Black race.

Garnet was first and foremost a proud Black man. He had a deep sense of Black consciousness and love for his race. While a Northern free Black, he realized that the status of free Blacks was inextricably bound with Southern Blacks. He expressed this view in his famous "Address to the Slaves:" "While you have been oppressed we have also been partakers with you; nor can we be free while you are enslaved. We therefore unite to you as being bound to you."

In addition to Garnet's bond with Southern Blacks, was his bond with Africans as well. He felt a special kinship to his African brothers and sisters: ". . .for although. . .my habitation were fixed in the freest part of Victoria's dominions yet it were. . .worse than vain for me to indulge the thought of being free while three millions of my people are waiting in the dark prisonhouse of oppression."

Fundamentally, Garnet believed in the God-given humanity and sacredness of the human person. He told the Congress of the United States that: "Our poor and forlorn brothers [and sisters] whom thou has labelled 'slaves' are also [persons]. [Their] God and thine has stamped on [their] foreheads [God's] title to [God's] inalienable rights. . .God made [them] such and you cannot unmake [them]." Thus, in spite of America's attempt to deny African-Americans access to their being, Garnet encouraged them to hold to their inalienable rights of personhood.

In addition to emphasizing their dignity as persons, Garnet called attention to the glories of the African past. He began the account always by reminding them that their foreparents were brought to American against their wills:

Two hundred and twenty-seven years ago, the first of our injured race were brought to America. They came not with glad spirits to select their homes in the New World. . . . But they came with broken hearts, from their beloved native land, and were doomed to unrequited toil and deep degradation.

He argued that when the Africans were in a high state of achievement, the ancestors of the slave-owners were still in caves:

When these representatives of our race were filling the world with amazement, the ancestors of the now proud and boasting Anglo Saxons were among the degraded of the human family. They abode in caves underground either naked or covered with the skins of wild beasts. Night was made hideous by their wild shouts and day was darkened by the smoke which arose from bloody altars upon which they offered human sacrifice.

It was thus the intent of Garnet to impress upon the Black race that low achievement and slavery were not their natural inheritance.

Emphasizing the horrors of slavery, Garnet focused on cross-generational Black suffering. He brought this idea to the attention of the slaves to further motivate them to seek their freedom: "Years have rolled on and tens of thousands have been borne on streams of blood and tears. . .nor did the evil of their bondage end at their emancipation by death. Succeeding generations inherited their chains. . .and have returned again to the world. . .ruined by American spirits."

In an effort to instill pride in a broken and an enslaved people, Garnet emphasized the Black contribution to America. He pointed to the American Revolution where many Black persons had fought for their country to win freedom from the British: "Sir, in consideration of the toils of our [parents in the war], we claim the right of American citizenship. We claim it, but shall we ever enjoy it? Our ancestors fought as wise[persons], but I will leave it to you to decide whether they are deserving [men and women]." He mentioned the contributions of the slaves whose unrequited toil had helped to build the Southern economy: "the South. . .is indebted to us (African-American slaves) for every breath of agricultural prosperity that she draws." For these reasons Blacks were to press America for their share of citizenship.

Finally, Garnet told the slaves that they were to take the initiative for their freedom. Some Blacks argued for a gradual, non-threatening, accommodating approach to liberation. According to this view, slavery was a declining institution, failing because of its economic infeasibility and its immoral foundation. In time, Whites would acknowledge the error of slavery and happily emancipate their slaves. The invention of the cotton gin, however, strengthened the economics of slavery and the White Church continued to support a theology of slavery. Garnet realized that if Blacks were to be free then they had to strike the first blow. He thus advocated a more aggressive approach to liberation including violence if necessary.

Closely related to Garnet's concept of Black consciousness was his belief in the Christian faith. He argued that the proper interpretation of the Christian faith provided one the strength to resist and overthrow the institution of slavery. Indeed, Garnet believed it the Christian duty of the slaves to revolt against slavery: "In every [person's] mind the good seeds of liberty are planted and [the person] who brings his [or her brother or sister] down so low as to make him [or her] contented with a condition of slavery, commits the highest crime against God and [humanity]."

What then was Garnet's eschatological direction for African-Americans? Armed with the knowledge of their storied past, an abhorrence for the slave-system, and the belief that God sided with the oppressed, African-Americans were thus equipped to fight for their freedom. Indeed, the Christian faith encouraged them to resist evil and to fight for liberation.

Was Garnet referring to a physical fight? Not necessarily. Indeed, he asked the slaves to plead with their owners for a peaceful emancipation. Yet, if the peaceful appeal to the slave-owners failed, then Garnet argued that they would be better deceased than slaves.

What of the thought of Crummell on the nature and destiny of the Black race? Crummell believed that Blacks were called to suffer for a noble end. He hastened to make the point, however, that he did not mean that Blacks were under a curse. The act of slavery did not single out Blacks, rather it was a part of a general social evil.

Much like Irenaeus, Crummell believed in the theology of development. Irenaeus maintains that humankind began in a childlike condition open to growth.

Continuing this line of thinking, Crummell reasoned that the African rejection of God was due to their social and theological immaturity. And yet, God took their evil and turned it to good. In God's providence, God provided a plan of suffering, redemption, and greatness for the Black race.

For Crummell, men and women are social beings-- integral parts of societal and institutional structures. Men and women tend towards group existence as opposed to individual existence. This theory is applied to races as well. A race of people, therefore, belong both to the human family and to their race family.

Crummell had to answer the question posed by the amalgamation theorists who proposed that Blacks inter- marry and assimilate into the White race and culture to alleviate the race problem. Realizing that Black discrimination was in many instances correlative to skin color, the amalgamationists sought to lose the color identity. Crummell rejected the theory of amalgamation because it went against the evolutionary process of nature. He wrote: "Amalgamation would be an impossibility. It would take generations to make the American people homogeneous in blood and essential qualities." Crummell thus believed that amalgamation was a genetic improbability.

Even if amalgamation were genetically possible, Crummell felt it undesirable because it would force the Black race to deny itself in terms of God's purposes. Crummell reasoned that all races should reach their potential. Indeed, races ought to be sensitive and tolerant of each other's differences, thus allowing the races to prosper and live in harmony. The race problem for Crummell was not a problem of amalgamation, but a moral one.

What then is the ethical duty for the Black race to resolve the moral issue of the race problem? Crummell's answer is tied to his theory of providence. He believed that all history is directed by God towards God's goals. Thus, one's ethical imperative must be consistent with God's goals, if it is to have success. Crummell wrote: "But it is to be observed in the history of [humankind] that, in due time, certain principles get their set in human society, and there is no such thing as successfully resisting them. Their rise is not a matter of chance or hap-hazard. It is God's hand in history."

Crummell recognized two principles that were integral parts of God's plan for the alleviation of the race problem: the concepts of brother/sisterhood and democracy. Both principles are rooted in the Scripture. Crummell wrote:

> When I speak of the spirit of democracy I have no reference to that spurious, blustering, self-sufficient spirit which derides God and authority on the one hand, and crushes the weak and helpless on the other. The democratic spirit I am speaking of is that which upholds the doctrine of human rights; which demands honor to all men [and women];. . .which uses the state as the means and agency for the unlimited progress of humanity. This principle has its root in the Scriptures of God, and it has come forth in political society to stay!

When properly understood and practiced, Crummell argued that democracy was the solution to the race problem in America and the ideal form of government.

Crummell saw the eschatological pilgrimage for Black America through the dual perspective of Africa and America. The two-fold perspective was tied to his persistent theory of Providential Design. He firmly believed that a remnant of talented Black Americans were to return to Africa to redeem the homeland. On the other hand, the bulk of Black Americans were to remain in the United States to benefit from Western Civilization. He further argued that the Black race in America would serve to keep the country on trial. Indeed, America stood or fell on the basis of its relationship with Black America.

What of the thought of Turner concerning the nature and eschatological future of the Black race? Turner was a consistent advocate for the personhood rights of Black Americans. His conversion experience, the transformation from a lost person to one who came to know the saving grace of Christ, provided a theistic affirmation of himself. This experience gave him a new level of consciousness, self-hood, and identity. He knew that as a creature of God he was entitled to his God-given personhood rights. Applying the idea of theistic affirmation to the African-American race, Turner fought throughout his life for the elimination of racism, injustice, and oppression.

Turner coupled the idea of personhood with the concept of full societal participation. The one could not exist without the other. He spoke against the systematic exclusion of African-Americans from the mainstream of American life. A strong advocate of African-American political participation, he wrote: "If the Negro is a person in keeping with other persons, why should he [or she] be less concerned about politics than anyone else?" Turner further argued:

For the Negro to stay out of politics is to level himself [or herself] with a horse or a cow. . . . If the Negro is to be a [person] full and complete, he [or she] must take part in everything that belongs to [personhood]. If he [or she] omits a single duty, responsibility, or privilege to that extent, he [or she] is limited and incomplete.

Believing that personhood is God-given, Turner refused to beg White America for his rights. In his unforgettable speech to the Georgia legislature, Turner vigorously argued that he was not present in the Assembly to beg for his rights; nor was he there to "fawn and cringe before any party"; nor was he there to "appeal to the sympathy of any member of the opposition party." He was there to "demand" his "rights" and "to hurl thunderbolts at the persons who dare to cross the threshold of his [personhood]."

Turner reasoned that God had a liberating and redemptive purpose for Black people both in America and wherever they could be found. Convinced of a divine mission, he wrote: "God has [God's] hand upon our race. God will give us means and marvelous agencies." God thus had a providential purpose for slavery: "God intends that [God's] degraded race which had been dwarfed through centuries of heathenism shall imbibe your White civilization with its religion and when sufficiently sobered through generations of self-possession will return to Africa and bring its millions to Christ and heaven."

Turner saw the problem of Black people in its broader perspective--in the European partition of Africa for its riches. Turner claimed that African-Americans had an important role in solving the problem. He said:

> Let [humankind] see and recognize the hand of God in the institution of slavery and dispose of its remains as God directs, and endless blessings will flow alike to White and Black. The Christianized Negro will be a blessing to the millions of Africans and the wealth of that great continent will be a blessing to the White race. Slavery has been a dark providence, but behind it God hides a smiling face if [humankind] will only see its duty and adjust themselves to it.

Turner reasoned that African-Americans were to use Western culture and Christianity to redeem and uplift African peoples from around the globe. He thus had a broad focus for Black liberation.

At home in America, wherever Turner tried to achieve success in the integrated society, he experienced racial prejudice, however. He experienced the harshness of racism as an Army Chaplain, as an agent for the Freedpersons Bureau, and in his position as Post person for Macon, Georgia. In addition, he was refused a seat in the Georgia General Assembly. These and many other negative experiences caused Turner to concentrate on Africa as an eschatological future for Black Americans.

Having refocused his concentration to Africa as the eschatological future for Black liberation, Turner argued: "I am taking the ground that we will never get justice here, that God is and will [continue to] withhold political rights from us for the purpose of turning our attention to our [parentland]." Turner became so negative about the American experience that he encouraged Blacks to return to Africa. He argued that Africa would be a place to seek refuge from the hostilities of America. He believed that the Black race could find its true self only in Africa.

What of the differences and similarities among the three men concerning their position on the nature, thought, and eschatological future of the Black race? All three thinkers believed in the God-given humanity and the sacredness of the person. Refusing to believe that Blacks were created for eternal slavery, this empowering idea became the fundamental starting point for their efforts towards liberation.

The race problem for the three thinkers was a moral one. It was an ethical problem for the White race in choosing between excluding African-Americans from equal citizenship or allowing them their full citizenship rights.

For Garnet, the forced labor of African slaves, the efforts of Black veterans of the Revolutionary War, and the countless contributions of free African-Americans earned a people brought to America against their wills a share of free citizenship. For Crummell, the true practice of democracy that included the concepts of brother/sisterhood and equality provided the means through which African-Americans would join the American mainstream. For Turner, the recognition of the personhood rights of African-Americans would ensure their full participation at all levels of American society.

The differences in the eschatological future for African-Americans in the thinking of the three men is in their response to White resistance to Black liberation. Garnet, realizing that Whites were not so willing to surrender to the moral approach of ending slavery through peaceful means, concluded that violence was a viable alternative. He further reasoned that some African-Americans would have to emigrate to other Black nations in order to fulfill their potential and to help uplift their race abroad. He was not an advocate of full emigration, however.

The final plan of Black liberation for Crummell focused both on America and Africa. Like Garnet, he believed that there ought to be a plan for redemption on both continents. They arrived at the plan for African redemption through different theories, however. The plan of Garnet for African redemption was based on an idea of humanitarian assistance. He believed that African-Americans equipped with a higher level of civilization had to answer the call for Macedonian help to wherever their brothers and sisters called. The plan of Crummell for African redemption, on the other hand, was based on his theory of providence: the idea that God predestined Africans for slavery so that they could acquire Western Civilization and the Christian religion to return to Africa and redeem their race.

Turner came to the realization that Africa would be the eschatological future for Black Americans. Initially, he, much like Crummell, believed it providential for African enslavement in order to acquire Western culture and religion to help redeem the Black race. There is an important difference in their theories of providence, however, and it will be further examined in the next section. Frustrated in his long efforts to secure liberation in America, Turner turned from an emphasis on America to a concentration on Africa as the only place where the Black race could attain true greatness.

Chapter VII: **COMPARISON AND ANALYSIS OF THE THEORIES OF GARNET, CRUMMELL, AND TURNER**

Garnet developed an idea of theodicy that included the elements of Providence and African-American Resistance. For Garnet, the causes of slavery and oppression were the misuse of free will by the White race and their economic greed for the economic benefits of the slavery-system. For Garnet, the making of slaves violated the sacredness of the human person and would bring about God's wrath.

An essential element in Garnet's theodicy was the idea of providence. In general, it refers to God's purpose and goal for humanity that concerns itself with the way in which God attempts to accomplish God's purpose in history. For Garnet, God's goal for the Black race was that of liberation.

Another important element in Garnet's Liberation model of theodicy was the idea of resistance. Resistance complimented Providence; Providence gave the hope, while resistance provided the efforts to actualize the hope.

Thus, while Garnet reasoned that God would break into history with a "future judgment and the righteous

411

retribution of an indignant God," he advocated an African-American working-hope towards liberation.

Unlike Garnet, who put the responsibility for slavery with Whites, who abused free will and were motivated by greed, Crummell put the cause of slavery on the African foreparents who refused to worship the Christian God. Employing a theory of Providential Design, Crummell reasoned that God allowed African enslavement for their failure to worship God and as a mechanism for African-American restoration.   Crummell equated the Hebrew captivity in Egypt and Babylon with African-American enslavement. Because slavery provided the opportunity for the Black race to acquire Western Civilization and to convert to Christianity, it had redemptive value. These qualities would be employed to restore Africa to union with the true God and to uplift Africa with Western Civilization. Actually, providence as it relates to God's will had different meanings for Garnet and Crummell. For Garnet, God's providence meant the goal of liberation.   For Crummell, God's Providence meant a design of slavery that included the dimensions of retribution and restoration for the Black race.

Turner, on the other hand, reasoned that God allowed slavery as a White duty to Africa, as a trust from

God, and as a part of God's Providential Design. Under this plan, the slave-owners were required to educate, Civilize, and convert the slaves to Christianity. The slave-owners misused God's trust, however, in refusing to elevate the slaves.

Slavery was also part of God's Providential Design. In this plan, slavery would be employed to elevate African-Americans, who upon emancipation would return to the parentland to redeem and regenerate Africa. Turner's idea of Providential Design differed from Crummell's idea of Providential Design in that Turner reasoned that Whites misused God's trust by developing and maintaining a barbaric system of slavery that denied both African-American personhood and the means of elevation.

For each of the three men, the specific idea of providence meant something different. As previously stated, Garnet's idea of Providence meant God's goal of liberation for the Black race. For Crummell, God's Providence meant a design of slavery that included the dimensions of retribution and restoration for the Black race. Turner's idea of providence, the most controversial of the three, claimed that "an omnipotent God intimately overseeing all human affairs would provide means for African-Americans to become wholly free and to find fruitful arenas for their energies and talents." Turner's idea of providence appropriated parts of both Garnet's and Crummell's ideas with a significant difference. Like Garnet's providence, Turner held that God was ultimately in control of life and would in God's own time liberate the Black race. Like Crummell's providence, Turner held that God instituted a system of Providential design that allowed the enslavement of the Black race in order to convert them to Christianity and to elevate them with Western Civilization. Crummell reasoned that Whites, in enslaving Blacks, were merely fulfilling their roles in God's plan. Turner, on the other hand, reasoned that Whites misused God's trust in refusing to honor the essential element of the plan: the elevation, Christianization, and ultimate liberation of the Black race.

While Garnet put the responsibility for slavery squarely upon the free will of Whites, Crummell puts the responsibility upon God through God's Providential Design and upon Africans for their failure to worship God. Turner, like Crummell, puts the responsibility for slavery upon God's Providential Design, but as previously stated, distinguishes his idea from Crummell's, in reasoning that Whites abused God's trust in refusing to elevate the slaves.

Turner, like Garnet, did not believe in a futuristic-eschatological hope, but in African-American Uplift and African-American Emigration for the here and now. While Crummell retreated from his original idea of African-American Emigration to Africa, Turner remained committed to Crummell's original Emigration position. In the final analysis, Turner's African Emigration ventures were failures, due to a lack of financial support, and his efforts on behalf of African-American Uplift experienced serious setbacks due to the hostilities of White America during the last quarter of the nineteenth century. Attempting to give African-Americans hope through a God who identified with their struggles for liberation, Turner's Liberation model of theodicy was the only one of the three to identify God as an African-American.

Analytical Summary
The View of God and Evil, 414

The twin themes of a just God with the corresponding power to support and enforce the will of God have been identified in the thinking of Garnet, Crummell, and Turner. The importance of this view cannot be understated because the concept of an omnipotent God enhanced the plausibility of their theodicies. For an enslaved and oppressed people of the nineteenth century, the idea of impotent goodness had little appeal. Acceptable theodicy had to appeal both to the "reasons of their hearts" and the "reason of their heads." The belief in an all-good God provided the theoretical hope of liberation. The belief in an omnipotent God provided the means through which the hope of liberation would be achieved.

The three mean refused to provide a rational explanation for the origin of evil. They seemed to accept evil as a given. Crummell and Turner, however, provided the answer for the evil of slavery through their concepts of Providential Design. While the two theories of Providential Design are different, both absolve Whites from the liability for slavery. For Garnet, and most contemporary Black theologians, this is an unacceptable idea. In the idea of Crummell the slavery is punitive. Indeed, he convicts the African foreparents of an imaginary sin--the sin of refusing to worship the Christian God--a God that they did now know. In the idea of Turner, slavery became the means for Christian evangelism and the elevation of the Black race. Was this the best means through which God could achieve God's purposes? Because the ideas of Providential Design for Crummell and Turner are fraught with problems they were unacceptable for Garnet. Indeed, he argued that if slaves had believed the providential idea of their slavery, they would have had less of a religious hope for their freedom.

Nature and Destiny of the Black Race

The three men found their authentic self-hoods through a theistic affirmation of themselves. The conception of themselves as persons made in the image of God gave them a sense of self-worth and identity. They reasoned that as individuals created in the image of God, they shared in God's universal love and respect. Applying the concept of personal theistic affirmation to the Black race, the men argued that Black people were also members of the universal human family. Had God created the Black race for slavery? Certainly not, argued the men, every race is to be respected because God created and loves them.

The three thinkers developed a theory of humankind not unlike the twentieth century Boston University Personalist who argued that the clue to ultimate reality is found in personality. Professor Paul Deats, a Boston Personalist, explained the Boston tradition:

> Personalism is a philosophical perspective for which the person is the ontological ultimate and for which personality is the fundamental explanatory

417

principle. Walter Muelder has expressed its essence as holding that truth is of, by, and for persons (not isolated but in community) are the clues to reality with the Divine Person.

Professor Deats further explained Boston Personalism through the thinking of Borden Parker Bowne: "In all our thinking when critically scrutinized we find self-conscious and active intelligence the presupposition not only of our knowledge but of the world of objects as well." There is thus a premium placed on the inherent worth of the person. The idea of the sacredness of the human person became the fundamental starting point for the efforts of Garnet, Crummell, and Turner towards liberation.

The problem of slavery for the three thinkers was a moral one. They argued that Whites had the opportunity to choose between African-American emancipation and liberation or African-American slavery and second-class citizenship.

The abolitionists of the nineteenth century thus made the fight for freedom a moral crusade. The genius of a moral crusade was the ability to turn the professed faith and beliefs of White America into outright challenges to the slavery system. The abolitionists used the natural rights doctrine, the faith of the Revolutionary War, the pieistic Christian faith, indeed every historical document and religious or philosophical belief to their advantage in helping to overcome slavery. Many historians argue that this approach was perhaps the greatest single element that helped to break the back of slavery.

Interestingly, the Civil Rights Movement of the next century used a similar approach: a moral crusade turning the professed faith of White America into outright challenges to the system of segregation. Dr. Martin Luther King, Jr. developed the philosophy of Nonviolent Resistance, an idea that combined the concept of Christian love with direct action to force the opponents to come to grips with their evil. Much like the abolitionists of the nineteenth century, Dr. King used the egalitarian principles embodied in the Constitution, the Declaration of Independence, and the Judeo-Christian faith to break the back of segregation.

The theories of Providential Design and Pan-African Uplift were central in the eschatological concepts of Crummell and Turner. Crummell proposed both America and Africa as places for the eschatological future of the Black race. Journeying to Africa as a missionary-teacher, he spent over twenty years redeeming and elevating the Liberian people. Crummell was unsuccessful in beginning a massive emigration movement to Africa, however.

Initially, Turner was an ardent spokesperson for the successful integration of Blacks into American society. In addition to his integrationist position, Turner argued that a small contingent of African-Americans ought to return to Africa to elevate and evangelize their race. After long frustrated attempts to secure full Black participation in America, Turner turned to Africa the place where Blacks could achieve their most success.

The eschatology of Garnet is based more on the theory of Pan-African Uplift. Having contributed so much to America, and having been forced to come to America against their wills, Garnet argued that the prime location for the future of African-Americans was their adopted land. On the other hand, he proposed that a small group of Black Americans relocate to Black countries to help redeem and elevate their kinspeople. After making a great contribution to Jamaica, Garnet was called back to the United States to assist in the Civil War effort.

The different emigration positions among the three thinkers reflect the diversity of emigration opinions among nineteenth century Black Americans. In general, most Black Americans preferred to stay in America.

Theodicy

Fundamentally, Garnet's theodicy puts the blame for slavery at the doorsteps of the Europeans. Slaves were thus unburdened with a deserved suffering mentality. The Garnet system of creation provided humankind with ultimate earthly authority. Slavery was thus inconsistent with humankind's exalted status. Indeed, the Creator frowned on slave acquiescence to their oppressed condition.

Garnet proposed that God would alleviate the slave condition through God's future actions. This did not mean that slaves were to take a wait-on-God approach to oppression. Garnet's theodicy provided the oppressed with a working hope: both faith in God's future actions and self-liberative activities.

The idea of direct action was an extremely powerful technique. It inspired belief in a God who sides with the oppressed and self-liberative activities. These were extremely powerful beliefs that helped to sustain the slaves through the harshness of slavery.

Crummell, on the other hand, postulated that God allowed slavery because of the sins committed by prior African generations. Crummell's theodicy thus at the outset saddles Blacks with a deserved suffering mentality. While Blacks caused their own suffering, according to Crummell,

421

they were, nevertheless, given opportunities for redemption through their suffering. Crummell asserted that God provided opportunities both for African redemption and restoration through a return to the worship of the Christian God and the evangelization and "civilization" of Africa.

Garnet would vigorously oppose Crummell's idea of Providential Design because it absolves Whites from the liability for slavery and gives responsibility to God for ordaining the system. Garnet would further argue that if the slave Christians had believed that God ordained their slavery they would have had less of a religious hope for their freedom and would have easily acquiesced to their oppressed condition based on this religious idea.

Turner, the most controversial of the three, agrees in part with Crummell's idea of Providential Design and agrees with Garnet's idea of self-liberative activities. Under Turner's idea of Providential Design, much like Crummell, Whites were to institute a benign-type slavery and were to educate, civilize, and convert the slaves to Christianity. After a period of uplift, Whites were to emancipate and return the slaves to Africa to regenerate and redeem their homeland. Whites, however, misused God's trust in instituting a harsh-type slavery and in refusing to educate and civilize the Black race. Turner, like Garnet, believed it the duty of the slaves to rebel and free themselves from their oppressors.

While it is extremely difficult to accept Turner's account for slavery, the remaining thoughts in Turner's theodicy are more acceptable. For Turner, personhood was a God-given identity and a quality that could not be denied. He proposed that Blacks demand their rights as God required. In demanding their personhood rights, both African-American self-respect and self-uplift emerged. In his attempt to develop a religion that related to the African-American situation, Turner pronounced that God was a Negro. Turner's idea provided the Black community with a God who identified with their struggles for liberation. It was a symbolically powerful idea that provided an oppressed people the opportunity to identify with the Ultimate Sovereign.

Of the three theodicies, we find Garnet's theodicy, in general, the most acceptable. Both the theodicies of Crummell and Turner have the theory of Providential Design as an account for slavery that absolves Whites of liability. Both Crummell and Turner put the priority of Western Civilization and the Christian religion above freedom, Traditional African Religion, and African civilization. Garnet rightly puts the liability for slaves on the Europeans. So while he appreciates Western Civilization and certainly believed in Christianity, he seems to place freedom above Western Religion and culture.

Chapter VIII: **NEW UNDERSTANDING**

Is it Necessary for the Black Nationalists to Address the Issues of Unmerited Oppression of Black People by Developing the Theodicies Which Make the Suffering Contextually Bearable?

The book has provided an historical overview of the Black Church and Black Nationalism. Several of the historic relations between the Black Church and Black Nationalism were examined. Having set forth an historical and social context for the study, the next chapter comparatively focuses on the lives and theodicies of Garnet, Crummell, and Turner.

The comparative process has revealed three important concepts. Believing that God would alleviate the slave condition through God's future actions, Garnet proposed the ideas of Providence and African-American Resistance. It was a two-dimensional approach that affirmed belief in God's Providence and simultaneous self-liberative activities. Not only did Garnet speak in terms of a spiritual-hope but a working-hope as well. He felt that the oppressed could never dispense with their own efforts for liberation.

Crummell, on the other hand, postulated that God allowed slavery because of the sins committed by prior

African generations. He therefore proposed the doctrines of Divine Retribution and Divine Restoration. He asserted that God provided opportunities both for African Redemption and for African Restoration through a return to the worship of the Christian God and the evangelization and "civilization" of Africa. Armed with the English language, exposure to Western Civilization, and the knowledge of the true, Christian God, African-Americans were thus well-equipped for this task.

For his part, Turner, considered the father of "Black Theology," viewed slavery as a White duty to Africa as a trust from God and as part of God's Providential Design. For the former idea, the slave-owners in return for unremunerated labor were to educate and civilize the slaves. For the latter idea, the slave-owners were to use slavery as a temporary measure to facilitate the slaves' rapid transition from heathenism to Christianity. Turner observed, however, that Whites had misused God's providential plan for slavery in refusing to educate, elevate, and free the slaves. He thus proposed that African-Americans use whatever means necessary to achieve liberation.

Having set forth the theodicies of Garnet, Crummell, and Turner, in conclusion, the study focuses on the implications of their thoughts as they relate to a critically important issue: Is it necessary for the Black Nationalists to address the issues of the unmerited oppression of Black people by developing the theodicies which makes the suffering contextually bearable? The critical examination of this important issue is fundamentally dependent on the Black Nationalists' definition of self and the theistic-atheistic starting points: whether there is belief in God, what are the understandings of the God idea, and what are the desired relationships between God and persons and their relationships to each other?[733]

Central in the thinking of Garnet, Crummell, and Turner was their belief in an all-good and all-powerful God. They came to know their true personhood through their conversion experiences that provided theistic affirmation. Having met God, the three men were transformed from lives of sin and feelings of worthlessness to new creatures liberated from sin, complete with value and meaning in their lives. The God-encounter provided the fundamental basis upon which the three men affirmed themselves and other African-Americans as authentic human beings. Thus the

---

[733]*Atheist* as used in this study refers to one who does not believe in the existence of God. *Theist* as used in this study refers to one who believes in the existence of God.

ideas of God-given personhood and the universal brotherhood and sisterhood of humankind were extremely important.

Once identifying the three men's theistic starting points, then the answer to the first question is an obvious and resounding: No! Cone raises the important question: "[h]ow do we explain our faith in God as the liberator of the oppressed when Black people have been oppressed for more than three centuries in North America?"[734] Based, thus, on the Garnet-Crummell-Turner models of Black Nationalism in relation to God's justice, a serious Black Nationalist focuses on the questions posed by theodicy.

Having established the idea that a theistic Black Nationalist ought to have a theodicy, the conclusion turns to the thinking of the atheistic Black Nationalist. While an atheistic Black Nationalist has "no external living God to blame for the existence of evil,"[735] if the atheistic Black Nationalist is to be taken seriously, he or she must take the

---

[734] *God of the Oppressed*, 179.
[735] Major Jones, *The Color of God: the Concept of God in Afro-American Thought* (Macon: Mercer University Press, 1987), 68.

God concept into account because religion is extremely important in the African-American experience.[736]

The importance of Black Religion cannot be underestimated. Indeed, Wilmore reasons that Black Religion provided the principle means for African-American survival and liberation through a distinctive spirituality that enabled them to survive slavery and oppression.[737] He reasoned further that their denied access to other forms of "self-affirmation and group power caused African-Americans to use religion and religious institutions as the principle expression of their peoplehood and their will both to exist and to improve their status."[738] The power and continuity of Black Religion transcends both regional differences and economic class.[739] Both religion and religious institutions are therefore extremely important for African-Americans.

Even where one takes great pains to find the religious presence, the issues of humankinds' justice for the atheist are still important for the Black Nationalist. The importance lies in the opportunity to continuously challenge

---

[736]Ibid., 63; *God of the Oppressed*, 188.
[737]Wilmore, *Black Religion and Black Radicalism*, 202-221.
[738]Ibid.
[739]Ibid.

the structures of evil and to work creatively for change. Without such a focus there would be less reason to fight against the odds. Indeed, one of the ideological bases of Black Nationalism is the uplifting and liberating survival of the race which is bolstered by the idea of hope, and for the African-American community, the concept becomes a religious hope.[740]

There are several implications for the contemporary African-American situation:

(1) The dualistic explanation for the problem of evil is totally unacceptable for the Black Nationalist because the idea that attempts to portray reality in terms of good and evil is directly opposed to the prevailing African-American norm of an omnipotent and all-benevolent God.

(2) William Jones' humanocentric model of theodicy is generally unacceptable for the Black Nationalist because the idea overlooks the crucial African-American element of faith. There has been, and continues to be, the idea of an eschatological hope in the historic faith of the African-American community. The resurrection event serves as a dynamic act of faith upon which is built the idea of a working-hope for liberation.

---

[740]Cone, "Epilogue: An Interpretation of the Debate Among Black Theologians," in *Black Theology: A Documentary History, 1966-1979*, 620-622.

(3) The Christian religion, the predominate faith of Black Americans which offers an all-powerful and all-good God, must respond to the problems posed by theodicy. In addition, the theodicy ought to provide both the faith and the spirituality to make the suffering contextually bearable. Finally, the theodicy ought to provide the idea that the Divine will provide the final eschatological resolution to suffering.

In addition to the preceding implications, the conclusion focuses on the Nation of Islam and its theodicy. While the majority of Black Americans are Christians, a focus on the Nation of Islam provides the opportunity to develop implications for ministry through both a non-Christian and a Black Nationalist religion.

Image Ownership: Public Domain
Fard Muhammad

The appearance of Fard Muhammad (1895?-1934?) in Detroit during the Great Depression of the 1930's marks the beginnings of the National of Islam or the Black Muslim Movement.[741] Claiming to be a messenger of the Islamic God Allah, Farad Muhammed said that he came to America

---

[741]C. Eric Lincoln, *The Black Muslims in America* (Boston: Beacon Press, 1963), XV; Henry Young, *Major Black Religious Leaders Since 1940,* (Nashville: Abingdon, 1979), 66-72.

to teach Blacks their true identity and to prepare them for the final confrontation between the Black and White races. After establishing a temple in Detroit, Farad Muhammed mysteriously disappeared.

Image Ownership: Public Domain
Elijah Muhammed
Not long thereafter, Elijah Muhammed (1897-1975) assumed the leadership of the new movement. Developing momentum, the Nation of Islam spread to several key cities in the Midwest and Northeast. Elijah Muhammed

developed a philosophy of Black Nationalism based on religious principles. He vigorously opposed the Christian teachings about God as spirit. To further refute the Christian claim about God, Elijah Muhammed claimed that God had made God known to African-Americans in the person of Farad Muhammed. Elijah Muhammed believed Allah to be the One True God. "He also believed that Islam is the true religion of the world and that Black America would never be free until they recognized Allah as the true God, Islam as the true religion, and Elijah as the messenger of Allah."[742]

The theology of the Nation of Islam is best expressed by Malcolm X (1925-1965), one of the group's most popular spokespersons.[743] Fundamentally, Malcolm X followed the teachings of Elijah Muhammed. Malcolm X argued that just as the evils of slavery had caused the destruction of ancient Egypt, Babylon, Greece, and Rome, so in this generation America's enslavement of twenty-two million Blacks would bring her to her hour of judgment and her downfall as a respected nation. He felt it was God's divine will and power that destroyed the slave empires of

---

[742]Young, 69.

[743]Ibid., 73-81; Alex Haley, *The Autobiography of Malcolm X,* (New York, NY: Ballantine Books, 1965).

ancient times and that same force would also bring about the destruction of White America.[744]

Continuing this line of reasoning, Malcolm X claims that before God could bring about God's destruction, the oppressed must be separated from the oppressor. At this point Malcolm X begins a religious philosophy based on separatism. Believing that the White race would fall, he proposed the separation of the races. Indeed, he believed that all Whites were devils and would never respect the Black race. Believing Christianity to be the religion of the White race, he did not think that Blacks would be saved from the wrath of God through Christianity. The true route of salvation for the Black race was through the acceptance of Allah.

The Nation of Islam grew in size and stature and has taken a seat (albeit, a very small one) alongside the Christian Church as an established religion in the Black community. Like the Christian Church, if the Nation of Islam is to be taken seriously, it must speak to the issues of unmerited oppression of Black people by developing a theodicy that makes the suffering contextually bearable.

---

[744]Young, 76-77.

The Nation of Islam has accomplished this goal through a theodicy that puts the liability for slavery and oppression on the White race. In addition, the eschatology of the Nation of Islam foresees the destruction of the White race by Allah. Salvation for Blacks is for those who accept Islam. This kind of thinking is extremely attractive to vulnerable people looking for self-identity, hope and something to guide them through the harshness of oppression. Unfortunately, the theodicy of the Nation of Islam refuses to offer a hope of reconciliation between the races. The theodicy is therefore unable to build bridges between the races and work toward the goal of the beloved community.[745]

The *Black Nationalism and Theodicy: Emphasizing Henry Highland Garnet, Alexander Crummell, and Henry McNeal Turner* concludes that the Black Nationalists must address the issues of unmerited oppression of Black people. Besides, the Black Nationalists have to develop theodicies

---

[745]This is a term that I borrowed from Dr. Martin Luther King, Jr. He envisioned the beloved community as the place where the members would allow the spirit of agape to direct all their individual and social relationships; hence they would manifest a persistent willingness to sacrifice for the good of the community and for their own spiritual and temporal good. See John J. Ansbro, *Martin Luther King, Jr.: The Making of a Mind* (Maryknoll, NY: Orbis Books, 1986), 187-197.

that make the suffering contextually bearable. Furthermore, there must be hope of final relief. Ultimately, the theodicy has to provide means for the reconciliation of the races and the promise of universal brotherhood and sisterhood.

Chapter IX: **BIBLIOGRAPHY**

Primary Alexander Crummell Sources

Published Writings and Speeches of Alexander Crummell
Crummell, Alexander. *Africa and America: Addresses and Discourses by the Rev. Alex Crummell.* Springfield, Massachusetts: Wiley and Company, 1891; Reprint, New York, N.Y.: Negro University Press, 1969.

_____ *The Duty of a Rising Christian State.* London: Wertheim and Macintosh, 1856.

_____ *The Future of Africa: Being Addresses, Sermons, Etc., Etc., Delivered in the Republic of Liberia.* New York, N.Y.: Charles Scribner, 1862; Reprint, Detroit: Negro History Press, 1969.

_____ "The Solutions of Problems: The Duty and Destiny of Man." Microfilmed, Schomburg Collection of Negro Literature and History, New York Public Library.

Moses, Wilson, ed. *Destiny and Race: Selected Writings 1840-1898/Alexander Crummell.* Amherst, Massachusetts: University of Massachusetts Press, 1992.

Manuscript Collections

George W. Forbes Papers (Rare Book Department, Boston Public Library)

Moorland-Spingarn Collection (Howard University)
Schomburg Collection (New York Public Library)

Other Crummell Sources

Dubois, W.E.B. "Of Alexander Crummell." *In The Souls of Black Folk*. Greenwich, CT: Fawcett, 1961.

Heath, Robert. "Alexander Crummell and the Strategy of Challenge by Adaptation." *The Central Speech Journal* XXV 3 (Fall 1975): 178-187.

Moses, Wilson. "Civilizing Missionary: A Study of Alexander Crummell." *Journal of Negro History* 60 (April 1975): 229-251.

Wahue, Kathleen O'mara. "Alexander Crummell: Black Evangelist and Pan-Negro Nationalist." *Phylon* 29 (Winter 1968): 338-395.

Dissertations and Master's Theses

Earl, Riggins. "Toward a Black Christian Ethic: A Study of Alexander Crummell and Albert Cleage." Ph.D. diss., Vanderbilt Univ., 1978.

Primary Henry Highland Garnet Sources

Published Writings and Speeches of Henry Highland Garnet

Garnet, Henry Highland. *The Past and Present Condition, and the Destiny, of the Colored Race: A Discourse.* Washington, D.C.: Moorland Foundation, 1848.

Walker's Appeal, With a Brief Sketch of His Life. New York, N.Y. Humanities Press, 1965.

Ofari, Earl. "Selected Speeches and Writings of Henry Highland Garnet." In Let Your Motto Be Resistance: The

Life and Thought of Henry Highland Garnet. Boston: Beacon Press, 1972.

Smith, James. *A Memorial Discourse by Henry Highland Garnet*. Philadelphia: Wilson, 1865.
Manuscript Collections

Schomburg Collection (New York Public Library) Gerrit Smith Papers (Syracuse University)

Andrew Johnson Papers (Library of Congress)

Minutes of Various Abolitionist, National Liberty Party, and Negro Conventions

Bell, Howard, ed. Minutes of the Proceedings of the National Negro Conventions, 1830-1864. New York, N.Y.: The New York Times and Arno Press, 1969.

Minutes of the Fifth Annual Convention of the Colored People of the State of New York, Held in the City of Schenectady. New York: Kneeland, 1844.

Minutes of the National Convention of Colored Citizens; Held in Buffalo, on the 15, 16, 17, 18, and 19 of August, 1843, for the Purpose of Considering Their Moral and Political Conditions and American Citizens. New York: Piercy and Reed, 1843.

Proceedings of the National Convention of Colored Men Held in the City of Syracuse, New York, October 4th, 5th, 6th, and 7th, 1864. New York, N.Y.: Wesleyan Methodist Church, 1864.

Proceedings of the National Liberty Convention, Held at Buffalo, New York, June 14th and 15th, 1848; including the

Resolutions and Addresses Adopted by That Body, and Speeches of Beriah Green and Gerrit Smith on That Occasion. Utica, N.Y.: S.W. Green, 1848.

Newspapers

African Repository and Colonial Journal
American and Foreign Anti-Slavery Reporter
American Missionary
National Anti-Slavery Standard
The Liberator

Other Garnet Sources

Abzug, Robert. "The Influence of Garrisonian Abolitionists' Fears of Slave Violence on the Antislavery Argument, 1829-1840." *Journal of Negro History* 55 (Jan 1970): 15-26.

Bauer, Raymond and Alice Bauer. "Day to Day Resistance to Slavery." *Journal of Negro History* 27 (Oct 1942): 388-419.

Bell, Howard. "National Negro Conventions of the Middle 1840s: Moral Suasions vs. Political Action." *Journal of Negro History* 17 (Oct 1957): 247-260.

Brewer, William. "Henry Highland Garnet." *Journal of Negro History* 13 (Jan 1928): 36-52.

Crummell, Alexander. Eulogy on Rev. Henry Highland Garnet, D.D. in Africa and America, 1882.

Dick, Robert C. "Negro Oratory in the Anti-Slavery Societies: 1830-1860." *Western Speech* 28 (Winter 1964): 5-14.

"Rhetoric of Ante-Bellum Black Separatism." *Negro History Bulletin* 34 (Oct 1977) 133-137.

Edmonds, Irene C. "An Aristotelian Interpretation of Garnet's Memorial Discourse." *Research Bulletin: Florida A&M College* 5 (Sept 1952): 20-28.

Gross, Bella. "The First National Negro Convention." *Journal of Negro History* 31 (Oct 1946): 435-443.

Hirsh, Leo H. Jr. "New York and the Negro, from 1738 to 1865." *Journal of Negro History* 16 (Oct 1931): 382-454.

Kennicott, Patrick C. "Black Persuaders in the Antislavery Movement." *Journal of Black Studies* 1 (Sept 1970): 5-20.

Levesque, George A. "Black Abolitionists in the Age of Jackson: Catalysts in the Radicalization of American Abolitionism." *Journal of Black Studies* 1 (Dec 1970): 18-202.

MacMaster, Richard. "Henry Highland Garnet and the African Civilization Society.
" *Journal of Presbyterian History 48* (Jan 1970): 95-112.

Mann, Kenneth. "Nineteenth Century Black Militant: Henry Highland Garnet's Address to the Slaves." *Southern Speech Journal* 34 (Fall 1969): 11-21.

Quarles, Benjamin. "Ministers Without Portfolio." *Journal of Negro History* 39 (Jan 1954):
27-42.
Rosen, Bruce. "Abolition and Colonization: The Years of Conflict: 1829-1834." *Phylon* 33 (Sum 1972): 177-192.

Schor, Joel. "The Rivalry Between Frederick Douglass and Henry Highland Garnet. " *Journal of Negro History* 1 (1979): 30-38.

Shiffrin, Steven H. "The Rhetoric of Black Violence in the Antebellum Period: Henry Highland Garnet." *Journal of Black Studies* 2 (Sept 1971): 45-46.

Smith, Arthur. "Henry Highland Garnet: Black Revolutionary in Sheep's Vestments. " *The Central States Speech Journal* 2 (Sum 1970): 93-98.

Wesley, Charles H. "The Negro in the Organization of Abolition." *Phylon* 2 (Fall 1941): 223-235.

"The Negroes of New York in the Emancipation Movement. " *Journal of Negro History* 24 (Jan 1939): 65-103.
"The Participation of Negroes in Anti-Slavery Political Parties. " *Journal of Negro History* 29 (Jan 1944): 32-74.

Master's Theses

Hunton, William. "What a Negro Preacher Did in 1865" Master's thesis, Howard University, 1925.

Miller, Ernest. "The Anti-Slavery Role of Henry Highland Garnet." Master's thesis, Union Theological Seminary, 1969.

Primary Henry McNeal Turner Sources

Published Writings and Speeches of Henry McNeal Turner
Turner, Henry McNeal. African Letters. Nashville: AME Sunday School Union, 1893.

_____ The Barbarous Decision of the United States Supreme Court Declaring the Civil Rights Act Unconstitutional and Disrobing the Colored Race of All Civil Protection, The Most Cruel and Inhuman Verdict Against a Loyal People in the History of the World (Pamphlet). Atlanta, 1893.

_____ The Black Man's Doom: The Two Barbarous and Cruel Decisions of the United States Supreme Court, Declaring the Civil Rights Act Unconstitutional and Disrobing the Colored Race of All Protection (Pamphlet). Philadelphia, 1896.

_____ The Civil and Political Status of the State of Georgia and her Relations to the General Government Reviewed and Discussed in a Speech Delivered in the House of Representatives of the Georgia Legislature, August Il, 1870 (Pamphlet). Atlanta: New Era Printing Establishment, 1870.

_____ Emigration of the Colored People of the United States: Is it Expedient? If So, Where To? Prepared by Request for the Colored National Conference to Meet in Nashville, Tennessee, May 6, 1879 (Pamphlet). Philadelphia, 1877.

_____ The Genius and Theory of Methodist Polity Practically Illustrated Through a Series of Questions and Answers. Philadelphia: AME Book Concern, 1877.

_____ The World's Exposition (Pamphlet). Atlanta, 1884.

_____ Comp. The Hymn Book of the African Methodist Episcopal Church. Philadelphia: AME Book Concern, 1883.

_____ "Correspondence." AME Church Review I (July 1884): 45-48.

_____ "The Democratic Return to Power - Its Effect. " AME Church Review I (July 1885): 213-250.

_____ The Negro in All Ages: Lecture Delivered in the Second Baptist Church of Savannah, Georgia, April 8, 1873 (Pamphlet). Savannah, 1873.

_____ The Negro in Slavery, War, and Peace. Philadelphia: AME Book Concern, 1913.
Only for the Bishop's Eye (Pamphlet). Atlanta, 1907.

_____ Only for the Bishop's Eye (Pamphlet). Atlanta, 1907.
_____ A Speech on the Present Duties and Future Destiny of the Negro Race (Pamphlet). Savannah, 1872.
_____ Turner's Catechism: Being a Series of Questions and Answers Upon Some of the Cardinal Topics of Christianity. Ed. by B. T. Tanner. Philadelphia: ANIE Book Concern, 1917.
_____ "My Trip to South Africa." AME Church Review 15 (April 1899): 808-812.

_____ "Reminiscences of the Proclamation of Emancipation. " AME Church Review 29 (Jan 1913): 211-214.

Manuscript Collection

Henry McNeal Turner Papers. Moreland-Spingarn Research Center, Howard University. Washington, D.C.
Minutes of AME Church General Conferences
and Annual Conferences

AME General Conference 1872, 1876, 1880, 1884, and 1888.

Georgia Annual Conference, 1868-1895.

South Carolina Annual Conference, 1865-1875.

Newspapers and Periodicals

AME Review
Christian Recorder
The Southern Christian Recorder
Voice of Missions
Voice of the People

Other Turner Sources

Articles

Bacote, Clarence. "Negro Officeholders in Georgia Under President McKinley." *Journal of Negro History* 44 (July 1959): 217-237.

Batten, Minton. "Henry M. Turner, Negro Bishop Extraordinary." *Church History* 8 (Sept 1938): 231-246.

"Bishop H.M. Turner's Twenty-Fifth Anniversary." *AME Church Review* 22 (July 1905): 1-11.

Coan, Josephus. "Henry McNeal Turner: Fearless Prophet of Black Liberation." *Journal of the Interdenominational Theological Center I* (Fall 1973): 8-20.

"The Colored Chaplain." *American Phrenological Journal* (March 1864): 76-78.

Coulter, Merton. "Henry M. Turner: Georgia Negro Preacher Politician During the Reconstruction Era." *Georgia Historical Quarterly* 48 (Dec 1964): 374-410.

Cummings, Melborne S. "The Rhetoric of Bishop Henry McNeal Turner." *Journal of Black Studies* 12 (June 1982): 457-470.

Dittmer, John. "The Education of Henry McNeal Turner." In *Black Leaders of the Nineteenth Century*. Edited by August Meier and Leon Litwack, 253-274. Urbana, Ill.: Univ of Illinois Press, 1988.

Herndon, Jane. "Henry McNeal Turner's Africa Dream: A Re-evaluation." *Mississippi Quarterly* 22 (Fall 1969): 327-336.

Ramsom, Reverdy. "Bishop Henry McNeal Turner." *AME Church Review* (July 1915): 45-47.

Redkey, Edwin. "Bishop Turner's African Dream. " Journal of American History 54 (Sept 1967): 271-290.

_____ "The Flowering of Black Nationalism: Henry McNeal Turner and Marcus Garvey." In *Key Issues in the Afro-American Experience*. Edited by Nathan Huggins, et. al., vol. 2, 107-124. New York, N.Y.: Harcourt Brace Javonovich, 1971.

_____ "Rocked in the Cradle of Consternation. A Black Chaplain in the Union Army Reports on the Struggle to Take Fort in Fisher, North Carolina, in the Winter of 18641865." *American Heritage* 31 (Dec 1980): 70-79.

Singleton, Richard. "Bishop Turner His Birth, Rearing, and Education." *AME Church Review* 22 (July 1903): 8-11.

Dissertations and Master's Theses

Angell, Stephen. "Henry McNeal Turner and Black Religion in the South, 1865-1900." Ph.D. diss., Vanderbilt Univ, 1988.

Bacote, Clarence. "The Negro in Georgia Politics, 1880-1908." Ph.D. diss., Univ of Chicago, 1955.

Coan, Josephus. "The Expansions of Missions of the African Methodist Episcopal Church in South African, 1896-1908." Ph.D. diss., Hartford Seminary Foundation, 1961.

Herndon, Jane. "Henry McNeal Turner: Exponent of American Negritude." M.A. thesis, Georgia State College, 1967.

Martin, Elmer. "The Life of Henry McNeal Turner, 1834-1870." M.A. thesis, Florida State University, 1975.

General Bibliography

Allen, Richard. The Life Experience and Gospel Labors of the Rt. Rev. Richard Allen. Nashville: Abingdon, 1960.

American Anti-Slavery Society. Southern Outrages Upon Northern Citizens. New York, 1860.

Angell, Stephen. Bishop Henry McNeal Turner and African-American Religion in the South. Knoxville: University of Tennessee Press, 1992.

Ansboro, John J. Martin Luther King, Jr.: The Making of a Mind. Maryknoll, New York: Orbis Books, 1968.

Apther, Herbert. One Continual Cry: David Walker's Appeal to the Colored Citizens of the World, 1829-1830: Its Setting, Its Meaning. New York, N.Y.: Humanities Press, 1965.

_____ The Negro in the Abolitionist Movement. New York, N.Y.: International Publishers, 1941.

Arnett, Benjamin, ed. Proceedings of the Quarto-Centennial of the AME Church of South Carolina, May 15-17, 1889. Charleston, S.C., 1890.

Asante, Molefe. Afrocentricity. Trenton, N.J.: African World Press, 1988.

Baldwin, Lewis V. Invisible Strands of African Methodism. New Jersey: Scarecrow Press, 1983.

Barnes, Gilbert H. The Anti-Slavery Impulse, 1830-1844. New York, N.Y.: D Appleton-Century Company, Inc., 1934.

Barret, Leonard E. Soul-Force: African Heritage in Afro-American Religion. Garden City, N.Y.: Anchor, 1974.

Beach, Waldo and Niebuhr, H. Richard. Christian Ethics: The Sources of the Living Tradition. New York, N.Y.: John Wiley and Sons, 1955.

Beckler, William H. "The Black Church: Manhood and Mission." Journal of the American Academy of Religion 40 (Sept 1972): 316-333.

Bell, Howard. "Expressions of Negro Militancy in the North, 1847-1853." Journal of Negro History 45 (Jan 1960): 11-20.

"Negro Nationalism: A Factor in Emigration Projects, 1858-1861." Journal of Negro History 46 (Jan 1962): 42-53.

"Some Reform Interests of the Negro During the 1850's as Reflected in State Conventions." Phylon 21 (Sum 1960): 173-181.

"The Negro Emigration Movement, 1849-1854: A Phase of Negro Nationalism." Phylon 21 (Sum 1959): 132-142.

Bennett, Lerone. *The Shaping of Black America*. Chicago: Johnson Publishing Co., 1975.

Blassingame, John. "Before the Ghetto: The Making of the Black Community in Savannah, Georgia, 1865-1880." *Journal of Social History* 6 (Sum 1973): 463-468.

Boles, John B. , ed. *Masters and Slaves in the House of the Lord: Race and Religion in the American South*, 1740-1870. Lexington: University Press of Kentucky, 1988.

Bourke, Vernon, ed. *The Essential Augustine*. New York, N.Y.: New American Library, 1964.

Bowen, James E., ed. *Africa and the American Negro and the Fatherland*. Atlanta, 1886.

Bowne, Borden Parker. *Personalism*. Norwood, Massachusetts: Plimpton Press, 1936.

Bracey, John; August Meier, and Elliot Rudwick, eds. *American Slavery: The Question of Resistance*. California: Wadsworth Publishing, 1970.

_____ *Black Nationalism in America*. Indianapolis: Bobbs-Merrill, 1970.

_____ *Blacks in the Abolitionist Movement*. California: Wadsworth Publishing Co., 1971.

Bragg, George. *History of the African-American Group of the Episcopal Church*. Baltimore: Church Advocate Press, 1922.

Brightman, Edgar Sheffield. *A Philosophy of Religion*. New York, N.Y.: Prentice Hall, 1940.

Brotz, Howard. *African-American Social and Political Thought,* 1850-1920. New Jersey: Transaction Publishers, 1992.

Carson, D.A. *How Long, O Lord?: Reflections on Suffering and Evil*. Grand Rapids: Baker House, 1990.

Cheek, William F. *Black Resistance Before the Civil War*. Beverly Hills: Glencoe, 1970.

Cleage, Albert. *The Black Messiah*. New York, N.Y.: Sheel and ward, 1968.
_____ *Black Christian Nationalism: New Directions for the Black Church*. New York, N.Y.: William Morrow and co., 1972.

Cone, Cecil Wayne. *The Identity Crisis in Black Theology*. Nashville: AME Publishing House, 1975.

Cone, James. *A Black Theology of Liberation*. Philadelphia: Lippincot, 1970.

_____ *Black Theology and Black Power*. New York, N.Y.: Seabury Press, 1969.

_____ *God of the Oppressed*. New York, N.Y.: Seabury Press, 1975.

Conway, Alan. *The Reconstruction of Georgia*. Minneapolis: University of Minnesota Press, 1966.

Coppin, Levi. *Unwritten History*. New York, N.Y.: Negro University Press, 1968.

Craven, Avery O. "An Unorthodox Interpretation of the Abolition Movement." *Journal of Southern History* 7 (Feb 1941): 57-58.

Cromwell, John. "The Early Convention Movement." *American Negro Academy*. Occasional Papers, No. 9 (1905).

Curtis, James and Lewis Gould, eds. *The Black Experience in America*. Austin, Texas: University of Texas Press, 1970.

Deats, Paul and Carol Robb, eds. *The Boston Personalist Tradition in Social Ethics, Philosophy, and Theology*. Macon: Mercer University Press, 1986.

Dittmer, John. *Black Georgia in the Progressive Era*, 1900-1920. Urbana: University of Illinois Press, 1977.

Douglass, Frederick. *The Life and Times of Frederick Douglass*. New York, N.Y. • Collier Books, 1962.

_____ *My Bondage My Freedom*. New York, N.Y.: The New York Times and Arno Press, 1968.

_____ *Narrative of the Life of Frederick Douglass*. Hartford, CT.: Park Publishing Company, 1882.

Drago, Edmund L. *Black Politicians and Reconstruction in Georgia: A Splendid Failure*. Baton Rouge: Louisiana State University Press, 1982.

Draper, Theodore. *The Rediscovery of Black Nationalism*. New York, N.Y.: Viking Press, 1970.

Duberman, Martin, ed. *The Anti-Slavery Vanguard*. Princeton: Princeton University Press, 1965.

Dubois, W.E.B. *Black Reconstruction in America*. New York, N.Y.: World Publishing co., 1962.

Dumond, Dwight. *Anti-Slavery*. Ann Arbor: University of Michigan Press, 1961.

Essien, Udom. *Black Nationalism: A Search for an Identity in America*. Chicago: University of Chicago, 1962.

Fadumah, Orishatukeh. *Defects of the Negro Church*. Washington, D.C.: American Negro Academy, 1904.

Fanon, Frantz. *The Wretched of the Earth*. New York, N.Y.: Grove Press, 1968.

Filler, Louis. *The Crusade Against Slavery*, 1830-1860. New York, N.Y.: Harper and Row, 1963.

Fladeland, Betty. "Who Were the Abolitionists?" *Journal of Negro History* 24 (April 1964): 99-115.

Foner, Eric. *Free Soil, Free Labor, Free Men: The Ideology of the Republican Party Before the Civil War*. New York: Oxford University Press, 1970.

Foner, Phillip. *History of Black Americans*. Westport, CT.: Greenwood Press, 1975.

Foster, Charles I. "The Colonization of Free Negroes in Liberia, 1816-1835." *Journal of Negro History* 27 (Jan 1953): 41-66.

Fox, Early L. *The American Colonization Society*, 1817-1840. Baltimore: Johns Hopkins, 1919.

Frazier, E. Franklin. *The Negro Church in America*. Liverpool: The University of Liverpool, 1963.

Freire, Paulo. *Pedagogy of the Oppressed*. New York: Continuum, 1984.

Gaines, Wesley J. *African Methodism in the South*. Chicago: African-American Press, 1969.

Gara, Larry. "The Fugitive Slave Law: A Double Paradox." *Civil War History* 10 (Jan 1964): 229-240.

Gardiner, James. *Quest for a Black Theology*. Philadelphia: United Church Press, 1971.

Geach, Peter. *Providence and Evil*. New York, N.Y.: Cambridge University Press, 1977.

Genovese, Eugene. *Roll, Jordan, Roll: The World the Slaves Made*. New York, N.Y. • Pantheon, 1974.

Gesterle, Jean, trans. *Thomas Aquinas on Evil*. Notre Dame, Indiana: University of Notre Dame, 1995.

Gravely, William B. "African Methodism and the Rise of Black Denominationalism." In *Perspectives on American Methodism*. Edited by Russell Richey, Kenneth Rowe, and Jean Schmidt, 108-126. Nashville: Kingswood Books, 1993.

_____ "James Lynch and Black Christian Mission During Reconstruction." In *Black Apostles at Home and Abroad: Afro-Americans and the Christian Mission from the Revolution to Reconstruction*. Edited by Richard Newman and David Wills, 161-188 Boston: G.K. Hall and Company, 1982.

Gregg, Howard. *History of the AME Church*. Nashville: AME Sunday School Union, 1980.

Griffith, Cyril E. *The American Dream: Martin R. Delany and the Emergence of Pan-African Thought*. Pennsylvania: Pennsylvania State University, 1975.

_____ *Clarion Call: The History and Development of the Negro Peoples Convention Movement in the United States*, 1817-1840. New York: Bella Gross, 1947.

Gwaltney, Grace. "The Negro Church and the Social Gospel from 1877-1914." Master's thesis, Howard University, Washington, D.C., 1949.

Haley, Alex. *The Autobiography of Malcolm X*. New York, N.Y.: Ballentine Books, 1965.

Hanson, Geddes. "Black Theology and Protestant Thought." *Social Progress* (Sept - Oct 1969): 128-139.

Harding, Vincent. "Religion and Resistance Among Ante-Bellum Negroes, 1800-1860. In *The Making of Black America*. Edited by Elliot Rudwick and August Meier, Vol. I, 184-187. New York: Athenaeum, 1969.

_____ *There is a River: The Black Struggle for Freedom in America*. New York, N.Y.: Harcourt Brace Javanovich, 1981.

Hart, Albert. *Slavery and Abolition*: 1831-1841. New York, N.Y.: Negro University Press, 1968.

Herskovitts, Melville. *The Myth of the Negro Past*. Boston: Beacon, 1958.
Hick, John. *Evil and the God of Love*. San Francisco: Harper and Row, 1966.

Huggins, Nathan. Martin Kilson and Daniel Fox, eds. *Key Issues in the Afro-American Experience*. New York, N.Y.: Harcourt Brace Janovich, 1971.

Idowu, Bolaji E. *African Traditional Religion*. Maryknoll, N.Y.: Orbis, 1973.

Jacobs, Donald. "David Walker: Boston Race Leader, 1825-1830." *Essex Institute Historical Collections* 107 (Jan 1971): 94-107.

Jennifer, John T. *Centennial Retrospect of the AME Church*. Nashville: AME Press, 1915.

Jones, Lawrence. "Black Churches in Historical Perspective." *Christianity in Crisis* 30 (Nov 1970): 226-228.

Jones, Major. *Black Awareness: A Theology of H*ope. Nashville: Abingdon, 1971.

_____ *The Color of God: the Concept of God in Afro-American Thought*. Macon: Mercer University Press, 1987.

Jones, Miles J. "Toward a Theology of the Black Experience." *Christian Century* 87 Sept 1979): 1088-1091.

Jones, William. *Is God a White Racist?* New York, N.Y.: Anchor Press, 1973.

_____ "Theism and Religious Humanism: The Chasm Narrows." *Christian Century* (May 1975): 520-524.

_____ "Theodicy and Methodology in Black Theology: A Critique of Washington, Cone, and Cleage." *Harvard Theological Review* 64 (Oct 1971): 541-557.

_____ "Theodicy: The Controlling Category for Black Theology." *Journal of Religious Thought I* (Spring-Summer 1973): 28-38.

_____ "Toward an Interim Assessment of Black Theology." Christian Century 89 (May 1972): 513-517.

Jordan, Artishia. *The AME Church in Africa*. New York: ANTE Press, 1960.

Kennicott, Patrick C. "Black Persuaders in the Antislavery Movement." *Speech Monographs* 37 (March 1970): 15-24.

Killian, Charles. "Daniel A. Payne and the AME Conference of 1888: A Display of Contrasts." *Negro History Bulletin* 1969, 32 (July 1969): 11-14.

King, Jr., Martin Luther. *Strength to Love*. Philadelphia: Fortress Press, 1981.

Klim Keit, Hans-Joachin, trans. *Gnosis on the Silk Road: Gnostic Textsfrom Central Asia*. San Francisco: Harper, 1993.

Kushner, Harold. *When Bad Things Happen to God People*. New York: Schocken Books, 1982.

Lampton, Edward W. *Digest of Rulings and Decisions of the Bishops of the AME Church from* 1847-1907. Washington, D.C., 1907.

Lincoln, C. Eric. *The Black Muslims in America*. Boston: Beacon Press, 1963.

Litwack, Leon. *Black Leaders of the Nineteenth Century*. Chicago: University of Illinois Press, 1988.

_____ *North of Slavery: The Negro in the Free States*. Chicago: University of Chicago Press, 1961.

_____ "The Federal Government and the Free Negro, 1790-1860." *Journal of Negro History* 43 (Oct 1958): 261-278.

Long, Edward. *A Survey of Recent Christian Ethics*. New York: Oxford Press, 1982.

Lynch, Hollis. *Edward Wilmot Blyden: Pan-Negro Patriot*, 1832-1912. London: Oxford University Press, 1978.
_____ "Pan-Negro Nationalism in the New World, Before 1862." In *Boston University Papers on Africa, II*.

Madden, Edward. *Evil and the Concept of God*. Springfield, Illinois: Thomas Publisher, 1968.

Maritain, Jacques. *St. Thomas on the Problem of Evil*. Milwaukee: Marquette University Press, 1942.

Mays, Benjamin E. *The Negro's God*. New York: Athenaeum, 1973.

Mbiti, John S. *African Religions and Philosophy*. London: Heinemann Educational Books, Ltd., 1969.

_____ *Concepts of God in Africa*. New York, N.Y.: Praeger, 1969.

Mcadoo, Bill. "Pre-Civil War Black Nationalism." *Phylon* 6 (June-July 1966).

McCall, Emmanuel L., ed. *The Black Christian Experience*. Nashville: Broadman, 1972.

McCloskey, Henry. *God and Evil*. The Hague: Nijhof, 1974.

McManus, Edgar. *Black Bondage in the North*. Syracuse, N.Y.: University of Syracuse Press, 1973.

Meier, August. *Negro Thought in America*, 1880-1915: *Racial Ideologies in the Age of Booker T. Washington*. Ann Arbor: University of Michigan Press, 1963.

Miller, Floyd J. "The Father of Black Nationalism." *Civil War History* 17 (Dec 1971): 91-92.

Moses, Wilson. *Alexander Crummell: A Study of Civilization and Discontent*. New York, NY.: Oxford University Press, 1989.

_____ *The Golden Age of Black Nationalism*, 1850-1925. Hamden, CT.: Archon Books, 1978.

Myers, John L. "American Antislavery Agents and the Free Negro 1833-1838." *Journal of Negro History* 52 (Jan 1967): 200-219.

_____ "American Antislavery Society Agents and the Free Negro, 1833-1838. " *Journal of Negro History* 52 (Jan 1967): 200-219.

Payne, Daniel. *History of the African Methodist Episcopal Church*. New York: NY Times and Arno Press, 1969.

Pease, William H. and Jane Pease, eds., *Bound With Them in Chains*. Westport, CT.: Greenwood Press, 1972.

_____ *The Anti-Slavery Argument*. Indianapolis: Bobbs-Merril, 1965.

_____ "Black Power: The Debate in 1840." *Phylon* 29 (Spring 1968): 19-26.

_____ "Negro Conventions and the Problem of Black Leadership." *Journal of Black Studies* 2 (Sept 1971): 29-44.

_____ *They Who Would Be Free: Blacks Search for Freedom*, 1830-1861. New York, N.Y.: Athenaeum, 1974.

Perdue, Robert. *The Negro in Savannah*, 1865-1900. New York: Exposition Press, 1973.

Ponton, Mongo. *Life and Times of Henry McNeal Turner*. Atlanta: A.B. Caldwell, 1917.

Quarles, Benjamen. *Black Abolitionists*. New York, N.Y.: Athenaeum, 1968

_____ *Frederick Douglass*. Washington, D.C.: Publishers, Inc., 1948.

Raboteau, Albert. *Slave Religion: The Invisible Institution in the Antebellum South*. New York, N.Y.: Oxford University Press, 1978.

Rankin, James O. "The Missionary Propaganda of the AME Church. *AME Review* (Jan 1916): 81-89.

Redkey, Edwin. *Black Exodus: Black Nationalist and Back to Africa Movements*, 1890-1910. New Haven, CT: Yale University Press, 1969.

Richardson, Harry V. *Dark Salvation: The Story of Methodism as it Developed Among Blacks in America*. Garden City, N.Y.: Anchor Press/Doubleday, 1976.

Roberts, J. Deotis. *A Black Political Theology*. Philadelphia: Westminster Press, 1974.

_____ "Black Theology and the Theological Revolution." *Journal of Religious Thought* 28: 1 (Spring-Summer 1971): 5-20.

_____ *Black Theology in Dialogue*. Philadelphia: Westminster Press, 1987.

_____ *Liberation and Reconciliation: A Black Theology*. Philadelphia: Westminster Press, 1971.

Rosen, Bruce. "Abolition and Colonization, The Years of Conflict: 1829-1834." *Phylon* 33 (Summer 1972): 177-192.

Ruchames, Louis, ed. *Racial Thought in America: From the Puritans to Abraham Lincoln*. Amherst: University of Massachusetts Press, 1969.

Schor, Joel. *Henry Highland Garnet: A Voice of Black Radicalism in the Nineteenth Century*. Westport, CT: Greenwood Press, 1977.

Shanks, Caroline L. "The Biblical Anti-slavery Argument of the Decade 1830-1840." *Journal of Negro History* 16 (April 1931): 132-157.

Sherwood, Henry. "The Formation of the African Colonization Society." *Journal of Negro History* 2 (1917): 209-228.

Singleton, John. *The Romance of African Methodism*. New York, N.Y.: Exposition Press, 1952.

Smith, Charles. *A History of the AME Church*. Philadelphia: AME Book Concern, 1922.

Smith, James M. *Sketch of the Life and Labors of Henry Highland Garnet*. Springfield, Massachusetts: 1891.

Smith, Kenneth and Ira Zepp. *Search for the Beloved Community: The Thinking of Martin Luther King, Jr*. Valley Forge, Pennsylvania: Judson Press, 1974.

Smith, Timothy. "Slavery and Theology: The Emergence of Black Christian Consciousness in Nineteenth Century America." *Church History* 16 (1972): 497-512.

Sorin, Gerald. New York *Abolitionists: A Case Study of Political Radicalism.* Westport, CT.: Greenwood Publishing Corp., 1971.

Staudenraus, P.J. *The African Colonization Movement*: 1816-1865. New York: Columbia University Press, 1961.

Stuckey, Sterling. *The Ideological Origins of Black Nationalism.* Boston: Beacon Press, 1972.
Tanner, Benjamin. *An Apology for African Methodism.* Baltimore, 1867.

Ullman, Victor. Martin R. *Delany: The Beginnings of Black Nationalism.* Boston: Beacon Press, 1971.

Viner, Jacob. *The Role of Providence in the Social Order.* Philadelphia: Philosophical Society, 1972.

Walker, Clarence. *A Rock in a Weary Land: The AME Church During the War and Reconstruction.* Baton Rouge: Louisiana State University Press, 1982.

Walker, Theodore. *Empower the People: Social Ethics for the African-American Church.* MaryKnoll, N.Y.: Orbis Books, 1991.

Wander, Phillip C. "Salvation Through Separation: The Image of the Negro in the American Colonization Society." *Quarterly Journal of Speech* 57 (Feb 1971): 57-67.

Washington, Booker T. "The Mission Work of the AME Church." *AME Church Review* 1 (Jan 1916): 71-81.

Waymon, Alexander. *Cyclopedia of African Methodism.* Baltimore: AME Book Depository, 1882.

West, Cornel. *Prophesy Deliverance! An Afro-American Revolutionary Christianity*. Philadelphia: Westminster Press, 1982.

Wheeler, Edward. *Uplifting the Race: The Black Minister in the New South*, 1865-1902. Maryland: University Press of America, 1986.

Williams, Walter. *Black Americans and the Evangelization of Africa*: 1877-1900. Wisconsin: University of Wisconsin Press, 1982.

Wilmore, Gayraud. *Black Religion and Black Radicalism*. Maryknoll, N.Y.: Orbis, 1983.

Wimberly, Edward. *Pastoral Care in the Black Church*. Nashville: Abingdon, 1979.

Woodson, Carter G. *The Mind of the Negro as Reflected in Letter During the Crisis* 1800-1860. Washington, D.C.: Associated Press, 1926.

Wright, Richard R. *Bishops of the AME Church*. Nashville: AME Sunday School Union, 1963.

_____ *Centennial Encyclopedia of the AME Church*. Philadelphia: AME Publishing House, 1916.

Young, Henry. "Black Theology and the Work of William Jones." *Religion in Life* 44 (Spring 1975): 14-28.

_____ "Black Theology: Providence and Evil." *Journal of the Interdenominational Theological Center* 40 (Spring 1975): 87-96.

_____ *Major Black Religious Leaders*: 1755-1940. Nashville: Abingdon, 1977.

_____ *Major Black Religious Leaders Since* 1940. Nashville: Abingdon, 1981.